D1474026

Blind Journey

A Journalist's Memoirs

Jack Hawn

Strategic Book Group

Strategic Book Group
P.O. Box 333
Durham CT 06422
www.StrategicBookClub.com

ISBN: 978-1-60976-011-3

Contents

To my wife Charlene and our children—
Patty, Linda, Barbara and John

Acknowledgments

Returning from the nearby grocery market and discovering he had forgotten to buy ice cream for dinner that night, an aging retiree decides to go back, telling his wife he won't be long.

"OK, honey," his wife says, "and don't forget the chocolate topping. Better make a list."

"That's ridiculous," he says, "vanilla ice cream and chocolate syrup. Be right back."

He returns and sets a small bag on the kitchen counter. Reaching into it, the man's wife withdraws the only item—a dozen eggs.

"I told you to make a list," she grumbles. "Where's the bacon?"

Although my wife and I haven't regressed to that point, frequent searches for misplaced car keys and eyeglasses are aggravating. Yet, with intense concentration, particularly when lying awake at night in the dark, I was able to recall memories stored in my brain undisturbed for decades—names, incidents, anecdotes—but not *everything* recorded in this book.

Among those who confirmed, expanded or corrected my recollections of yesteryear and to whom I am forever grateful include:

Boxing promoter Don Fraser; former Los Angeles Times and Orange County Register sports columnist John Hall; former Times Sports Editor Bill Dwyer; former Times assistant sports editor Chuck Garrity; my ex-boss in the Times View and

Calendar section, Don Alpert; syndicated cartoonist and former View makeup editor Steve Moore; and the late Jerry Clark, a former Times reporter who headed an L.A. club known as OFS (Old Farts Society) that keeps ex-newsmen updated on current events and never allowed the golden era of journalism to die.

Especially helpful were L.A. Times Librarian Robin Mayper and Presidio of Monterey, Department of the Army, archivist Caroline Cantillas, both of whom provided invaluable research.

Thanks also to my cousin Robin Leslie, with whom I had not been in contact for years, for documented information about her father, Jack Lewis, a prisoner of the Japanese during World War II who was killed years later when his private plane crashed into a mountainside in Southern California.

Although I took liberties quoting people, I believe I captured the essence of their words as best as I could remember. Some quotes were unforgettable, such as those emanating from the lips of a corporal relaying a message from a colonel who headed the Fort Ord Public Information Office.

"He told me to tell you that you have one week to prove yourself," the corporal said. "If you don't, you'll be on your way to the front lines in Korea as soon as he can have orders cut. And that's quick, soldier."

Just when I thought my manuscript was ready for print, along came Cherie Lee, a gifted editor who assured me after browsing through a few pages it definitely was not.

Cherie's perceptive eye not only identified glaring inconsistencies, but also infinitesimal typos ("heat attack or heart attack?"). She noted style violations and questioned my logic, continuity, meandering prose and a dearth of my emotional reactions when "it cries for them."

She adored commas, but not too many, frowned on my excessive use of dashes and broke rambling sentences into one-liners, if possible.

She was a godsend. Thank you, Cherie.

"How would you like to be in PIO?" the colonel asked. *"I'm the public information officer. You would write stories about Fort Ord recruits to send to their hometown newspapers....We'll teach you."*

"OK," I replied. *"I'll give it a try."*

Introduction

Don King's hair stood at attention—stiff, pointed at the ceiling as if suddenly jolted by electricity. When he spoke three-inch porcupine-like needles quivered.

"Make me famous, Jack," the relatively unknown boxing promoter's voice bellowed, followed by uproarious laughter as only Don King can roar.

A devious scoundrel on a pugilistic prowl for fame and fortune when we first met, Don King recently had served four years at Marion Correctional Institution in Cleveland, Ohio. Convicted of manslaughter for fatally injuring a man in a street fight, King was paroled in 1971 on a reduced charge.

Self-educated behind bars, he literally read the dictionary to increase his vocabulary. He would string together long words and phrases, delivering them in machine-gun spurts to drive home his point, seldom permitting interruption. Occasionally, he would misfire with an incorrect or inappropriate word, but press on unabashed. Once his mouth was in motion, it was almost unstoppable.

One night, King invited a small group to a gourmet restaurant at the Sahara Hotel in Las Vegas. He was in his glory, commanding attention from one and all with a boisterous monologue that must have lasted five minutes. Finally, he paused a second too long.

"Don," my wife Charlene quickly interjected, "you took the words right out of my mouth." The flamboyant promoter couldn't contain himself. He nearly burst with laughter.

He had an eye for my wife—an attractive blond who frequently accompanied me on out-of-town assignments—and once offered to buy her an expensive evening gown to wear at a formal party he was giving.

Of course, it was an offer I *could* refuse—and immediately did. I covered boxing for the Los Angeles Times then. Had my sports editor, Bill Shirley, known King had even made the offer, I suspect I would have been pulled off the beat and relegated to a desk job at best.

Early on, King was good for professional boxing, good for sportswriters. Gregarious, energetic and street-smart, he generated large headlines, tossed lavish parties, made his inner circle of friends and hangers-on laugh and predicted great things for himself and the title-hungry boxers he controlled.

I didn't make Don King famous, but many of my Times articles and columns in the 1970s contributed to his monumental—and controversial—rise to fame and wealth.

But this book is not about Don King. It's an autobiography focusing on my journalistic career, laced with memories of my life with Charlene—tough times, wonderful times—and our four children.

Anecdotes about other famous, and infamous, people whose lives I touched professionally are chronicled in this book—humorous, embarrassing, tragic incidents, some of which made headlines.

For more than half a century, I worked in the shadow of fame as a journalist—primarily at the Hollywood Citizen-News and Times, also in radio and television. I covered sports and entertainment, freelanced as a wire service stringer, wrote for L.A. sportscasters and scripts for dramatic TV series—*12 O'clock High, Gunsmoke, FBI* and others.

I never studied journalism in school, never aspired to be a writer, never considered it. So how did I land in this profession and spend most of my life doing what I was never trained to do?

Looking back, I can't explain why a chance meeting on a Greyhound bus set in motion a seemingly predestined future in journalism, why certain people crossed my path when they did and why they had such profound influences on my life.

Actor Matthew Broderick once made a statement on the TV

show *60 Minutes* that impressed me. Apparently, Broderick didn't struggle a great deal to gain stardom as do most in his profession. He explained that his career just seemed to fall in place. He listed a few examples, then said, "All of these things have to line up that are out of your control."

As my wife told Don King, Broderick took the words right out of my mouth—at least most of them.

Like a blind man being helped across a street, I believe God simply took my hand when I strayed from life's journey and pointed me in the right direction.

But unlike Broderick's experiences, mine would take decades to "line up" before achieving any measurable degree of success.

Part One

THE ARMY

Chapter 1

A Nostalgic Farewell

Los Angeles Times columnist Jack Smith, a plain, unpretentious man with a common name that fit his relaxed James Stewart-like mannerisms, was hanging his jacket on a clothes rack when I spotted him.

"Hi, Jack," I said. "How are you?"

I hadn't seen Jack for awhile, merely spoken briefly a few times on the phone to discuss items in his column. My mindless greeting—normally eliciting a mindless response from anyone else—was a mistake.

I should have been specific. "How's your general health, Jack? How's your state of mind this morning? How are you feeling compared to yesterday morning or perhaps last week when you had a cold?"

Jack turned to me, pondered my greeting, then replied, "You know, I'm never quite sure how to answer that question. Do you mean...?"

Not uncharacteristically, Jack launched into a broad dissertation about insincere phrases people use daily, such as "Have a nice day," "Take care" and, well, "How are you?"

I wouldn't swear to it, but I believe one of his ensuing columns addressed that very topic.

Author of 10 books, Jack Smith's columns poked gentle fun

at Los Angeles, himself and his family, mostly chronicling small moments. He might focus on the birdbath in the backyard of his Mount Washington home, his wariness of cats, a visit to the Getty Museum's garden, and contradictions of the English language or thoughts that flitted through his mind while driving the freeways.

Once, Jack wrote of a gruesome incident during his days as a Marine combat correspondent—the precise moment an enemy shell decapitated the soldier kneeling beside him on the beach of Iwo Jima.

Shockingly inconsistent with his style, Jack's descriptive words of that bloody scene were horrifying. They may have faded over the years but that column remains one of my most memorable.

I don't remember what inspired that piece. I also don't recall much of what Jack said on the afternoon of June 28, 1991, when he addressed about 50 writers and editors who had assembled to wish me well in the blazing Arizona desert where my wife Charlene and I had chosen to retire. As dreadful as that might sound, for us it would be a long-awaited departure from the congested San Fernando Valley, where we had lived for half a century.

I'm not averse to the spotlight, but I do remember being uncomfortable that day when co-workers delivered rehearsed lines

Charlene and friends Evelyn and Jewett Conradson help Jack get through the unavoidable retirement ceremony.

intended to be humorous, showered me with silly gifts—a flexible rubber-shafted golf club, jock strap and other useless items—and lied about how I would be missed after 21 years at the paper.

Were it not for the cake and champagne—a vintage of lesser quality than the The Times served at Pulitzer Prize winners' parties I attended—I suspect the turnout would have been noticeably fewer.

The gift I still cherish is a silver-framed cover page of the View section, which normally featured articles dealing with lifestyles and trends. This page consists of a four-column by nine-inch mug shot of a smiling 61-year-old retiree, boldly headlined *Jack's New Beat*, a bit of nonsense about me in the Highlights column and Jack Smith's column, where it frequently appeared below the fold.

Whereas Jack's faithful readers numbered in the thousands, this specially written tribute may have had a readership of 10. That would include the unknown editor, a proof reader, my wife and four kids, our lifelong friends, Jewett and Evelyn Conradson and, of course, myself.

"If there are any typos, misspelled names, error of grammar or fact, ambiguous syntax or dubious opinions in this piece," Smith wrote, "it will be because it was not edited by its subject: Jack Hawn.

"For some years now, Jack has been my catcher—the steady, imperturbable, heroic man on the flying trapeze…

"We have developed a symbiotic relationship," he rambled on. "Because I work at home, I am almost always available by phone—much more so than writers who have a desk at the office but who can never be found there. Thus, I almost always get a call from Jack in the morning, asking me if perhaps I meant something else beside what I seem to be trying to say. He is usually right."

Had I edited that, I certainly would have questioned that last sentence. Jack was never stubborn about suggestions for changes, but he was a good negotiator. Often, we would strike a compromise.

"…It must be a pain in the ass (he would have asked if there wasn't some other way I could say that) for a writer to have to read someone else's copy," his column continued.

It was, in fact, a pleasure. Jack's work needed little editing

5

until age caught up with him resulting in a few typos or factual errors now and then. His column ran for 37 years in The Times almost until the day he died in 1995 at 79.

Jack Smith's career was kick-started when, as a rewrite man at the Los Angeles Daily News, his story about Elizabeth Short's murder made the front page.

The police beat reporter phoned in the bulletin to Smith, who described in his book *Jack Smith's L.A.* what was "perhaps my finest hour as a newspaperman."

"Within the minute," he recalled, "I had written what may have been the first sentence ever written on the Black Dahlia case. I can't remember it word for word, but my lead went pretty much like this: 'The nude body of a young woman, neatly cut in two at the waist, was found early today on a vacant lot near Crenshaw and Exposition Boulevards.'"

His editor added one adjective, making Short "a *beautiful* young woman."

"Our city editor, of course, no more knew what the unfortunate young woman had looked like than I did," Smith later wrote. "But the lesson was clear. On the Daily News, at least, all young women whose nude bodies were found in two pieces on vacant lots were beautiful. I never forgot it."

Published accounts reported that Elizabeth Short's body was drained of blood, her face slashed from the corners of her mouth toward her ears and that she was posed with her hands over her head and elbows bent at right angles.

It's unknown exactly who labeled the victim the "Black Dahlia," but Jack Smith didn't. According to other newspaper reports, she received the nickname at a Long Beach drugstore a year before she was killed as a word play on the then-current movie *The Blue Dahlia*.

However, the Los Angeles County district attorney investigators' reports state the nickname was invented by newspaper reporters covering the crime. In either case, Short was not generally known as the "Black Dahlia" during her lifetime.

The unsolved murder occurred in January of 1947. As a 17-year-old high school senior at the time, I knew nothing about Elizabeth Short. I know I would never have recognized a dahlia had I seen one, particularly were it black. I did, however, have a

6

basic knowledge of flowers, having planted a few gladiola, iris and other seeds in a small bed near our front porch one spring.

As a journalist, I looked back on that murder and regretted not having taken an interest in what became one of Los Angeles' most famous homicides.

Shortly after the woman's mutilated corpse was discovered — probably as newspapers continued to sensationalize the story — my parents sold our house in the San Fernando Valley and with my 13-year-old sister moved 50 miles north, leaving me with a neighbor for three months until I graduated.

It would be years later that I realized what monumental effect that temporary living arrangement would have on my life. Meanwhile, I had other roads to travel on my blind journey.

Chapter 2

An Impulsive Commitment

My father, John Michael Hawn—nicknamed Sham—labored all his life.

Born Jan. 22, 1904, on a small farm outside of Dunlap, Iowa, he was one of 10 children (six beautiful sisters and three younger brothers).

An infant boy died shortly after birth, and Harold—a handsome, athletic young man and family favorite, I was told—was killed in a freak auto accident when he was 21. Driving a Model-T Ford home from a dance with friends, Harold struck a tree and was thrown out of the vehicle. He landed on a tree stump and died instantly. His friends were uninjured.

I don't know at what point dad broke away from his family, but I suspect it was long overdue. As the oldest son he had been saddled with a heavy workload at the farm starting at an early age. He was intelligent but not formally educated. I don't believe he completed high school.

My mother, Thelma Tucker Hoover, was born July 29, 1909, in Kearney, Nebraska, where her father, a doctor, practiced medicine. She had three sisters and a brother, Albert, the youngest.

I never heard anyone call mom Thelma. My sister Bonnie says she believes mom picked up the name Jean in school and it stuck through her lifetime. To close friends, she was Jeanie. To her youngest sister Maurine, she became "Hawnie" after mom married my father.

Mom was well-educated, some college, sang briefly on a radio program and, from the time I could talk, corrected my grammar.

When quite young, she and her sister Maurine attended a small dance in Omaha, where the band's relatively unknown singer asked my mother to dance to recorded music during a break.

"I turned him down," she recalled. "I don't know why. He wasn't very handsome, and I guess I just didn't feel like it."

Some time later, she learned she had snubbed Fred Astaire, who lit up dance floors with Eleanor Powell, Ginger Rogers and so many others, sadly, not my mother.

"Any regrets, mom?"

"Not really," she replied with a shrug.

I'm still not sure about that.

At age 18 or 19 my mother met dad on a blind date, arranged by one of his sisters, Bessie, who shared an apartment with her in Omaha. My parents ended up at the altar in November of 1928, when dad was 24.

Living in Omaha when it came time for my birth, mom returned to Kearney.

"I wanted dad to deliver you," she told me, "but he was too nervous. He got the doctor across the street to do it."

I came into the world in January of 1930, as America was crashing financially in the wake of the stock market's collapse. For a young couple embarking on a lifetime journey with one child and another to come a few years later, it was devastating.

Jack's parents celebrate purchase of their new home in 1940.

I never heard about my father standing in bread lines during the Great Depression, but I do remember eating meals at a union hall of some sort and receiving second-hand Christmas toys.

Somehow dad managed during those desperate years. He worked on President Franklin Roosevelt's WPA program, toiled with a heavy electric grinder on an automobile assembly line in the Midwest and worked hard at Lockheed Aircraft during World War II.

When times improved, my parents could afford some extras.

I took trumpet lessons, tried to emulate Harry James' versions of *Deep Purple, Sleepy Lagoon* and others and randomly punched the instrument's three valves in rapid succession to produce sounds I thought resembled *Flight of the Bumble Bee.*

My mother was a gifted pianist. She couldn't read music but kept herself and our family entertained with boogie, blues, ragtime and whatever anyone could hum.

When the gold-plated Martin horn didn't pan out for me, I pretended I was Gene Krupa. But the second-hand drum set my parents purchased led to nothing more than complaints from our next-door neighbor about my practice sessions.

Several months before the war ended, my father signed a short-term lease to operate a gas station. Mom worked alongside him, and I helped when I could.

Working in a service station brought the war into focus, with the rationing of fuel determined by windshield stickers. There were only two gas prices—18 cents per gallon for regular; 20 cents for the higher octane.

Service stations truly were that. Besides pumping gas, I filled tires, checked oil and washed windshields. Once, while bending over an engine, I cringed in pain as a front tire slowly rolled over my toes. I don't think the customer behind the wheel even noticed. No bones were broken, but my foot was sore for days.

I hated working in that station, but not nearly as much as my father. He often labored 12-hour days as his health deteriorated.

The day an American plane dropped the first of two atomic bombs on Japan, dad sent me to a nearby parking lot to change a customer's flat tire. The date was August 6, 1945, my sister's 11th birthday.

While changing the tire, I overheard a shocking news bulletin on a car radio. The city of Hiroshima was an inferno of death, but there were few details. I didn't attach much significance to it. Not until Nagasaki, Japan, was bombed three days later, did I and most Americans realize what historic events had taken place.

Finally, dad was able to unload his service station lease in 1947. He sold the house, moved and embarked on his second business venture, the fulfillment of his lifelong dream. A heavy drinker since his early teens, dad couldn't have made a worse choice.

As the new proprietors of a neighborhood beer and wine tavern in Oak View, four miles from the historic town of Ojai, my parents hung the Shamrock Inn shingle over the front door.

They opened it to paying customers on St. Patrick's Day, March 17, 1947. Meanwhile, I was left behind with a neighbor, Beatrice Lamb, until I graduated from high school in June and joined my parents for the summer.

Dad introduced me to a young man who became an instant friend. Together we found work building a reservoir, but the job didn't last.

I can still see the fat straw boss sitting under a shade tree, reading a newspaper and sipping on a can of beer while my friend and I labored below under a blazing sun. We operated a tamper, a jackhammer-like machine that jarred my body so much my teeth chattered.

Every now and then, fatso would peer over the edge of the deep hole, pick up a clod of dirt and toss it to a high spot he wanted smoothed. So we would hustle over and tamp it to his satisfaction. After a week or so, we quit.

It didn't take long for me to get bored, hanging around the Shamrock each day with little to do. I was too young to work behind the bar, but I swept out, cleaned the outdoor bathroom and did what I could.

At 10 cents a glass for draft beer, my parents barely eked out a living, especially considering dad's generosity. He seemed to set up drinks more frequently than he rang up the cash register. At least, my mother thought so.

Many steady customers became dad's good friends. Some competed against him in tavern shuffleboard tournaments he organized and usually won. They laughed at each other's stories and spent leisure time together away from the Shamrock, playing pool or merely having a few drinks in Ojai or Ventura. Dad quickly became well known and liked in that friendly rural community.

Besides drinking too much, dad also loved to gamble. He obtained a license to operate small poker games in an adjoining room. I sometimes watched the action through a service counter from the bar area.

One afternoon, I saw a player steal two $25 chips off dad's

stack when he stepped away to get a new deck from a wall cabinet.

I thought of telling my father what I had seen, but as soon as he sat down, he rippled his chips and looked up at the man on his right, a semi-regular customer.

"Somebody's taken chips off my stack."

"Don't look at me, Sham," the man replied, his elbows on the chair arm rests, hands cupped against his stomach. As he spoke, he attempted to drop the chips onto his lap. Instead, one fell between his legs onto the wooden seat and bounced to the floor.

Wham! In an instant, the man was on the deck, blood trickling from his cut lip. Unhurt, he sheepishly arose, apologized and shamefully exited out the side door.

After dad closed the game and cashed out the remaining players, he returned to the bar and told my mother what had happened.

"He just left," my mother said, "charged a six-pack."

Dad could only shake his head, knowing he had been taken again.

That was my summer. I was ready to move on.

For lack of something better to do, I enrolled at the University of California at Santa Barbara in September. I never gave my future much thought, but my parents were willing to pay the tab, so I drove 40 miles or so up the coast to give it a try.

"Your major?" the college counselor asked.

Law sounded interesting. I signed up for such pre-law courses as bowling, football and music appreciation. I obtained respectable grades that semester and next, but nothing akin to law was part of my curriculum.

In 1948, talk of resuming the selective service program hovered over young men my age, and in 1949 Congress revived the draft to prepare for an ugly war that initially was labeled a "police action."

Some were convinced it was only a matter of time before they would be called to fight in Korea. A few friends joined naval reserve units; some enlisted; others sought shelter from the draft in school.

As the UC Santa Barbara semester was drawing to a close in June, I planned to return in September. It had been a happy year.

I had acquired a girlfriend with a bubbly personality and, certainly significant, an attractive figure. Shirley seemed different than many girls on campus. Even the spelling of her last name was uncommon—Read.

Living in a dormitory complex that had been converted from U.S. Army hospital barracks, Shirley and I enjoyed good times with other couples, participating in group activities, without any serious commitments. Nonetheless, we all had steady partners, and Shirley Read clearly was mine.

A long central hallway provided access to male and female living quarters, a cafeteria and other rooms. Occasionally, we would hear about a male student opening the "wrong" door late at night, resulting in a screech or two. If there was any hanky-panky going on in those dormitories, I never heard about it.

The most popular meeting spot was the Santa Barbara Public Library, where we gathered in groups, ostensibly to study, which some frequently did. With my curriculum, I was never hard-pressed to cram for exams. For me, it was just another social get-together. Coffee and pie usually followed at one of many restaurants in that college-oriented city.

Although I still had no long-range plans, I did envision a summer romance with Shirley, whose parents lived in North Hollywood—a 90-minute drive from Oak View. At least, I looked forward to dating her, sans the group.

As classmates prepared to scatter, bidding emotional good-byes, a sports car arrived in front of the dorms. A handsome young driver asked for Shirley, who suddenly materialized, bags in hand. Introducing him as a senior who attended the University of California at Berkeley, Shirley apologized for not having mentioned him earlier.

Oh, and by the way, she added, "We're engaged."

I can't recall what foolish words I must have uttered or the expression on my face, but it must have been one drained of blood. I was stunned.

Shirley and Joe College piled into the car and sped off, not unlike a final scene of an old Warner Bros. movie in which the happy bride and groom dash off to paradise.

That was the last I saw of Shirley Read.

Not wanting to go home immediately, I stayed in Santa

13

Barbara an extra day to sulk, ponder my future and see an afternoon movie.

A fan from the time I was a boy, I used to ride my bike seven miles every Saturday afternoon to see Tom Mix, Buck Jones, Ken Maynard and other Western heroes outdraw the bad guys.

As I dejectedly trudged out of the theater on State Street, I spotted an Army recruiting office and peered through the window. Why I immediately stepped through the doorway, I can't say. I simply did. Attribute it to one of those sudden impulses that propel you without consideration of the consequences.

An impeccably uniformed sergeant smiled warmly as might an optimistic car salesman welcoming a hot prospect into his cubicle.

"Hello, young man. What can I do for you?" the sergeant asked, or some such innocuous greeting. Within minutes, I had signed the enlistment papers, thereby removing troubling thoughts about my future, at least for me, if not my parents.

In three years, I would decide on a career in law, or whatever.

I can't say for certain that Shirley and her fiancé led me to that recruiting office, but I sometimes think about that fateful day in 1948 and wonder what happened to that good-looking brunet with the bubbly personality.

I wish I could recall the movie I saw. It wasn't a western, probably a romantic love story with a sad ending.

Chapter 3

The Colonel

Awaiting my first breakfast at Fort Ord, I inched along the street toward the front door of the company mess hall behind a line of recruits, shivering in my newly issued Army fatigues and stomping the pavement in stiff combat boots.

A chilly breeze blowing in from the Pacific Ocean made the wait uncomfortable as the first signs of daybreak were at least an hour away.

Finally at the serving counter, I picked up a cold metal tray. A line of KP servers slapped on two thick pancakes, molasses, scrambled eggs and a generous portion of potatoes that should have fried longer. The coffee was ink black and bitter, but drinkable with cream and sugar. Later in life, I preferred it black, no sugar.

After breakfast, our barracks again emptied onto the street, where an arrogant, foul-mouthed corporal called us to attention.

Although daylight by then, a misty fog hung over us as we assembled for Sunday church services. Mandatory or not, no one voiced an objection.

"Awright," the corporal shouted, his booming hillbilly twang slicing through the fog like a banjo wire cutting through butter. "Ah want all you f'n Catholics to fall in over heah. On the double."

We mackerel-snappers—as Catholics sometimes were labeled when the church considered it sinful to eat meat on Fridays—hustled to the designated area. We quickly formed a couple of lines, leaving the majority in place.

"You f'n Protestants, line up over theah. Move yeah asses. Ya got lead in 'em?"

That done, a small group remained at attention.

"The rest a you f'ers, we gonna *larn* ya a f'n religion."

What immediately followed has been long forgotten, but that first mess hall breakfast and our introduction to six miserable weeks of Army life remain indelibly etched in my memory.

THE DRIVE from San Francisco to Fort Ord, Calif., was about two hours by Greyhound bus—a scenic ride during the day, but past midnight, the only view through the windows was an occasional set of approaching headlights.

I had spent the weekend with a college buddy, Doug McCune, at his family home in St. Francis Wood, an affluent residential neighborhood in San Francisco.

Taking full advantage of Doug's hospitality, I enjoyed a gourmet meal Friday evening and was treated to a swinging party in my honor Saturday night. All I can remember about that party was meeting an attractive girl. We seemed to click, but the next morning I couldn't remember her name. I also had a hangover.

Dead tired and not eager to face another week of military drudgery, I moved toward the rear, found a vacant seat next to someone and settled in for a snooze. There wouldn't be much sack time when I got to the barracks.

"Hi, soldier," the man next to me said. "Enjoy the weekend?"

My friendly seat companion was considerably older and wore metallic oak-leaf clusters on his Army tunic. In the semi-darkness, I couldn't be sure—major or lieutenant colonel?

On a Greyhound bus? Don't they travel in staff cars? Driven by corporals?

"I'm Colonel Flemings," he said.

I introduced myself and soon felt as comfortable conversing with him as I might be chatting with a civilian stranger. I had stored up a barrage of complaints about the Army for anyone willing to listen. And there I was, mouthing off to a high-ranking officer who seemed genuinely interested.

Among other things, I suggested a more civil indoctrination to military life, better oversight by company commanders during basic training, instructors with a semblance of intelligence and Lord knows what else.

The colonel let me ramble on without interruption, then finally hit me between the eyes with an unexpected offer.

"How would you like to be in PIO?" he asked. "I'm the public information officer. You would write stories about Fort Ord recruits to send to their hometown newspapers."

I suppressed a chuckle. Write newspaper articles? As a youngster, I scribbled steamy gossip items about neighborhood schoolmates having boy-girl crushes, and other tidbits. I distributed the sheets at the bus stop each morning until my sources ran dry—or, more likely, lack of interest.

I also wrote letters from time to time and got straight-A report cards from Mrs. Opal Oliver, my high-school English teacher. But I couldn't envision myself bent over a typewriter attempting to compose an acceptable news story.

Experience, however, was not an Army prerequisite at Fort Ord's Public Information Office in 1948.

Colonel Amos W. Flemings, director of public relations at Apple Valley Country Club in Victorville, California, was a reserve officer given an assignment he relished. Seemingly, he was in the process of creating a media conglomerate. And the "help-wanted" sign was out.

"We'll teach you," Colonel Flemings continued. "I think you will find the job interesting."

"OK," I replied without hesitation, "I'll give it a try."

STATIONED ON the picturesque Monterrey Peninsula, the 4th Infantry Division was under the command of General Robert T. Frederick, at 42, the youngest major general in the United States Army at the time.

I entered post headquarters, a large, impressive building where daily decisions by the general and his staff affected the lives of thousands of young recruits. Many went directly to Camp Stoneman in northern California en route to Korea. I had lucked out.

As I moved down a hallway, looking for Colonel Flemings' office, my mind was "rehearsing" what I planned to say.

I had second thoughts about changing jobs after talking to my barracks buddies the morning after I met the colonel. They knew no more about PIO than I did, but they convinced me a transfer was risky. What if I didn't work out? Would Korea be next?

My friends reminded me of the good duty I had checking baggage of GIs being sent to installations around the country. I worked regular hours, often short days, got every weekend off and pulled no kitchen police duty. That was about as good as a buck-ass private could expect.

After a few sleepless nights, I decided I would not become a journalist.

I found the sign on the door—"Colonel Flemings, Public Information Office"—and stepped inside. A second lieutenant, seated behind a desk in a small outer office, looked up from some papers. No one else was present.

"Good morning, solider. What can I do for you?"

I introduced myself and told the young officer about having met Colonel Flemings on the bus, etcetera.

"I'd like to speak to him, sir, if possible. Is he available?"

"Colonel Flemings won't be in until tomorrow," his adjutant said. "Can I give him a message?"

What a relief!

"Just tell him, sir," I continued, "that I've changed my mind. Tell him thanks for the offer to join his staff, but I think I'll stay where I am."

I don't remember the lieutenant's reply, but I recall feeling instantly uncomfortable by whatever he said despite his promise to deliver my message.

Exiting the office, I immediately regretted how I had mishandled that delicate situation. I prayed I wouldn't run into Colonel Flemings—in the hallway or ever!

My thoughts focused on how I *should* have handled it. I could have been appreciative, certainly not as haughty as I must have sounded. I could have explained that I was satisfied with the job I had, knew nothing about writing newspaper articles and might not live up to his expectations. In short, I could have used diplomacy.

"Just tell him…"

What arrogance. A private doesn't *tell* a colonel anything. But those are the words I chose, and that was that.

A week later, while checking baggage, I was summoned to my company Orderly Room, handed papers and told to pack my bags.

"You're on orders, private," the first sergeant barked. "You're moving to PIO. I'll have a driver for you in 15 minutes. Be ready."

I was shocked. I had almost forgotten about Colonel Flemings.

"I guess the colonel didn't get my message," I started to explain, but was cut short: "Move it, soldier. I've got work to do."

I left the Orderly Room, eyed the orders in my hand and shook my head in disbelief.

Dressed in my Class A uniform with my belongings stuffed into a duffel bag, I reluctantly climbed into the Jeep waiting for me for the five-minute ride up the hill. It seemed like an hour. What now? To say I was nervous or apprehensive would be a colossal understatement. If my driver spoke, I can't recall a word.

Exiting the Jeep, I didn't even glance at the view sprawled below me—part of a 20,000-acre installation on the shores of the Pacific Ocean. I did, however, note press cards on windshields of several staff cars and Jeeps parked in front of a converted two-story bachelor officers' quarters. The sign in front: PIO Headquarters.

A heavy-set, sloppily dressed corporal with a sweaty face greeted me, took the paperwork I had brought and showed me to my room.

My room! My mouth must have remained agape all the way up the stairs. Opening a door from a long hallway, I saw two bunk beds with rolled-up mattresses, one next to a window overlooking the entrance, which I selected. A clothes rack sufficient for two people, shelves and two sets of dresser drawers impressed me.

My room! Already I was perking up.

Before unpacking, I immediately got the grand tour. Besides private living quarters, the BOQ had a large recreation room, dominated by a Ping-Pong table; newsroom; storage for broadcasting equipment, and a wire-service teletype machine.

Next came a staff-car ride with Charlie Amussen, the overweight corporal. A friendly, cheerful man, Charlie probably was in his mid-20s, but looked older. He casually flashed his ID at the main gate and was waved through by a stoic MP, who apparently was accustomed to seeing press cars.

It was a short drive to My Attic, a Monterey bar so narrow overweight patrons sometimes had to push forward on their stools to make room for customers passing behind them.

But Charlie and I were My Attic's only customers that afternoon. It was as quiet as an empty church. Settled at the bar with a glass of beer in front of us, Charlie immediately got to the point. He told me that Colonel Flemings had gone directly to the general's chief of staff to expedite my transfer.

"When he heard you didn't want to come," Charlie said, pausing dramatically to shake his head while searching for the proper words, "well, he was pissed." Charlie took a sip of beer, lowered the glass and stared at me as if he were about to deliver a death sentence.

"He told me to tell you that you have one week to prove yourself. If you don't, you'll be on your way to the front lines in Korea as soon as he can have orders cut. And that's quick, soldier."

After all these years, I can still remember those frightening, penetrating words, the sudden panic attack that produced a cold sweat on my forehead and the silence that followed.

What could I have been thinking? I alienated a staff officer who had offered me a career in journalism, and now, I'm in serious trouble. I had only just learned to type, seldom read a newspaper and certainly never tried to write articles for one.

Worse, I didn't like guns, barely qualified with the M-1 rifle on the firing range and didn't even know where Korea was located. I could picture myself in some muddy foxhole, fumbling to load a rifle and the horrors of battle.

What if I...? Oh, my God!

Prove myself? In one week?

How could I do that?

Chapter 4

The Staff

"Stay in your lane," Pete instructed, "more to the left…
Good. Stop sign coming up. Slow it down. Easy, easy…
now stop… STOP! I said."

Pete Schwartz, a slightly crazy civilian photographer with an
abundance of nervous energy, sat beside me as I drove a press
Jeep down Fort Ord's main street. We were headed for a company
mess hall to cover a story for the post newspaper, the Panorama.

Anyone observing my erratic driving must have thought I
was blind. Well, I was… temporarily. It's a wonder the MPs didn't
spot us and pull me over. I may have entered the Army *emotionally* blinded, but this childish stunt was stupid, not to mention
dangerous.

"Pete," I implored, reaching for the cloth covering my eyes,
"this is nuts. We could get killed or kill somebody else."

Pete laughed. He had had his fun. I removed the blindfold
and continued toward the mess hall.

A chain-smoking professional who also got his kicks pho-
tographing weird people with weird stories, Pete liked teaming
with me because, well, "weird" was my beat.

After my panic attack at My Attic, I must have "proved myself," whatever that meant, because I didn't get another call to
the Orderly Room as I had feared. I don't recall seeing Colonel

Flemings during that "tryout" week, but I'm sure he received a report about my attitude and how I was fitting in.

Lord knows I didn't impress anyone with my work. Despite an ongoing struggle to put two intelligent sentences together on paper, I suppose I was handling my assignment satisfactorily.

My PIO job meant sifting through stacks of questionnaires to select recruits with interesting backgrounds for interviews. I'd write a press release about them and send it along with their photograph to their hometown newspapers. The Army wanted to depict these young men as having made a smooth and happy transition from civilian life.

Managing Editor Monty Ash and Stewart Bennion, two civil service newsmen with impressive journalistic credentials, headed the staff that produced the post's weekly newspaper, the Panorama. They tutored me and usually rewrote most of my articles. Were it not for their patience, well...

A widely used Army acronym, RHIP, meaning rank has its privileges, didn't apply in PIO in 1948. Keith Moon was a good example.

A cocky private first class who wrote a weekly column titled "Column Left," Moon was clever, had a sharp wit, good contacts and often printed items that sometimes proved embarrassing at post headquarters. Yet, he managed to stay out of serious trouble.

Moon may have been the most privileged single-striper at Fort Ord. A favorable mention in his column opened doors for him and helped remove the barrier that separated the staff's enlisted men from commissioned officers in the field.

Daily courtesy patrols that strolled the main street—a second lieutenant and sergeant—nabbed GI's out of uniform and those who failed to salute the officer.

To my knowledge, Moon never was cited for breach of regulations. A sloppy dresser, he almost always wore his tie loose below an unbuttoned collar and paid little attention to military protocol.

To a lesser extent, I enjoyed preferential treatment from most company commanders eager to publicize themselves, their unit or both. A phone call from the Panorama to arrange an interview opened doors and broke down barriers. It was my introduction to the "power of the press," and, admittedly, I liked it.

Bing Crosby's annual golf tournament received major coverage in the post newspaper. The Crooner invited PIO staffers to play complimentary rounds at Pebble Beach, Spyglass Hill and other prestigious Monterey Peninsula courses a week prior to his Clambake—an event now titled AT&T National Pro-Am.

Even though I had little interest in the game, I did cross paths with Crosby early one morning. He strolled toward a group of us whistling a tune and appeared to enjoy the scenery. It was, in fact, breathtaking.

He greeted us with a broad smile. "Hi, fellas," he said in his resonant, incomparable voice that made him a music icon. "Beautiful morning, isn't it?"

Golf was Crosby's passion. He played the game to the very end—literally. On Oct. 14, 1977, while enjoying a round with friends at the La Moralejo Golf Club outside of Madrid, Spain, Crosby suffered a massive heart attack. He died en route to a hospital at age 73.

KEITH MOON quickly paired up with a young civilian society editor—Cleo Chase, a perky and flirtatious blond from Washington state who authored "Column Right."

Since I paired mostly with Pete Schwartz on stories, I can recall working only occasionally with another staffer, Tech Sergeant Andy Hawkins, a well-liked black photographer whose private room was near mine.

That was significant in 1948, when the Army segregated troops. Once while sharing a Jeep with Andy on a hot afternoon, we approached a Non-Commissioned Officers Club.

"Let's stop for a beer, Andy," I suggested, licking dry lips.

"Well, you know, we've got our own club," he replied matter-of-factly.

I think both of us were embarrassed. Andy apparently didn't want to point out he wasn't allowed inside. I knew it, too, but literally had forgotten I was working with a black man.

Staff Sergeant Ernie Brickman, a PIO sportscaster, gained some notoriety years later in Palm Springs, Calif., where he had his own radio sports show. He contacted me once when I was in a position to help him break into the Los Angeles market. I tried, but it didn't work out. Ernie died at a relatively young age.

23

Probably the most interesting PIO character was Corporal James McKinley, the Sergeant Bilko of the office.

A career soldier, McKinley knew nothing about journalism and contributed nothing to the Panorama, but he knew where and how to obtain anything the colonel needed or wanted. A spit-and-polish dresser, Mac also knew Army regulations explicitly. He knew what rules could be bent and how far they'd bend without serious consequences. He shared that advice with me and the Panorama staff. He was irreplaceable.

Weekends were special.

Often a small group would take off in an Army staff car for a quaint little bar in Carmel, cruise the scenic, lightly traveled 17-mile drive or go for a delicious burger at The Nepenthe on Highway 1 in Big Sur, where views are spectacular.

Perched on the edge of the continent, high above the Pacific, the restaurant opened April 24, 1949, when we helped christen the place. In 1963, The Nepenthe was selected as the site for a folk-dancing scene used in the movie *The Sandpiper*, starring Elizabeth Taylor and Richard Burton.

The family-owned-and-operated business, which has served poets, artists, travelers and vagabonds for more than 50 years, became one of the most popular tourist stops in Big Sur. But in 1949, it was our secret little hideaway.

While PIO personnel had special privileges, there were limits. Occasionally, a reporter would encounter a problem attempting to interview a high-ranking officer. Someone suggested that on certain assignments, enlisted men be allowed to wear civilian clothes. I don't know who vetoed that idea, but it didn't fly.

As a civilian, Pete Schwartz was not bound by military regulations and occasionally would jerk people into position to set up his photo. Although Colonel Flemings received complaints from time to time, to my knowledge, Pete was never reprimanded.

Early in our working relationship, Schwartz and I were assigned to cover a special entertainment program for GIs at the Soldiers' Club. The relatively new facility was impressive, built on the beach by General Joe Stilwell. A Japanese prisoner during World War II, the general was nicknamed "Vinegar Joe" for his acetic characteristics.

I never met Stilwell, but the general in charge of that show must have been his twin when it came to a sour disposition. After stumbling through an inept interview with Tommy Dorsey and xylophone master Lionel Hampton, I asked the musicians to pose with the general for a photo.

In his typical rough manner, Pete grabbed the general by his arm and pulled him into position for the shot. It was obvious the officer resented such crude treatment but said nothing. I told Pete we would hear from the colonel about that.

"Relax, kid," he said. "The general wants his picture in the paper."

As expected, Pete's photo of Dorsey, Hampton and the unsmiling general made the front page of the following issue. If Colonel Flemings received a complaint from the general, we never heard about it.

I PARKED the Jeep in front of the company mess hall and headed inside to interview the recruit—a circus performer in civilian life who, according to his questionnaire, ate razor blades, broken pieces of light bulbs and such items in his act.

"God, where do you find these guys?" Pete said as he grabbed his equipment.

Schwartz's adrenaline was pumping. A creative genius, Pete envisioned his set-ups long before arriving on the scene. For this assignment, he instructed the mess sergeant to wear a chef's hat and apron over his uniform and hold a salt shaker over a plate of broken bulbs in front of the seated soldier. Pete told the recruit to scoop up a spoonful and hold it in front of his opened mouth.

Flash! Flash! Another angle. Flash! And another...

"OK, son, let's see you eat that," Pete said.

Unflinchingly, the soldier placed the spoon into his mouth, slowly crunched and swallowed, quickly washing it down with a gulp of water.

Schwartz continued shooting, the flash bulbs popping with each crunch. Finally, Pete set his camera on the table, looked at the young man, laughed and shook his head in disbelief.

"You're weirder than he is," Pete told him, nodding toward me.

I suppose I learned something from Pete, but no one taught me the value of good timing. I learned that on my own.

One of the Panorama's most popular series was *Recruit of the Month*, which generated major competition among company commanders. For a coming issue, I had selected a handsome, clean-cut young soldier and, for once, suggested the photo setup.

A well-known liquor ad that appeared in magazines and on billboards across the country showed an impeccably groomed middle-aged gentleman in a red plaid smoking jacket, standing beside a high-backed chair draped in velvet. He held a cocktail glass said to contain a popular brand of whiskey. The ad was labeled "Man of Distinction."

What could be better, I thought, than to copy that ad, substituting a bottle of Coca-Cola for the liquor and labeling it "Recruit of the Month"?

Pete bought the idea, got the required props and shot the kid's photo at the plush, relatively new service club as a crowd of GIs watched. Not only was the photograph published prominently in the Panorama and mailed to the soldier's hometown newspaper, it also appeared in a Sixth Army Headquarters publication, and, no doubt, elsewhere.

It might have been premature to expect a promotion, but I was proud of our project… until we received a phone call from a lieutenant at the Fort Ord military police headquarters who had seen the photo in the Panorama.

The officer informed us a fight had erupted the previous night at a sleazy Monterey bar. Several intoxicated soldiers apparently had argued over a prostitute and several people had been injured.

Among those arrested was our "Recruit of the Month."

Unbelievable! Not only was it a major embarrassment for Col. Flemings, but it seemed certain Gen. Frederick, the post commander, would hear from Sixth Army Headquarters at the Presidio of San Francisco.

I had picked the soldier based on his photograph and company commander's recommendation. I didn't perform a background check. Was it my fault the "Recruit of the Month" got into a barroom brawl? Schwartz wasn't about to take the blame.

"You sure can pick 'em, kid," he said, laughing.

To me, it wasn't a joke. I was worried for weeks, but, officially, the incident was never mentioned.

MY ROOM was private for a few months until one morning I woke and saw an unmoving ape-figure on the other cot. A mass of black hair protruded above the blanket. An Ike jacket with many hash marks, stripes and service ribbons hung next to mine on the clothes rack. My jacket had a four-leaf clover patch on the shoulder designating the 4th Division, nothing more. My new roommate was a tech sergeant.

Hoping he might stir soon, I remained in bed. Finally, I dressed noisily, went to the latrine and returned. The sergeant still slept.

Having seen a couple of people lying in coffins in my youth, a fleeting thought crossed my mind that perhaps he had suffered a fatal heart attack during the night. I wished he had snored. Finally, biting the bullet, I gently tapped his shoulder.

"Sergeant, time for breakfast." I paused, then added, "Or, would you rather sleep longer?"

When he didn't move or answer, I poked his shoulder again. He grunted and rolled onto his back, exposing a shriveled right forearm. I immediately noticed the ugly scars.

Looking up at me with one eye closed, he yawned, exhaling with a guttural bellow: "What time is it?"

I don't recall the time only that it was too late to eat at the mess hall.

"We can have breakfast at the service club, if you like. No rush."

When properly scrubbed and his hair combed, Sgt. Bob Stevens' transformation was remarkable.

About five-feet, 10 inches tall with a thick neck, broad shoulders and a handsome moustache that spread across his face when he smiled—and that was often—Stevens bore a striking resemblance to Clark Gable.

While chatting over breakfast, I inquired about his background in journalism.

He chuckled.

"You kidding? I don't know anything about writing. Maybe you can give me some lessons."

A World War II hero who made headlines diving into Okinawa caves with a knife clenched between his teeth to extract the enemy, Bob was marking time for an early retirement. Under special regulations, he was allowed to virtually choose his assignments.

He was not required to perform routine functions that involved use of his right arm, which included saluting.

He explained that when he arrived at Fort Ord, a corporal in Classification and Assignment asked him where he wanted to be assigned.

"Where I don't have to do anything," he said.

"How does PIO sound to you?" the corporal asked.

"Pie-oh. What's it mean?"

"Public Information Office. They don't do much."

"Let's try it."

So, there he was, paired with someone who knew no more about writing for a newspaper than he did. What a team.

The first time we approached the courtesy patrol on a sidewalk, Bob kept his right hand pocketed while I saluted the officer.

"Mornin' lieutenant, sergeant," Stevens said, flashing his Clark Gable grin as we passed. Turning back, the officer stopped us as I knew he would.

Relishing the moment, Stevens was ready when admonished by the young lieutenant for failing to salute.

"Sergeant," he said, in a high-pitched voice. "Don't you recognize an officer when you see one?"

I knew what was coming and loved it. By the time Stevens had cited the special Army directive that covered his exemption from saluting, the officer had had enough of Bob Stevens.

"Carry on," the lieutenant said, quickly walking away. The non-com at his side also seemed to have enjoyed what probably was a refreshing turnabout.

The more I became acquainted with my roommate, the more I liked him. Bob Stevens soon became my fatherly role model.

I was given the task of accompanying a war hero to Post Headquarters, where Gen. Frederick and his staff seldom talked to Panorama reporters.

With his cloth cap tucked under the epaulet of his Ike jacket, a dress-code violation, Stevens would poke his head into open doors and greet whoever was behind a desk. Often he would be ignored and respond with a sarcastic comment.

It was obvious Stevens' assignment was a mistake. Not only was it non-productive in terms of acquiring news stories, Bob's haughty manner annoyed members of the general's staff.

I was never comfortable touring the building every morning in search of non-existent stories and relieved when we were pulled off the beat. Thereafter, Stevens mostly did what he wanted.

One night after we had shared a few beers in our room, Bob showed me an old Stars & Stripes clipping he had saved. Below a six-column headline that read *No. 1 Jap Killer in the Pacific*, he was described as a fearless jungle fighter who had cheated death more than once, single-handedly killing scores of Japanese troops.

Stevens' war stories were fascinating and, at the same time, horrifyingly atrocious. His admissions of unspeakable acts he and other Americans committed during the insanity of battle remain vivid to this day. However, as years passed, I suspected they were embellished during that drinking session.

Stevens believed he was indestructible and attempted to prove it one night when he sat with a mess hall sergeant in his friend's room. A loaded revolver lay next to an opened bottle of whiskey and two half-filled glasses. Russian roulette? My God! I didn't know what to do. Somehow I persuaded Bob to give up the gun and helped him back to our room.

Some time thereafter, Stevens and his sergeant buddy visited a mutual friend one afternoon for a drinking party in the Santa Cruz Mountains. Why I accompanied them, I don't know.

When Bob climbed behind the wheel to head back to the post, I guess I didn't realize he was in no condition to drive. I realized it moments later. All three of us were nearly killed.

Pulling out of the driveway onto a narrow road, the car blew a tire and skidded onto a gravel shoulder. The front and rear wheels on the driver's side became slightly airborne, sending the car against some small trees growing just below the road. It finally stopped against a skinny one.

Seated between Stevens and his friend, I looked out the passenger-side window. The car was teetering against the trunk, threatening to slide off it and roll down the steep embankment.

I was afraid to move but knew we had to exit the car immediately.

In no hurry to escape, Stevens and his buddy merely sat there and laughed.

Finally, we eased out, phoned for a tow truck and inspected the damage, a few scratches and a small dent caused by the tree.

To my knowledge, Bob Stevens wasn't a religious man. I'm not sure he even believed in God.

I thanked the Lord for saving all three of our lives.

Chapter 5

The Girl Next Door

Beatrice Lamb, an attractive, extraordinary woman, wrote for a small newspaper in San Fernando. That impressed me when I stayed at her house for three months in 1947, even though I never envisioned a similar occupation, much less a professional writing career.

I admired Bea's independent lifestyle. Far ahead of her time, she raised three children on her own after two marriages ended early. Onalee Ayres and her older brother Don, two years apart, were teenagers when Bea remarried and gave birth to Charles Lamb, who became a multimillionaire real estate executive in the San Fernando Valley.

Extremely generous, Bea again offered me Don's room when I got my first three-day pass from the Army. Her son was away in the service, due home on leave soon. I had planned to visit my neighborhood buddies who lived within a few blocks of my old house. At least, that was my intention.

As I sat at Bea's piano tapping out *Elmer's Tune* with one finger on a late Friday afternoon, the prettiest girl I had ever seen walked into my life.

The lot next to Bea's house was vacant during the seven years I lived across the street. After I left the neighborhood, a two-bedroom tract house built on my childhood playground was

31

purchased by John West, a struggling, hard-working mechanic at Lockheed Aircraft. He and his wife Dorothy had four children— Mary, Don, Jack and Charlene, the oldest.

Carrying a few school books, Charlene had stopped on her way home from a nearby bus stop to show Bea's daughter Onalee her new black and gold senior sweater.

Onalee introduced us. Charlene smiled and we exchanged a few meaningless words. Then she acted as if I were invisible. I couldn't take my eyes off her.

Charlene West, encouraged to enter her high-school beauty pageant, was too shy.

Shapely, long-legged with dark hair and light, unblemished skin, Charlene surely would have been a top contestant for the San Fernando High School beauty pageant that night had Bea been able to persuade her to enter. She was too shy.

"Would you and Lee like to go?" Bea asked, referring to her daughter. "It should be fun. I'll drive you."

"Thanks," Charlene replied. "I can't. I just stopped in to show Onalee my sweater. I have to get home."

As she headed for the front door, I told her how pleased I was to have met her and suggested we might see each other over the weekend.

"I'm going steady," she said abruptly. "He's in the Air Force, away for awhile."

She was, of course, referring to Bea's son. Although Don and I had been friendly when growing up, we were not close. We once wrestled in the street during a violent argument. I also recalled being tossed from his frisky horse in his next-door lot. Suddenly, I considered him my rival.

The following morning, Bea and Onalee had plans that didn't include little Chucky, as Bea called her young son. He needed supervising for a few hours, she said, so I volunteered.

"Maybe you and Charlene could take him up to Hansen Dam," Bea suggested. "There's sort of a picnic area there. Chuck would like that. You could take my car. I won't need it."

"Do you think Charlene would go with me?" I asked. "She hardly said hello yesterday."

"That's because of Don," Bea replied with a smile. "I'll call her."

Not wanting to refuse Bea's request to baby-sit, Charlene reluctantly accompanied me to Hansen Dam. She remained aloof throughout the afternoon. But later that evening, I received a big surprise.

Thanks again to Bea, Charlene accepted my invitation to attend a movie in North Hollywood. It was our first real date.

"Remember," Bea reminded me when she again loaned me her car, "she's Don's girl."

I don't recall the movie we saw or what we talked about, but I'm certain there was little improvement in our frosty relationship.

It was several weeks later, I believe, when I finally got around to visiting my buddy Jewett Conradson, who worked for a swimming pool company.

It was a Saturday, and Jewett had to make a few leftover stops on his route.

"Why don't you come with me?" he suggested. "We can catch up on things."

Good idea. I had hitchhiked with a barracks buddy from Fort Ord the night before, got stuck in Santa Maria for 13 hours before getting a ride and was dead tired. I figured I could relax beside some pools while Jewett brushed them down.

The backyard at our first stop was beautifully landscaped, dominated by a large pool with several inviting lounge chairs on the decking. I stretched out on one.

"Hey," Jewett yelled minutes later, "wake up. I thought you were going to keep me company."

Right. I lifted my eyelids. We visited, sort of, for the next few hours.

Among other things, we talked about getting together for a beach party the next time I could get a pass.

"It'll be a couple's thing. I'll bring Evelyn. Maybe you could bring your new girlfriend."

"She's Don's girlfriend, Jewett. I told you that. Charlene won't give me the time of day."

"Don's gone. Ask her. Maybe she'll go."

I did. To my surprise, Charlene said she'd think about it.

Jewett, who helped me celebrate my retirement, and Clinton McElhenny, another neighborhood pal, resurfaced often during my career. I occasionally think about the early days when we and others in our group owned cars, shared girlfriends, joys and tragedies.

Mac and I drove four-cylinder Model A's.

Mine was jet black, a shiny 1930 jewel. Fifteen years old when I bought it, the car looked as if it had just rolled off the showroom floor after I lowered the frame and replaced the wheels with 1940 chrome hubcaps. The interior was impeccably redone with bright red leather seats, stitched by my grandmother Stella Hoover, padded paneling to match and a black-and-white enamel dash board.

Awesome, as young people like to say.

Mac was unconcerned about the appearance of his 1929 model. But its engine purred. He seemed to spend more time under it than behind the wheel.

Each morning before school, our group assembled at Jewett's house to talk about our cars, girls and plans for the weekend. Then we rumbled off, leaving barely enough time to make our first class.

Arriving at school, we would cruise past a cluster of girls in a low gear. A popping growl and puffs of black smoke from the chrome-plated exhaust pipes turned heads. Occasionally a flirtatious smile would make our day.

While racing one morning, Mac and I had a close call.

Traveling inches apart at maximum speeds—perhaps 60 miles an hour—our cars were taking up the whole road. Suddenly, I felt a severe thump and thought I was going to flip. My heart leaped as I fought for control and finally stopped.

Mac also stopped, jumped out and together we looked at what I considered a total wreck. I was angry. His car had hit a bump, bouncing a front wheel onto the passenger-side running board. The chassis was so lop-sided I couldn't drive it.

"You shouldn't have tried to pass me," I said. "I almost got killed. Look what you've done to my car."

"No problem. C'mon, grab hold."

We grabbed under the front and rear fenders, lifted and straightened the chassis. Model A's seemed indestructible.

"See, like new," Mac said as if nothing had happened.

When I got home that afternoon, I took a closer look. I couldn't find anything bent, but I was still angry. To this day, I think Mac believes I should have slowed to allow him to pass.

It wasn't long before both of us were under my car tinkering with something Mac thought might improve its performance. He was convinced he drove the faster vehicle. I always argued the point, but he probably was right.

Despite the running-board incident, I wouldn't say Mac and I were reckless drivers, nor was anyone in our group. We simply were typical teenagers. But sometimes accidents seem unavoidable. One involved Jewett.

When I arrived at his house one morning, I found him and Dick McCrillis in the driveway, grimly eyeing the front end of Jewett's Ford. The fender and grill were dented, the chrome stripping blood-stained.

About dusk the previous evening, Jewett's car had struck a man in his 50s who had been jaywalking across nearby Lankershim Boulevard—a wide, thoroughfare with few stoplights.

Jewett was behind the wheel, Dick beside him. Dick explained that a car in front of them had blocked their view of the pedestrian until it was too late. In an instant, it was over. Struck head on, the man died at the scene. Jewett was not cited after investigators determined the victim had been drinking.

Jewett never talked to me again about that horrible night, but I'm sure he has never forgotten it.

When a date was set for the beach party, I reminded Charlene she promised to give it some thought.

"Come on. It's just a bunch of my friends," I told her. "It'll be fun. Your mom said it would be okay."

"You asked my mother?"

"Well, I thought she might ... you know."

"She doesn't want me going with Don. She likes you a lot."

"Come on. I don't get down that often. Plan on it, okay?"

Thanks this time to *her* mother, Charlene consented. The party was at Zuma Beach near Malibu. Considered a special hideaway by our neighborhood gang, it was, that night at least, private. It also was cold, but with a roaring fire and heavy blankets to warm us, no one complained.

After that memorable night, I made trips from Fort Ord whenever I could get away. Charlene wasn't ready to drop Don Ayres entirely, but his absence and the fact her mother, all Irish and a strong Catholic, favored me continued to prove a big advantage.

I hitchhiked south at every opportunity, soon started sleeping on a front-room sofa at Charlene's house and took the Greyhound bus back. When I ran out of money, which was often, she bought the tickets.

Although I never forgot what Bea said—"Remember, she's Don's girl"—as time passed, I was convinced the girl next door didn't necessarily agree.

Chapter 6

A Timely Injury

Fullback Frank Cassara, my San Fernando High teammate who went on to play for the San Francisco 49ers in the National Football League, always performed at full throttle, even in practice.

During an afternoon scrimmage one day, I chased Frank, the ball carrier, as he rounded end near the dirt running track. He was coasting when I slammed into him. We collided at the edge of the grass, skidding onto the hard surface, Frank beneath me. It was one of the few times I ever stopped the hard-charging Casarra. It was a good feeling.

"What're you doin'?," the coach angrily yelled from the sideline, "tryin' to kill him?"

Casarra bounced up, unhurt, flashed a smile and jogged back onto the field. Despite his complimentary nod on the tackle, my "good feeling" immediately vanished.

My rapport with the coach didn't improve during league play when I made another colossal blunder. Barreling into a pile of players after the whistle had blown, I cost our team a critical penalty and was benched the rest of the game.

For months after the season ended, I harbored a deep resentment toward that coach. Had I played in one additional quarter, even a single play, I would have qualified for a letter.

Having come up short the two previous seasons, I had worked at a brickyard most of the summer to get in shape for my senior year. After another near miss, I avoided certain classmates and felt like an outsider.

Especially discomforting was when my friends wore their prestigious Lettermen's Club sweaters to class. Dick McCrillis, Dave Zollinger and Clint McElhenny, a high-energy dynamo and smallest player on the squad, lettered in football. Jewett won a letter in tennis.

I got through all of that, graduated and left those memories behind.

When I started college in a new environment with new friends, I signed up for a junior varsity team.

The squad, for the most part, was a cast of uncommitted misfits, coached by a graduate student younger than some players. A few overweight service veterans seemed to train on beer.

Again, I saw little action, but at least made the traveling squad and had opportunities. Much of that season is a blur, but a few lowlights linger.

Playing some JC team on the road at night in a hard rain, our rag-tag squad had a chance to pull out a victory as time was expiring.

"Hawn," the coach barked. "Get in there for Jordan. Hurry up."

I was so excited, I raced onto the field without my helmet, sent Jordan to the sideline and joined the huddle during a time out. The play choice was obvious. We needed a short field goal to win.

Oops! There was a problem. I had just sent Jordan, our regular place kicker, off the field.

"It's a chip shot," I told the quarterback. "I can make it."

At last, a chance for redemption. A chance to be a hero. I had never even *practiced* field goals, but how difficult could this one be?

Apparently, the officials didn't immediately notice I was bareheaded as I lined up behind the holder. Before a whistle was blown, the ball skidded off the side of my foot, missing the uprights badly.

Cited for not wearing a helmet, I caused our team a penalty

and was recalled to the bench. A longer field goal attempt, probably by Jordan, also failed, resulting in another disheartening defeat.

Our opponent in the season finale was the Santa Maria American Veterans, a winless team we thought we could beat even though we, too, were winless.

It was a night game in Santa Maria, where a former girlfriend lived. I hadn't seen or spoken to Trish since high school and hoped she might attend the game. Surprised to hear from me when I phoned a week earlier, she said she would try to be there.

As the game progressed, I kept looking for Trish in the stands. When it ended, my uniform as spotless as when our team took the field, I assumed she hadn't come and was glad. It was embarrassing enough sitting on the bench the entire game in front of strangers.

As our team headed toward the dressing room, I heard someone call me. Leaning over a chain-link fence about 20 yards away, Trish was waving, trying to get my attention.

"Jack," she yelled repeatedly, "over here."

I spotted her, smiled a forced smile and approached.

"Hi, Trish. Great you could make it," I lied.

Whatever was said, the conversation had nothing to do with the football game or the fact I didn't play in it.

Fortunately, there wasn't much time to talk before boarding a bus back to Santa Barbara. She seemed disappointed; I wasn't. We said our goodbyes and met only one other time about two years later.

The outcome of that season finale was another disappointment. It ended in a tie, once described by a famous coach as something "like kissing your sister."

This "kiss" was more like a peck on the cheek. It was a *scoreless* tie.

I was happy the season was behind me and I could forget about football. It hadn't been my long suit, I guess. So when I joined the Army and learned the Fort Ord team was holding try-outs, why did I show up that first day of practice?

Maybe I had something to prove. Maybe it was another impetuous decision, like when I signed those enlistment papers. I honestly don't know.

The fact is, I found myself competing against a horde of other hopefuls. After several sessions of being ignored by the coaching staff, I arrived wearing a white tee shirt over my pads and jersey. Spread across the front and back were four giant letters— H A W N.

Professionally labeled by my friend, Panorama staff artist Wylie Nielsen, the garish lettering worked. The head coach turned to a cluster of linemen on the sideline, scanned unfamiliar faces, then focused on my shirt.

"Hawn," he shouted, "get in there."

Helmet in hand, I hustled onto the field, pointed at the right guard who had been knocked on his butt in the previous play and thumbed him off. I was ready. On two successive plays, I bolted through the line and dropped the ball carrier for a loss. Like in high school, when I tackled Frank Cassara, it was a good feeling.

But that jolt of adrenaline was fleeting. A few plays later, while chasing a spurting back, I came up short and hit the ground hard, on my belly. Finished for the afternoon, I never returned to practice.

For days, I suffered abdominal pains that became excruciating. After a sleepless night, I told Bob Stevens, my roommate, maybe I should report on sick call. He told me to get dressed.

"You're going to the hospital, kid," he said as we pulled out of a parking space in a press Jeep and sped down the hill.

There were military procedures to go on sick call, and I reminded Bob that GIs simply don't take off for the hospital when they get a bellyache.

"Bellyache my ass. You can't even button your pants."

I didn't argue.

Arriving at the admissions desk, we faced an unsmiling female civilian who asked Bob a lot of questions, got no answers she liked, handed him forms to fill out and told us to be seated.

Stevens erupted.

"Can't you see this kid can hardly stand up?" he barked. "The forms can wait. Get a doctor."

Those words, I'm sure, are a mild version of what Bob actually told the shocked young woman. I have no recollection of what transpired after that until I awoke hours later in a recovery room.

"How do you feel?" a bird colonel asked me. "We nearly lost you. Your appendix burst. Your abdomen looked like a bowl of jelly...."

The colonel and two other Army surgeons, a major and captain, had saved my life, but recovery was a long way off. Two subsequent operations resulting from poison that had spread through my system kept me hospitalized for two months.

Time passed slowly and uneventfully with few visitors and little news from PIO. Bob visited early on, then stopped coming. I thought I was forgotten.

While I dozed early one morning, in walked Charlene, Mac and Dave Zollinger, another longtime buddy. Was I dreaming? What a surprise!

"Hi, honey," Charlene said with a bright smile as she leaned over to kiss me. "How are you feeling?"

If Don Ayres was still in the picture then, his image had faded considerably. I was floating on a cloud and couldn't wait to spend my next free weekend in L.A. with the girl I expected to marry. They had driven all night to spend maybe an hour at my bedside before immediately heading back to Southern California, another eight-hour trip.

My second surprise came when the Fort Ord football coach and his assistant showed up shortly before I was discharged from the hospital. With the season nearly over, they were desperate to fill vacancies created by players who had been transferred, some to Korea.

"How ya doing?" the coach asked. "How long before you're out of here? We need you."

Need *me*? I was surprised he remembered my name, but I guess that T-shirt left a lasting impression. Their offer boosted my morale, but I knew my football days were gone. I thanked them for coming and wished the team luck. They wished me well and left.

Out of the hospital, I reported to my company as ordered, expecting to immediately head up the hill to my old room and resume my PIO job.

"You're not going anywhere," the first sergeant said. "Things in PIO have changed, and so have your living quarters. Forget that BOQ on the hill. You're staying right here. Report to Barracks

41

C, grab a bunk and get settled. Here's a copy of your reassignment."

Stunned? Shocked? Words can't describe my reaction. It was back to formations, the mess hall, soldiering, maybe even kitchen police duty, heaven forbid. Private rooms, perks, press vehicles and Class A passes were gone. So was Colonel Flemings, along with most of his PIO staff, including Pete Schwartz and Sergeant Bob Stevens.

A manpower commission from the Department of the Army in Washington had been looking into the colonel's excessive expenditures and staff buildup for some time. Finally, the axe fell.

The entire PIO operation was downsized. A captain headed a drastically reduced staff at a smaller office. I was ordered to report to him the next day.

The draft, in effect for a couple of years, was drawing many prominent and professional people into the service, replacing the less qualified for combat duty. Thousands of young men from Fort Ord were leaving on a regular basis. Reportedly, 90 percent of the United Nations forces in Korea were composed of Americans.

When I arrived to begin a regular eight-hour shift (or thereabouts), I was greeted by the captain and introduced to his staff.

Among my new co-workers was Ben Svere, who had been with the Associated Press. Don Bedard was a high school English teacher, and Jimmy Dodd had written for the Baylor University newspaper.

Svere, a wiry nervous type who could pound out stories quickly and accurately, clearly was the best writer in the office. Bedard, likeable and easy-going, also was well-placed, as was Dodd, an outgoing energetic sports editor.

I never saw Bob again or others I had worked with and never learned their fates even though I inquired. Corporal Jim McKinley had survived the purge and remained vital to the organization.

"They were reassigned," Mac said, "probably transferred to other posts. Lucky you weren't carried on the active duty roster. You might've gone with them."

I thanked God for the timeliness of that hospitalization.

My new co-workers made me feel welcome, if not secure. At the outset of my new assignment, I felt vulnerable.

I also thought about my girlfriend. What if I were shipped overseas? Would she wait for me?

It wasn't long after I left the hospital when I proposed. Well, sort of.

It may have been a moon-lit night, maybe not. It was late, certainly not romantic, not sitting on a slab of cold cement on Charlene's front porch.

"Honey," I said, "you know how I feel about you. I've still got about two years before I get out. I could be shipped anywhere. Tell me, will you wait for me?"

That was the gist of it. No bended knee. No gushy words. No ring. Not even a real commitment. That, I decided, would come later.

"Yes," she replied. And we kissed. That seemed to clench it. Don Ayres was out; I was in.

Having "locked in" my future, I relaxed to some extent.

My ability to sniff out weird stories and follow them up with interesting Panorama articles kept the captain off my back and gave me a little breathing room.

As time passed, my writing skills improved and more of my stories were appearing on Page 1. When I was promoted to corporal, I no longer worried about an overseas transfer.

TIRED OF hitching rides to Southern California to be with Charlene, I had saved enough money for a down payment on an old Buick convertible. It ran well despite a rusted exhaust pipe that needed replacing.

Bedard, who lived in Orange County, often accompanied me on weekend trips, along with two or three recruits, who helped pay expenses.

Like many teachers, Don was conservative, certainly not a risk-taker. He expressed concern about a hole in the rusted tail pipe that emitted exhaust near the gas tank.

"Don't worry about it," I told him. "It's not that close to the tank. Besides, it doesn't get that hot."

Don worried.

As we headed south on a Friday afternoon under a blazing mid-summer sun, I was at the wheel. Don sat in front, three recruits in back, all sleeping soundly.

Drowsy from the monotonous hum of the engine and boring scenery, I fought sleep when, somewhere near Paso Robles, it happened.

Boom! I was sure the gas tank had exploded.

Jolted awake, my passengers screamed as I hit the brakes, sending the car skidding off the highway to a stop. The explosion, I thought, should have killed all of us. Incredibly, not only were we unhurt, the car was intact.

Exiting the vehicle, we expected to see at the very least a ruptured tank. Instead, a rear tire had exploded, probably overheated by the escaping exhaust.

"Just the tire, Don," I said with a shrug. "I told you not to worry."

DURING MORE than two years of weekend travel between Fort Ord and Southern California, my most frightening experience occurred about 2 a.m. one Monday. I was returning to the post after two days with little sleep.

Sticking my head out the window to remain alert, I suddenly saw a pair of headlights approaching fast on a narrow two-way road—in my lane. I braked, but the lights kept racing toward me.

Panic-stricken, at the last second I swerved onto the right shoulder just as the oncoming car whizzed past and kept going.

Later, I found a small, barely visible streak of paint along the left side of my car. I shuddered to think how close I had come to a head-on collision.

Whew!

Chapter 7

Back to School

A few weeks before Thanksgiving of 1950, the captain sent me to the Armed Forces Information School at Carlisle, Pennsylvania, to attend a six-week journalism course.

American Indian Jim Thorpe made the school famous half a century earlier with his athletic prowess in football, baseball and track and field. Playing for the Carlisle Indians, Thorpe led the team to exciting victories over major university squads and became an All-American.

Surrounded by a sprawling college-like campus near Harrisburg, the school bore no resemblance to a military installation. It provided high-level training for officers and enlisted personnel from every branch of the service, taught by senior officers, including generals and admirals.

The curriculum for professional journalism and photography merely skimmed the surfaces. I considered the school a waste of taxpayers' money.

On the plus side, being on the East Coast for the first time as a 20-year-old, this temporary "duty" came with no formations or responsibilities other than attending my classes. Ultimately I made friends with several enlisted men, including Johnny O'Brien, a fun-loving Army private from Brooklyn who had a car.

During six weekends, we visited Johnny's mother and aunt,

New York's Empire State building, the nation's Capitol, Gettysburg and other historic sites. Mostly, we ran wild and tried to avoid serious trouble.

The night before Thanksgiving, Johnny and I—in uniform—sat drinking beer at a Baltimore bar feeling depressed. Short on money and with no holiday plans, we were considering our next move when a friendly, nicely dressed man in his 40s appeared.

"Hi, fellas," he said with a pleasant smile. "Mind if I join you?"

He introduced himself as George P. Grow, a chef at an upscale Baltimore restaurant, bought us a beer and after a bit of small talk asked where we would be spending the holiday.

"I have a place not far from here, near the (Annapolis) naval academy," he said. "I'm going to have a few friends for dinner tomorrow. Would you like to join us? You could stay at the cabin tonight. There's plenty of room."

It was an offer we didn't think about twice.

"Sounds great," we said in unison.

Finishing our beers, we followed George in Johnny's car for about 30 miles before turning off the highway onto a winding dirt road to his spacious cabin nestled among trees.

Nice. Not what we had envisioned. What we also didn't expect was, in retrospect, obvious. We had been lured into a den of iniquity.

George's two gay friends arrived and before long made a few gestures. In a flash, Johnny and I exited to a bedroom, locked the door, and spent the night alone.

The following morning, we emerged from our room. We found a glowing fireplace, fresh-brewed coffee and George in the process of placing a large turkey into the oven. He and his two friends greeted us warmly.

"Good morning," our host said. "You boys must have been pretty tired. We've been up for a few hours."

It was as if nothing had occurred the night before. We spent a pleasant day sipping cocktails and munching on snacks while the gourmet chef prepared the most delicious Thanksgiving feast I've ever eaten.

George's friends left that evening. Johnny and I stayed, got up early, ate breakfast and thanked our host for a memorable Thanksgiving.

"I have to get going," the chef told us, "but you're welcome to stay as long as you want. Help yourselves to the leftovers and liquor. Just be sure to lock up when you leave."

Fantastic.

Hours later, stuffed with more turkey and dressing, we headed back to Carlisle, about 125 miles.

As we rounded a bend in some rural area, the tires slipped on a patch of ice. Our car ended up in a ditch, in front of a farmhouse.

What occurred immediately thereafter has been blurred by time. What I do recall is that we were unhurt, accused by the farmer of nearly hitting his dog and reported to Carlisle Barracks so late we missed several morning classes.

Technically we were AWOL. Worried at first, our fears gradually diminished when it became clear we weren't missed.

Unbelievable! This was the Army?

Those six weeks on the East Coast ended just before Christmas of 1950. When I reported back to Fort Ord to start the New Year, I was refreshed, eager to resume work.

First on my agenda was the weirdest discovery I had come across since joining PIO. Private Floyd O. Humeston's story was an absolute gem.

I received a tip that a company mess sergeant in the 6th Quartermaster Food Service (cook's) School was feeding a lion locked in a van parked near a barracks which housed inductees.

I don't know if the lion roared at night or if the mess hall suddenly came up short of meat for the troops, but the word was out and spreading fast. I called the company commander and made an appointment for an interview.

When Humeston turned 7, his grandfather gave the boy an unusual birthday present—a lion. It was the first of seven he acquired over the years, along with an alligator, falcon and boa constrictor.

Fearless Fagan, as the cat became known, was no ordinary lion, his master no ordinary trainer.

When drafted into the Army at age 24, Humeston sold six of his big cats but couldn't part with Fagan, having raised him as a cub. He had brushed the animal's teeth. He combed his hair daily and shared milk with him from the same bottle. Humeston also taught him a commercially profitable wrestling act and mastered a communication of gibberish that Fagan seemed to understand. On cold evenings, they slept together in a trailer, where Humeston and his mother lived.

Floyd and Fagan, Fort Ord's new arrivals, quickly made headlines, including the one on the front page of the Panorama. The Army, meanwhile, faced a dilemma. A search of regulations and Department of Army circulars failed to disclose authorization for quarters and rations for a dependent lion.

Pressured to solve the problem, a warrant officer ultimately granted Humeston a 14-day furlough to make living arrangements for his pet.

He visited circuses and zoos in search of a good home without success. Finally, the Humane Society of Monterey, only seven miles from Ord, agreed to take Fagan.

Humeston, of course, was overjoyed.

I can't swear to it, but I'm fairly sure the Monterey Peninsula Herald picked up my Panorama story and the wire services circulated it nationally. On Feb. 12, 1951, Life Magazine published a centerfold photographic layout.

One full-page shot showed Humeston in bed with his arm around Fagan, both covered by a spread (except for the animal's paws and their heads). Both appear sound asleep. Seven additional photos on the opposite page include one of Floyd taking his cat for a stroll on the beach.

The text is titled "Fearless Fagan Finds a Home."

I wish Pete Schwartz had been there with his camera. Who knows what he would've come up with?

Chapter 8

Marriage and Separation

As my three-year enlistment was drawing to a close, the Army decided not to let me and millions of others go so soon. Because the Korean War was escalating, my term of duty was extended one year. We set the wedding date.

So, there we were at the altar—Saturday morning, June 2, 1951.

As an Army corporal, I wasn't financially prepared to support a wife. But with a little money Charlene had saved working at Prudential Insurance Company in Beverly Hills following her graduation, and the Army allowance for a dependent, we decided a two-year engagement was long enough.

The ceremony at Our Lady of the Holy Rosary Catholic Church in Sun Valley, California, began at 9 a.m. It was much too early for Charlene to prepare for the most important day of her life. But whatever it took, she accomplished it with minutes to spare. Not many, as I recall.

She looked gorgeous in a white satin gown with a long flowing train, her veil held in place by a crown of seed pearls.

We began cutting expenses immediately. Among guests was a PIO photographer from Fort Ord who provided his services as a wedding gift. Included is his photo of Don Ayres, taken randomly with others.

Mr. & Mrs. Hawn, who vowed at the altar to share their lives together, start by sharing a knife.

Neatly attired in a sports coat and slacks, a stylish pipe clenched between his teeth, Charlene's former boyfriend is bent over the rear bumper of my 1940 Plymouth coupe. He is tying on a string of tin cans below a sign that reads "Jest" "Merried."

Charlene's ex-boyfriend Don Ayres ties one on.

I can describe that photo precisely, because it remains prominent in our Wedding Book. I wish I had been present when my PIO buddy snapped the shot. I might have pointed out the misspelled words to Don. Then again, probably not. It was thoughtful of Don to make the sign.

From left, church ushers Dick McCrillis and Jewett Conradson, Jack and his best man, brother-in-law Dave Walton.

When pondering a choice for my best man, I was torn between lifelong friends and my brother-in-law, Dave Walton.

I barely knew Dave, a sergeant assigned to Special Orders at Fort Ord. He called PIO one day, said he knew me and wondered if we might meet for a few beers at the NCO club.

Seated after the obligatory introductions, I was surprised to learn Dave was born and raised in Ventura, only a few miles from Oak View. More surprising was that he had been dating my sister for some time. That was for openers.

"What would you think about Bonnie and me getting married?" Dave asked.

Married? I couldn't believe he asked that question. I was speechless.

"Well," I finally stammered, "I think she's pretty young to get

51

married. She's only 16."

"I know she's young, but she's not a kid. Bonnie's been on her own for a few years. We love each other."

"I think you should wait, Dave. She's..."

Suddenly, a bombshell!

"We're already married," he interrupted. "We got married in Vegas two weeks ago."

My eyes bulged and my jaw must have dropped two inches. I didn't know how to respond.

"You're the first one I've told," he added.

According to Bonnie, she and Dave were married Sept. 8, 1950, "by a one-armed, intoxicated judge who performed our wedding with two of his staff that had to help David as he was very nervous."

She said she listed her age on the marriage license as 19, "and there were no questions. I always looked older than my age."

What could I do but accept it? I wasn't happy, but I liked Bonnie's choice for a husband. Bright, ambitious and straight-forward, Dave and I hit it off immediately.

As best man at our beautiful, well-organized wedding, I suspect he had regrets about his.

Charlene's parents and little sister Mary, left, join Jack's father and mother in the reception line.

A marvelous garden reception at the Burbank home of my aunt and uncle, Jack and Maurine Lewis, lasted longer than Charlene and I anticipated. It was late afternoon before we arrived at the luxurious blue-roofed Miramar Resort in Montecito, just south of Santa Barbara, to begin our honeymoon.

After a quick dinner and nothing more to drink, we retired to our spacious room. Charlene relied on me to make her first night as a married woman wonderful and memorable. Regrettably, it fell short of her expectations.

The next morning we attended early Mass at the historic Santa Barbara Mission and ate breakfast at a sidewalk café. We checked out of the Miramar without enjoying any of the amenities and drove north to Pismo Beach.

Day Two was more relaxing—unfortunately. Lying on a sandy beach in front of our motel, Charlene suffered severe sunburn and was virtually untouchable for the rest of our honeymoon.

Bummer!

As we traveled north, we took in a few tourist attractions, enjoyed some good meals and made the best of an unfortunate beginning. Arriving in San Francisco, we peeked inside the majestic Fairmont Hotel and decided we could afford at least one cocktail. We sat at the bar and pretended we were registered guests.

A friendly bartender congratulated us. I asked about dinner at the hotel, merely to make conversation. He recommended instead a trendy more affordable steakhouse nearby.

"Don't tell anyone I'm taking you out of the hotel," he said with a smile. "It's not far. Grab a cab and tell the driver to take you to Le Boeff."

For us, it was a special dining experience, a San Francisco highlight.

After free spending up the coast of California, it was Motel 6 and peanut butter sandwiches on the way back.

Having survived our honeymoon, I returned to Fort Ord and prepared to settle in for a happy summer on the beautiful Monterey Peninsula with my bride. It started well with an unexpected wedding gift from the Army. While on leave, I had been promoted to sergeant with a sizeable pay boost.

We moved into a comfortable, reasonably priced apartment in Seaside, a suburb of Monterey. It was directly across the street from Bonnie and Dave, who had rented the apartment for us when it became available.

After settling in, the four of us got together almost nightly. For six weeks, our social lives consisted almost entirely of pinochle games, which became intense at times.

Bonnie had given recent birth to her first of four girls. As my sister focused on the cards, she unconsciously rolled Kathy— sleeping in a bassinet with wheels under the table—back and forth with her foot. The distraction not only annoyed the three of us but sometimes resulted in Bonnie making a poor play.

Dave, an expert card player and fierce competitor, restrained himself to a point. More than a few games ended prematurely in heated arguments.

When it became clear Charlene was pregnant, not only did our card games end but also my tour at Fort Ord. Our lives were about to undergo drastic changes, starting with my voluntary transfer to a heavy-armored training camp near Barstow, California, that had just been reactivated.

"You'll be the ranking non-com in a new PIO office, working with a lieutenant," the captain told me. "You should make tech sergeant in no time. It's a great opportunity."

After three years at Ord, I was ready for a change and enticed by the captain's words, especially the possibility of a quick promotion. With a baby coming, we needed the extra money.

Charlene loved the peninsula, particularly the romantic Highlands Inn nestled in the towering pines above Carmel. We never stayed as guests, but the view from the balcony was spectacular.

Neither of us was anxious to leave, not knowing what to expect. But I concluded the longer I remained at Ord, chances of shipping out increased. It seemed unlikely the Army would send me overseas from Camp Irwin with so little time remaining on my enlistment. Also, setting up a PIO office was appealing.

The paper work didn't take long before we said goodbye to the beautiful peninsula with its rock cliffs, crashing waves and breath-taking scenery to travel to Barstow, our destination.

As I drove into that dusty desert town on a blistering August afternoon, my car radiator was boiling over. The trunk was loaded with wedding gifts, everything we owned. Charlene was nauseous, a puppy we had acquired a few weeks earlier was vomiting and most motels wouldn't accept pets.

Eventually I found a room so tiny we had to step over the bed to enter and leave. Sadly—a blessing, nonetheless—the puppy ran away.

The most serious issue we faced was lack of money. Because of a delay in processing a change in my payroll status, I wasn't receiving a dependency allotment, promised for weeks.

Now that our pet was gone, we qualified for a better motel, which required a deposit. Short only a few dollars, I decided to try my luck at poker up the street, where games were legal.

"You won't win," Charlene warned me. "You'll just make things worse."

"It's no big deal, honey," I replied. "If I win a few bucks we can check out of this dump. If I don't, we'll stay a little longer. I'll be getting paid soon."

At 21, I had never played poker in a professional game, but remember feeling confident as I took a seat in the back room of that Barstow bar, my young bride back in the sleazy motel, probably shedding tears.

Playing with older men, I managed to rake in a few small pots before being dealt a potential full house. When I hit, I tried to conceal my excitement, but my heart must have thumped like a beating drum. I was certain I had the winning hand.

After my final raise left me without any chips, a bearded old-timer who had been drinking heavily called. The pot was huge. I couldn't wait to rake it in, cash out and hurry back to Charlene and toss a fist full of bills on her bed.

I spread out my hand, revealing the full house, and reached for the pot.

"Hold it, soldier," the beard said. "Your cards don't beat these."

With that, he turned over four aces.

WEEKS PASSED before Charlene and I found a decent place to live—a new two-bedroom house we rented in a remote area several miles from Barstow. There were no stores or neighbors nearby, but plenty of wild life, including tiny lizards that occasionally found their way inside and slithered across the slab floor.

Charlene's "morning" sickness never left her. With no appetite and unable to retain food, she was becoming weak. Besides the oppressive heat and limited cooling from an electric fan, her days were long, lonely and uneventful. Occasionally on a weekend, we would attend a drive-in movie, her only times outside the house.

Our marriage had been on a downward spiral almost from the beginning, and I wondered if she privately questioned her decision to share her life with me.

Although relatively new, the house wasn't completely finished, furnished with only bare essentials.

When I arrived home from camp one late afternoon, I found a trail of stains on the floor from the kitchen to the living-room couch, where Charlene had been lying most of the day. Half a cup of cold tea was nearby.

The next morning I drove her to a hospital, where she was fed intravenously for several days before being discharged. Fearing a miscarriage, I drove her to her parents' home in Sun Valley, about a three-hour trip, and returned to Barstow alone.

We hadn't been married three months, and already we were separated—for how long, I didn't know.

I was alone, depressed and worried.

Chapter 9

Camp Irwin

If I hadn't realized my dreadful mistake when first rolling into Barstow, I was certain of it after driving 37 ½ miles northwest into the sun-baked desert to begin my new duties. Being ordered to Camp Irwin was one thing; volunteering for the assignment was the worst blunder I had made since donning a uniform. I couldn't blame God for that one.

My first glimpse of the tents, grungy GIs in plastic helmets, fatigues and combat boots, dirt roads and clouds of dust made me think about the cool, misty mornings, ocean breezes and that cozy Seaside apartment we had left behind.

The camp has a history dating back centuries, when Indians of the Lake Mojave period were believed to have lived in the area. In 1942, the Mojave Anti-Aircraft Range was renamed Camp Irwin in honor of Major General George LeRoy Irwin. Two years later it was deactivated and placed on surplus status.

The 673,000-acre camp was reopened in 1951 as an armored combat training site. Troops from regimental tank companies of the United States 43rd Infantry Division from Camp Pickett, Va., were the first to train at the facility.

The Public Information Office headed by First Lieutenant Milton Rosner—a reserve officer—was small, sparsely furnished with typewriters, a few desks and slat wood floors.

A successful Hollywood literary agent in civilian life, Rosner was well-placed by the Army and liked the challenge of his assignment with little or no interference from senior officers.

We got along well, but the lieutenant made it clear we were not buddies nor were any other enlisted men. He went by the book.

"Walk on the other side of me, sergeant," he once said as we strolled along discussing something.

He explained that in years past, enlisted men were required to walk next to the street when accompanying officers, should horses or carriage wheels splash mud on the boardwalks.

The lieutenant's uniform was always pressed and spotless, his silver bars glittering. Rosner maintained a sharp demeanor as well and ran the office efficiently, allowing me considerable freedom.

I reported directly to him each day, stood no formations and was not required to perform any duties unrelated to the dissemination of camp news, mostly to the local media.

Sergeant Frank Steele, a photographer, and I frequently wheeled around together in a Jeep, taking photos and gathering information for stories. Often in late afternoons we would cool off with a beer at the NCO club, killing time before I headed back to Barstow as early as possible.

The most familiar face at Camp Irwin was that of Private Richard Long, a good-looking young actor who had been drafted and assigned to PIO following basic training.

Entering films straight out of high school, Long—under contract to Universal Pictures—played juvenile leads in many studio productions. Among them was a recurring role as the son in *The Adventures of Ma and Pa Kettle*—a series in the late 1940s that starred Marjorie Main and Percy Kilbride. Long made his movie debut as Claudette Colbert's son in *Tomorrow Is Forever* in 1946 at age 18.

Despite his movies, many GIs who had seen Long's films couldn't place him. A typical conversation was one I overheard at the PX, where the actor was stopped by a soldier who seemed to recognize him.

"I know I've seen you somewhere," he said, suggesting various places where they might have met.

"No, I was never there," Long replied. "No, not there either."

Eventually the puzzled GI went away shaking his head.

Dick—as I soon began calling him—enjoyed playing his little game. It wasn't that he was modest; he wasn't. In fact, he had a rather haughty attitude, particularly around Rosner. They clashed from the outset.

On one occasion, the lieutenant ordered Long to extinguish a cigarette he was puffing and get busy as he sat idly in front of a typewriter. Wordlessly, Dick slowly took a final drag, inhaled, then defiantly flipped the butt onto the floor at Rosner's feet.

"Pick that up, private," the lieutenant said, "you're not on a movie set."

Long glowered at the officer, said nothing.

"I'm ordering you to pick that up!"

Again, no response.

"Sergeant," Rosner said, looking at me, "make him pick that up."

Eyeing Long's stony face, I was certain the smoldering butt would become a pile of ashes before the actor would bend over to retrieve it. The lieutenant probably knew it as well and had passed the buck to me. What was I going to do, call the MPs? I wished there had been a corporal in the office.

"Dick," I finally said with a disarming smile, attempting to shrug off the silly stalemate, "pick up the damn cigarette."

By then, we had become friends, but when he didn't make a move, I casually walked over, picked up the butt and crushed it in an ashtray.

"Now get going on that press release, Dick. I wanna get out of here."

I wasn't happy the way that ended. But the lieutenant was satisfied. It took him off the hook. Dick cracked a thin smile. He saved face, too. In the long run, it cemented our relationship.

BY OCTOBER, the desert was livable—pleasant days, chilly nights.

Besides the oceanic beauty of my former post, I missed the excitement Fort Ord offered, with its in-and-out flow of recruits with interesting backgrounds, their weird hobbies and friends I had left behind —unlike the day-to-day drudgery of grinding out routine news releases at Camp Irwin.

Typical was a two-column six-inch news story published in the weekly Barstow Printer Review bearing the headline "Tankmen Begin Second Training Cycle at Camp Irwin This Week."

The article probably impressed Army brass—including the camp commander, Colonel Maurice E. Kaiser of Sacramento—but made for dull reading otherwise.

One day a staff car pulled up outside PIO headquarters. The visit by the general officer was expected and Rosner was well prepared.

Press releases and photos, published news clippings of articles emanating from our office and other eye-catching displays were laid out like a school classroom's open house. The lieutenant had given us a dress rehearsal, the inspection went well and Rosner received high marks for a well-run Public Information Office.

I had a moment to chat with the general's driver, a corporal who recognized me from basic training.

"We were in the same company," he recalled, telling me his name. "What happened to you after basic?"

I told him how I had fallen into the PIO job and how the Army had opened the door for me to pursue a career in journalism.

I couldn't place him. I suppose he remembered me because I had been chosen to assist the first sergeant for some menial Orderly Room tasks despite my limited typing skills.

I had taken a class in high school. Practically rubbing shoulders with Barbara Hartman, a rosy-cheeked well-developed brunette who favored tight-fitting sweaters, I managed no better than a D on my report card. I suspect Barbara got an A, judging from her disinterest in me.

I learned to type reasonably well taking that Army course, but that class also had its distractions. I was assigned a bunk bed next to a young musician who said he had played piano in a small band. Taking our 10-minute smoking breaks together outside the classroom, we struck up an immediate friendship.

I soon discovered he smoked marijuana. One Sunday afternoon in the barracks, my friend produced a small recorder, placed a record of *Gloomy Sunday* on the turntable and lit up a marijuana cigarette. As Billie Holiday sang about the death of a lover, my bunk mate inhaled the weed, swaying moodily to the depressing lyrics.

"I gotta pick up a fresh supply in Monterey tonight," he said. "Want to come?"

Anticipating an adventure, I accompanied him to a rundown pool hall in a seedy section of town. Upon entering, I saw a lot of black eyes focusing on us, no Caucasions. After a few minutes, I was anxious to leave.

"He'll be here," my friend assured me, referring to his contact. "Let's play a game while we're waiting."

Besides poker, my dad had given me pool lessons.

As a teenager on the farm, my father would work all week for a quarter to spend in town on a Saturday night. I don't know how far a quarter went in those days, but it staked him to a few games of pool and soon he was winning money.

It seemed my buddy's contact would not be coming, but I was enjoying the game and didn't mind playing another.

Having seen dad bounce the end of a cue stick on the floor to summon an attendant to rack the balls, I did the same. Heads turned, but no one moved. I decided to use the men's room.

As I opened a door and entered a semi-dark hallway that led to the facility, I noted a giant black man lying motionless on a long table, his eyes shut.

Drunk? Dead? I didn't know or care, but upon returning, told my friend I would wait for him outside. Instead, we left together.

As we walked along the dark, deserted street, the delivery man appeared. He apologized for being late and the exchange was made—a sealed package costing $8.

When we arrived at our barracks, my friend was eager to light up and, perhaps, spin Billie Holiday's classic recording again. He opened the package, eyed it suspiciously, then sniffed the green weed.

"Alfalfa!" he exploded. "That bastard sold me alfalfa."

The general's driver laughed as we continued to chat beside the staff car parked in front of the PIO office.

"What happened to *you* after basic?" I wondered.

"Straight to Korea. Got these two fingers blown off right away," he said holding up the stubs. "They sent me back for reassignment. I've been bouncing around ever since, doing all kinds of stuff. Been driving for the general the last few months. Can't wait to get out."

"Yeah," I replied. "Me, too."

What else could I say? Eyeing those two stubs, I felt privileged but downplayed my good fortune. I know he must have been thinking that some people have all the luck. Was my chance meeting with Colonel Flemings on that bus a matter of luck? I don't think so.

A few days later, as I walked past open tents heading somewhere, I saw groups of GIs inside clustered around radios, all tuned to the same station. An announcer was reporting play-by-play action of a baseball game at the Polo Grounds in New York. It was as if his voice were booming over a loud speaker.

Suddenly, thunderous cheers burst from the tents along with an undercurrent of groans. The reactions came from—as later labeled—"the shot heard 'round the world." The date was Oct. 3, 1951.

I played most major sports in my youth and still followed college football closely but was not a baseball fan. I thought the season was too long and I had not developed an allegiance to any major league team. What's more, Charlene had no interest in sports of any kind.

So, I was not bent over a radio like millions of others around the country when outfielder Bobby Thompson slugged his famous home run off Brooklyn Dodgers pitcher Ralph Branca to give New York the National League pennant in the third game of a playoff series. The Giants' 5-4 victory that clinched a berth in the World Series is considered by most fans one of baseball's most dramatic games.

Although curious about the commotion, I wasn't particularly interested and, of course, didn't have a clue that reporting sports would become my profession.

I WAS thrilled to have Charlene back, looking much healthier than when she left to stay with her parents a week earlier. Her appetite had improved, but at five months, her pregnancy still was not obvious. Her doctor monitored her closely to guard against a setback. And I kept looking for a place to live closer to the camp. Charlene hated that rented house in the boondocks.

We soon found a perfect solution—a small house trailer.

Purchased for almost no money down and manageable

monthly payments, we hooked up to utilities in a crowded Barstow RV lot. Charlene, I thought, could get acquainted there and not be so lonely while I was at camp.

My enlistment was winding down. Only about eight months to go. We could handle that. Then, what we never saw coming, hit us between the eyes. A bombshell.

A month before Thanksgiving I received overseas orders.

Chapter 10

A Ticking Clock

Camp Stoneman, a Pittsburgh, California, port north of San Francisco, was a temporary stop for soldiers ordered overseas. I arrived in early December, 1951.

I immediately requested a deferment based on Charlene's complicated pregnancy and was transferred to a holding company to await the Army's decision.

Charlene, meanwhile, had gone to stay temporarily with my parents. She had found a doctor at a U.S. Navy medical facility about 25 miles from Oak View. That meant she had to drive, and I'd only given her a few lessons.

In one of her letters, she wrote that a friend of my parents drove her to the Department of Motor Vehicles. I had to laugh about how she described her test. The dialog with the young instructor probably went something like this:

"My husband's in the Army, at Camp Stoneman. He may be going overseas soon. I need to drive to Oxnard for my doctor appointments, so you see, I really need this license."

Pen and clipboard in hand, smiling, sympathetic, he tells her to relax, calm down. No way could my wife be calm. Nervous to the point of endangering anyone in the vehicle's path, she managed to avoid pedestrians, if not a couple of curbs, before bringing the car to a stop.

Almost in tears, she was certain she had failed the test.

"Well," the instructor tells her, pondering a decision. "You won't be driving much. Will you?"

"Oh, no," she replies, perking up with renewed hope, "just to Oxnard."

He looks at her, 21 years old, beautiful and pregnant. He smiles, checks the approval box and hands her a temporary license.

"Your permanent license will be mailed to you. Please drive safely."

Charlene and I sometimes talk about that day and share a laugh. I also remember how I worried and prayed for her safety.

When she suggested visiting me at Stoneman, I wrote back and advised her against it. An excerpt:

"As much as I want to see you, dear, I think it's better if you don't. First, the trip would be too long for you, and second, I can't even be sure I would be free when you arrived...."

She didn't insist, but I know she wasn't pleased. She was lonely and uncomfortable staying with my parents. Phone calls sometimes ended in arguments; our correspondence was sporadic. I walked to the mail room daily, about half a mile, once in heavy rain, and stood in line 15 minutes or longer.

I once criticized her for not writing and received six letters at mail call the next day. On another occasion, I became angry when she admitted she hadn't written because she was upset about something I had told her. By the time I got around to replying, I tore up my letter.

The longest letter I wrote was 14 pages. It was filled with rambling explanations of how I spent my time and money and unbridled expressions of love.

"...Just remember, honey, that I *do* love you. You know, sweetheart, I've lived with married guys in the barracks who go out every night with other girls, get satisfied, spend money like water, etc. If I were one of those kinds of men, you'd have something to worry about. I know I'm no prince, but I'd *never* do things like that—believe me. Trust me dear."

Charlene tolerated my gambling, knew I drank and smoked too much and hoped I was being faithful.

I related a story about a sergeant who was sent home from

Korea on an emergency leave to find his 25-year-old wife three-months pregnant after sleeping with a married man. Father of three small boys and deeply in love with his wife, he decided to stay with his family, even though he felt like committing suicide.

"It was after I heard this story and looked at this pathetic guy that I realized how fortunate I was to be married to you, Charlene. I would trust you to the end of the earth. I also realized that no matter where I am or how far we are apart, I will never destroy our marriage by doing anything to jeopardize it."

That December and much of January were extremely stressful. Charlene was six months along. Neither of us knew where she would deliver the baby. Both of us worried if it would be healthy, but worst of all, would I be at her bedside or would I be in Korea?

The interminable wait for the Army to rule on my request was agonizing for both of us.

Compounding the uncertainty was a ticking clock. I found a little known Army regulation that stated that enlisted personnel could not be sent overseas with fewer than six months service time remaining.

My letter to Charlene, dated Dec. 12, stated:

"I saw the major here who is the PIO. He is going to let me work in the office until I leave here—one way or the other. Actually, I only have 17 more days to sweat out now, and it seems like a lifetime."

A week later: "If anything happens that I don't get by these nine days, I want you to understand this: I will go to the adjutant here and tell him your condition is worse, as I had talked to you on the phone recently. And I'll need a few days to get a letter from your doctor as evidence. By the time the days elapse, I will be under the six-month mark. I just want you to know this in case they should check with you...."

As the deadline drew closer, I obtained a temporary job in the Special Orders section, where correspondence from Washington flowed. My job was to process incoming correspondence.

My orders finally arrived: *"Request for deferment denied. EM will comply with original overseas orders..."*

My heart sank. There was more but the only words that mattered were in that opening paragraph. Simply stated, they had the impact of a death sentence. Had my orders arrived two days later, I would have been home free. I would have been ineligible. Now...

How was I going to tell my wife?

Chapter 11

The City by the Bay

By the time the captain saw my orders, I had renewed hope. The directive had lain unseen for at least a week.

That black cloud that had hovered over my wife and me for so many weeks drifted away, replaced by rays of sunshine. I would be assigned to stateside duties for the rest of my enlistment.

As a bonus, I even got a leave to spend Christmas with Charlene—our first as a married couple. We both were elated that her condition had improved and looked forward to having a healthy baby.

"You will have to be reassigned, sergeant," the captain said. "You won't be leaving here for awhile."

Unknown to the officer, I was headed to Sixth Army headquarters at the Presidio of San Francisco, site of Letterman General Hospital. One of the Army's oldest and best-equipped medical facilities, it included an obstetrics ward for military wives. I had hoped Charlene could have our baby there.

Thanks to my old Camp Irwin boss, the transfer was virtually assured.

Lieutenant Milt Rosner had called me from Letterman, where he was visiting his wife, a patient at the hospital. He said he had arranged a "good deal" for himself on the Stars and Stripes newspaper in Tokyo, where I might have been assigned. Instead, the lieutenant had facilitated my transfer to the Presidio, which I had sought through normal channels.

"It is almost cinched," I wrote Charlene. "Rosner told the PIO officer, Colonel Sidle, that the Presidio was where I wanted to be stationed. You will probably enjoy living in San Francisco for a few months—I hope. Then, of course, as Rosner said, the work I will be doing there will be excellent to apply to civilian work."

I left Camp Stoneman Jan. 19. After reporting for duty, I was introduced to Colonel Sidle and shown around the PIO office. The colonel, aware of my wife's pregnancy, told me to take as much time as I needed to find a place to live off post before starting work.

After a quick housing search, I knew I needed money to make a deposit on an apartment. I wrote Charlene and asked her to send $100.

"It's bad around here, dear. You almost have to pay a rental agent here $10 or so just to find you a place. Then I figured I might have to pay up to $80 a month for a place. But I want to be with you regardless.

"The hospital is supposed to be the best," I continued. "The Presidio has many facilities for a married man. We can have a good time by going to the NCO Club to play Bingo. It's possible to win up to three or four hundred dollars, too. They also have dances and shows. Movies cost 25 cents per person. This is the Country Club of the Army. I'm sure we'll get settled and you'll enjoy being here. Remember, honey, it's only five more months."

Reunited shortly after writing that letter, we inhaled the morning fog as if it were a heavenly cure for what had ailed us and at Sunday Mass thanked the good Lord for sending us to the City by the Bay.

Wisconsin Street, like many in San Francisco, was a roller-coaster thrill ride. Our apartment, perched on a steep hill half a block below its crest, had a bay window over the front walk, providing a good view of the clustered structures below.

More than seven months along, Charlene looked forward to Sundays. We strolled along Fisherman's Wharf, peeked into windows of expensive restaurants, enjoyed movies on the post and stopped for pie and coffee before chugging back up Wisconsin Street in my worn-out Plymouth.

Weeknights we played cards, Chinese checkers and talked at length about our future together, making certain, however, never to miss our favorite radio programs.

Stretching out on the living room rug, we tuned to Jack Benny, Fibber Magee and Molly and blood-curdling thrillers such as *Inner Sanctum*, which always started with a an eerie squeaking noise followed by a resounding thud. You could visualize the swirling dust as a metallic coffin lid sealed the corpse inside.

Radio, with its talented actors and realistic sound effects, conjured up all sorts of exciting visions.

We seldom missed *I Love a Mystery*, which featured three soldiers of fortune who made up the A-1 Detective Agency—Jack Packard, the team leader; Doc Long, a likable Texan who had an eye for the ladies; and Reggie York, a prim and proper Brit.

Thirty-five years later, when I worked at the Los Angeles Times, Charlene and I met Carlton E. Morris, the creator of that series at his Woodside, California, home, about 40 miles south of San Francisco.

Agile, vigorous and slightly overweight when I interviewed him in 1987, he wore horned-rimmed glasses, had more hair over his lip than atop his head, and had just completed his fifth novel.

It has been said that Morse wrote more words than William Shakespeare, which may or may not be an exaggeration. Nonetheless, he estimated his output at 3 million words for *Mystery*. He told me he figured he had written 10 million words for *One Man's Family*, which he created in 1932, when family dramatic shows were non-existent.

"I wrote three episodes and presented them to the powers that be," he recalled. "They were dubious. They wanted action shows, but agreed to put it on the air for six weeks. That was April 29, 1932, and it ran 27 years."

He gave me a copy of *Killer at the Wheel*, his first novel published. He describes himself in the jacket as "...a thirty-year-old spirit trapped in an 86-year-old barrel."

Charlene and I still love a thrilling mystery and sometimes think of that exciting visit with Carlton Morse in his secluded Woodside hideaway nestled among the pines of northern California.

THE STRIPPED engine of my club coupe was hoisted two feet

above the frame. It hung precariously by heavy wires that ran through a hole drilled in a garage rafter, directly below our apartment.

Like the old days when we worked together on our model-A Fords, my school buddy was in charge.

Clint McElhenny was a naval reserve sailor on active duty in Alameda and visited us regularly. He quickly determined my car needed a new engine if we expected to keep driving it.

For Mac, if vehicles didn't purr, they needed instant attention from under-the-hood tinkering to major repair. I offered no argument.

I checked city bus schedules for convenient transportation times to and from the Presidio, and we settled on a time to begin the operation.

What I should have checked were reports of an imminent city bus strike. Predictably, once my car had been placed out of commission, city busses also stopped running.

While writing routine news stories in the office, I had formed a good relationship with the colonel. I explained the situation and the fact I couldn't afford daily taxis.

Complicating the issue was Mac's uncertain availability to oversee the project, which meant I might not have use of my car for weeks.

Aware my enlistment was running out and apparently in no great need of my presence in the office, the colonel had a simple solution.

"I'll arrange for a driver," he said. "He can pick you up in the morning and take you home when you're ready, sergeant. I know you're concerned about leaving your wife alone. I understand she's due soon."

"In March, sir... we hope."

It was settled. My driver arrived each morning, had coffee while traffic thinned, delivered me to the office and left early to avoid the evening rush hour.

Meanwhile, Mac showed up when he could. The engine replacement proceeded slowly while the bus strike showed no signs of settlement.

Mac's plan was to hoist the engine high enough to clear the front end of the car, which we would roll back, then slowly lower the block onto the floor. Although stripped, its shell must have weighed at least 200 pounds.

As we lifted the block, the rafter snapped. Almost simultaneously, the block plunged, sheering off the hood ornament as it dropped onto the concrete floor, inches from where we were standing.

Seated at a kitchen table above the broken rafter, Charlene heard the crash and rushed down the narrow staircase, no doubt swishing, if not jiggling, our unborn baby en route.

It's a wonder that didn't induce her labor.

When it came on March 30, the pain was excruciating. After 13 hours, she proudly presented Patricia Ann—a 5-pound, 6-ounce doll with a round perfectly formed face, big brown eyes and a full head of curly black hair.

Charlene's face beamed as she held our precious daughter. I passed out cigars, and our close friends Jewett and Evelyn Conradson paid us a surprise visit.

Despite the initial excitement, adjustment was difficult with Patty's incessant crying. Diapers kept clothes lines atop the roof full.

Charlene's mother came to help. She hadn't been with us long when my wife began to hemorrhage while I was at work. My mother-in-law used what diapers were available to stop the bleeding then rushed to the corner store for more. Many had floated over the windy city like tiny clouds.

The next two months passed quickly and uneventfully. I was discharged May 29, 1952, after three years, 11 months of Army service.

Part Two

HOLLYWOOD

Chapter 12

A Shaky Transition

Again a civilian, I was filled with wild ambition, bursting optimism and unshakeable confidence as I set out to conquer the world, starting with finding a job.

Now a 22-year-old family man without an income, a rented apartment costing $62.50 a month and mouths to feed other than my own, I was acutely aware of my need for immediate employment. However, I wasn't overly concerned.

An Associated Press writer, a reserve Army major on active duty in the Presidio's Public Information Office, had given me the name of a contact at a public relations firm in Hollywood, Carl Byers and Associates.

The major opened the door for me, but it shut quickly. My job interview may have been the company's shortest on record.

"We require at least five years writing experience on a major newspaper before even considering an applicant," the man behind a large desk said. "If you're still interested come back then."

There wasn't anything more to say, except "thank you for seeing me." However, I promised myself I definitely would return in five years. *Definitely*.

Meanwhile, I took part-time work, including a night service station job, so I could continue seeking employment on a newspaper.

Fortunately, I didn't need to go apartment-hunting. We had a "reservation."

Jewett Conradson's wife Evelyn managed an attractive apartment complex in Van Nuys. Upon arriving back in Southern California, we immediately moved into their next-door apartment.

It was difficult for Charlene, struggling, separated by seemingly paper-thin walls from our good friends who were long past the struggling stage.

Compounding my wife's discomfort was her close association with couples from our school days who lived in the same complex. Among the residents were her old boyfriend Don Ayres and his new wife. It was like living in an upscale commune. All could afford what we could not.

Jewett and Dick McCrillis were co-owners of a burgeoning pool-cleaning business. Their employees included Jewett's younger brother, four school buddies and my brother-in-law, Dave Walton. He and Bonnie lived directly behind us.

I'm sure I too could have gone to work for Jewett and Dick, but I wanted to pursue my so-called profession, at least give it a chance.

Despite our penny-pinching, I found an irresistible offer, a used black-and-white 12-inch TV set priced at $65. I paid $10 down with monthly installments.

As time passed and our bank account continued to shrink, I answered want-ads seeking employment. I learned that Dime-A-Line News in North Hollywood, a hole-in-the-wall advertising publication on Lankershim Boulevard, needed an office boy with a starting salary of $50 a week.

"You won't be doing any writing," the publisher, Bea Fredericks, said in reply to my question. "You will need a car. You'll be making several trips a week to our plant in Redondo Beach."

It was a start.

After almost two months of delivering proofs to local advertisers, sweeping out the office and performing other menial tasks in addition to frequent two-hour trips to Redondo Beach in pre-freeway days, I approached the publisher.

"As you know, Mrs. Fredericks," I began, "my wife and I have a baby daughter. We're really finding it difficult to get by on $50. I don't get mileage for using my car, and it's a long trip to Redondo. Sometimes I work overtime without pay. I really do need more money."

A cold, middle-aged woman, Bea Fredericks smiled an insincere smile.

"I can understand your predicament and would like to help you," she replied. "Maybe we can work out something. Does your wife do ironing?"

Shocked by her question, I instinctively replied, "Just for our family."

"Well, then," she added, "maybe you could come over on Saturdays to mow our lawn. Could you do that?"

It was clear I had no future at Dime-A-Line News. I don't remember what I told Mrs. Fredericks, if I responded at all. I simply had to find another job quickly.

Wasting no time to job search again, I saw a help-wanted ad placed by the Citizen-News, called and was granted an interview. The massive two-story building in the heart of Hollywood was impressive. So was Johnny Badovinac, the display advertising manager.

"The job pays forty-five dollars a week," he said. "I know you are earning a bit more, but you will be working on the copy desk and won't need a car."

"Will I be doing any writing?"

"No. The editorial department is upstairs. You will be handling display ads."

I knew almost nothing about display advertising and had no desire to pursue that field. But I needed a job and would, at least, have my foot in the door.

Small desks filled most of the lower floor, occupied by ad men talking on telephones or busy with paperwork. A few women at the front counter assisted walk-in customers with classified ads. Badovinac and Mr. T. Harwood Young, his boss, had private offices on one side of the room. The display copy desk where I would sit was isolated in the rear.

My impression of Johnny Bad as he was affectionately called by everyone, including Hollywood merchants who spent large sums of money at the Citizen-News, was favorable. He assured me $45 a week was temporary.

Charlene wasn't happy about a pay cut, but acknowledged the bottom line was an improvement. Our car, with its rebuilt engine, would last longer, and we would save on gas. It was settled. Still, I had mixed feelings.

I made friends with co-workers and a few ad men, but found the job dull, unchallenging. The friendly desk chief had been stuck in his job for two years and seemed content. By the end of six weeks, I knew selling ads had no appeal to me. I hadn't resorted to a kneel-down prayer, but God must have heard me, nonetheless.

An editorial copy boy's position became available upstairs. I immediately applied.

"The job pays forty dollars a week," Managing Editor Harland Palmer, Jr., the publisher's oldest son, said. "The Los Angeles Newspaper Guild represents editorial employees. That's the starting salary on the union scale."

Wow! I knew what Charlene would say. She was as predictable as a sunrise.

"Fifty? Forty-five? Now forty? You're going in the wrong direction."

My words, not hers, but close enough. I couldn't argue the point, but hoped I could convince her that the opportunity was worth another five-dollar gamble. Well, no, I wouldn't use *that* word.

"We can help you a little," Palmer continued. "Lowell Redelings, our drama editor, uses some of our staff from time to time for reviews—movies, plays, nightclub acts. We pay five dollars for each review."

Nightclubs? Ciro's, the Cocoanut Grove, Mocambo? Moulin Rouge? Sunset Strip nightclubs?

"When you review a performance, you and your wife would be invited to dinner. It's a nice evening out, and you'll be getting paid for it."

That clinched it. I always expressed strong opinions about movies I attended with anyone willing to listen but never thought I would become a professional critic. It was intriguing. Exciting.

I started immediately in my new job.

Dorothy's tumultuous departure from Kansas couldn't have been more exciting than when I climbed those steps each morning to enter a new world. The editorial department wasn't Oz, but it was vibrant, the thumping heart of any newspaper, especially for me. I felt I was on my way up that ladder of success.

It didn't take long to learn I was working for a unique conservative newspaper owned and published by Harland Palmer, a stern, straight-laced judge. The Citizen-News refused to accept cigarette and liquor ads, avoided controversial issues and focused almost entirely on Hollywood.

I was shocked when I heard that the judge's sister, Zuma Palmer, the radio and TV editor, had poured several bottles of expensive liquor down the ladies' bathroom toilet. Press agents, but apparently not all, knew the judge's policy and delivered gift baskets to writers' homes.

I was sorry I wasn't downstairs the day Bette Davis strutted through the front door to place a classified ad. Women at the front counter buzzed for days about meeting the famous actress.

Hard news seldom was found in the paper.

During an election year, a letter writer wondered why five days a week the editorial page favored Republicans, but on Saturdays, Democrats got preferential treatment. The truth wasn't made public, but I was told the regular slot man was a staunch Republican, replaced on Saturdays by a hard-line Democrat. The newspaper didn't publish on Sundays.

One day before a major earthquake shook Alaska, management called the news staff to a meeting to reiterate the paper's primary objective—to reach local readers with local news. If a story didn't have a local angle, management emphasized, it didn't belong in the Citizen-News.

When the Saturday slot man arrived early in the morning to begin work, he found reams of United Press (not yet UPI) and Associated Press wire copy reporting the Alaska quake piled behind the machines and continuing to spill out. Believing he was following strict orders, the slot man cleared stories from the City News Service machine, ignoring everything related to the quake.

The Citizen-News may have been the only daily in America that totally ignored the disaster that day.

To no one's surprise, the slot man was fired.

For most employees, it was a happy place to work with a casual environment. Annual picnics were held at the Los Angeles Police Academy, where families gathered for a full day of fun and food at the company's expense.

Charlene and I looked forward to them.

Chapter 13

Copyboy

When a seat became available on the news desk, Bill Kershaw was promised the job. He had spent months filling paste pots, running copy and performing other copyboy duties he considered demeaning.

Meanwhile, he was told to train me. I liked Bill, thought he was smart and could start me off on the right foot. I was wrong.

The copyboy's job wasn't difficult, but some duties were more important than others. For example, when editors spiked stories on a desk spindle attached to a base, they expected them to be picked up immediately and sent back shop in a vacuum tubing system to be set in type.

Ralph Palmer, the managing editor's younger brother, edited Valley stories. His spike, it seemed, was seldom empty and often overlooked.

"Copy!" he would bellow across the news room, sometimes more than once when not immediately picked up.

Bill Kershaw was not fond of that word, especially coming from the mouth of an editor he had grown to dislike immensely.

Related press releases were combined, edited for continuity and pasted together, forming long stories. It was time-consuming but effectively filled space when necessary. Valley pages usually contained a number of those rambling articles. Consequently,

Ralph Palmer's paste pot needed replenishing frequently. It was another task Bill Kershaw detested.

After clearing Ralph's spike of one of those long articles, I stepped across the room to the central copy desk, where the vacuum tubing system was located.

"Wait," Bill whispered, motioning me toward a back room, where photos and metal cuts were stored. "Let me have that."

Curiously, I handed him the rolled up copy and followed him to the morgue, which seldom was used by anyone other than the copyboy.

"Shouldn't we tube that, Bill?"

Kershaw ignored me. My mouth dropped to my chest when he unrolled the article, placed it in a metal container in a corner of the room, then struck a match.

"Are you nuts? We could get fired. Ralph must've worked on that for an hour. It should fill half his section."

Grinning like a drooling pyromaniac, Bill touched the flame to a corner of the story. In a matter of seconds it became a pile of ashes.

"You're crazy. I could be blamed for this."

"Relax. No one will ever know," he said. "The composing room misplaces copy all the time. In about 20 minutes you'll see Ralph get a call from composing when they can't find the copy. He'll slam down the receiver, jump up and rush back shop."

"What happens when they can't find it?"

"Nothing. Ralph will fill the hole with some of the crap he keeps around. I told you to relax."

I didn't.

After Kershaw destroyed the evidence, we reentered the editorial room. Ralph had spiked a final page dummy, which I removed and stepped away.

"That's it," he said, happy to have made another deadline.

As Bill had predicted, Ralph soon was on the phone, appearing perturbed. The conversation was brief. He slammed down the receiver, rose from his chair, strode across the room and disappeared through the swinging doors.

As far as Bill Kershaw and I were concerned, that ended the episode, except for a lingering fear that I would be blamed...and bad dreams.

After serving a relatively short "apprenticeship" at the Citizen-News, Bill moved on to the Los Angeles Times. We didn't keep in touch. I didn't miss him.

My sole contribution to the printed page was to send daily stock listings to composing—an important task that required no expertise.

The procedure was simple. A ticker tape of stock symbols in alphabetical order, followed by prices, arrived in the office at the same time five days a week. It clicked through the machine quickly and needed prompt handling.

The tape was inserted through a small plastic cylinder with a moistened sponge that gave it a sticky underside when pulled out. Easily cut by the device after each quotation, the tape listed the stock symbol and price. It was pasted on a printed pad alongside the name of the company it represented. A mindless job, I could zip through the process quickly.

Soon after the Citizen-News hit the streets one afternoon, phones began ringing off the hook. Virtually every stock listed on the business page had an incorrect quotation. Some readers were thrilled and called to verify the quotation; others seemed panic-stricken.

After retrieving the sheets from composing, the desk chief determined who to blame. I had pasted virtually every piece of tape alongside the wrong company. I couldn't explain how I could have committed such an enormous blunder. I was sure I would be job-hunting again.

Finally, the mystery was solved. I had opened a box of old, obsolete pads that listed companies not included on the updated pads. Had I been more alert, and recognized a few symbols, I would have realized I was pasting the tape incorrectly.

It was just one of many serious mistakes I would make in a profession that does its best to minimize them on a daily basis. Fortunately, I survived that one.

Considerably less stressful was a daily morning walk to Hollywood Boulevard to buy a Communist newspaper, the *People's World*, for Walter Scratch, our stuffy editorial columnist. He wore a bow tie daily, sat undisturbed in a far corner at an ancient desk with a roll-down top and seldom spoke to me.

Initially, I didn't have a clue why Walter wanted that paper and had never heard of it, but I did what I was told and delivered it to him.

A major news story made headlines across the country when I was in the Army. Julius Rosenberg was surprised by federal agents while shaving in the bathroom of his home. He was arrested July 17, 1950, charged with espionage. The news escaped me as did similar news three weeks later, when his wife Ethel Rosenberg also was arrested. The couple had been under an FBI microscope for years as suspected spies for the Soviet Union.

Coverage in the Citizen-News consisted mostly of Walter Scratch's editorials on the op-ed page.

Not only did I enjoy the short walk there and back, I found the assignment exciting. The periodical was never openly displayed and, I suppose, unavailable at most newsstands. At first, I felt guilty about asking for the Commie paper, almost as if I were being unpatriotic.

"It's for the Citizen-News," I explained the first time I purchased it.

After that, the vendor would have it ready when he saw me coming.

I took my time getting back, scanning articles about the spies along the way. On March 29, 1951, a jury had found the couple guilty of conspiracy to commit espionage. So, when I caught up with the cloak-and-dagger saga, the Rosenbergs were well on their way to the electric chair.

A few key dates: Jan. 10, 1952: "U.S. Court of Appeals gets the case..." Feb. 25, 1952: "Rosenbergs' appeal denied..." Oct. 13, 1952: "Supreme Court refuses to grant certiorari..." June 13, 1953: "Supreme Court denies stay of execution..." June 17, 1953: "Supreme Court Justice William O. Douglas grants stay..." June 19, 1953: "Supreme Court, in special session, vacates Justice Douglas' stay..." June 19, 1953: Julius and Ethel Rosenberg executed."

After coverage of the June 21 funeral, articles in the national press disappeared off front pages, but *People's World* continued to publish in-depth articles. Since Walter Scratch had no further interest in Communist propaganda, my trips to the Vine Street newsstand came to an end.

Unlike Walter's rigid work schedule, Drama Editor Lowell Redelings popped in and out.

I took a special interest delivering his mail, hoping some day I might become his assistant. Photos, press releases and unopened mail often stacked up. It was anyone's guess when you might find him there, shuffling through things, on the phone, laying out his section.

Always on the run, Redelings worked fast and wrote fast. Unlike other departments, drama pages were dummied well in advance of publication, providing the editor flexibility in his daily schedule. Redelings seldom, if ever, was hard-pressed to meet a deadline.

Typically dressed, a gaudy tie loosely knotted below an opened shirt collar, the lanky, middle-aged editor was scanning an embossed invitation when I approached one afternoon. Looking up, he handed it to me.

"Would you and your wife like to see Joe E. Lewis at the Mocambo?"

I beamed, glanced at the invitation addressed to Lowell and responded as always, graciously accepting, no questions asked.

Redelings liked on-the-spot decisions, saving him needless conversation and one less piece of mail to deal with. Based on previous assignments, he seemed confident I would turn in an acceptable review on time that required nothing more than proofing. For him, all that remained was dummying the Mocambo review with a circled "TK" (to come). I was penciled in.

When I again glanced at the invitation, I wondered why the former heavyweight boxing champion would be appearing at a swanky Sunset Strip club, but didn't want to expose my ignorance, so merely thanked Lowell and said nothing further.

Seated with my wife at the packed nightclub the evening of the show, I still didn't know what to expect.

Finally Joe E. Lewis stepped in front of a mike and waited for the thunderous applause to subside. Clearly, he was not the heavyweight boxing champion.

Holding a drink, he eyed his audience, grinned and proclaimed, "It is now post time." He downed it, smacked his lips approvingly and again waited for the laughter to end.

The date was June 2, 1953, our second wedding anniversary. We couldn't have planned a better celebration. The only downside was stopping afterward at the paper. The six-paragraph review took at least an hour to write while my wife snoozed on the cold leather couch in the reception area.

It really didn't matter who I reviewed at nightclubs. Charlene, I knew, would be thrilled. It always meant a wonderful night out, a delicious meal, drinks and a special table reserved for critics.

Lowell never wanted detailed reviews, six or seven paragraphs tops, which suited me fine. Moreover, the five dollars, which went to the baby sitter, would be added to my weekly take-home paycheck of $37.50.

Were it not for Lowell, our only night outings would have been at the nearby drive-in theater, where we saw movies almost weekly for less than a dollar a ticket. Charlene and I would cuddle undisturbed in the front seat while Patty slept in a bassinet in back. Like me, she could sleep through an earthquake.

We attended movie premieres, stage plays, musicals, whatever Lowell offered. I rejected nothing, but at times, wished I had been more selective.

Charlene sometimes also wished she had stayed home, especially when waiting for me in the ghostly editorial room.

None of my critiques came easy. A writer once apologized for turning in a long story, telling his editor he didn't have time for a shorter one. Sometimes, merely finding something favorable to write could be time-consuming.

An example was my review of *Love Rides the Rails,* an amateurish back-alley melodrama. It was dreadful. A bomb.

What got into print was far from reality. "It brought cheers for the hero and jeers for the villain," I began. "Lacking proper stage space, the three-act musical comedy was fair, but needs considerable 'polishing' to rank as a good production…"

Another time I reviewed a movie starring Virginia Mayo. The piece was headlined, *She's Back on Broadway: A Gay Musical.* The world then interpreted that to mean joyous, happy, light-hearted, merry, lively, blithe, sprightly, sportive, perhaps even hilarious.

Gay was a useful three-letter word editors favored, particularly one-column headlines because it had a broad meaning and easily fit the allotted space. Having been redefined, the word simply wouldn't work today for Virginia Mayo's movie.

Lowell took pride in his section which was sprinkled with articles bearing the byline Wylie Williams, a pseudonym assigned to me. Thank-you notes from performers included those from America's favorite pinup girl Betty Grable (whose shapely legs were said to have been insured for $1 million), songbird Anna Maria Alberghetti and the marvelous dance duo Landre and Verna.

Despite my disappointment that those notes weren't addressed to me, I treasured them.

As a copyboy, the only article published under my name appeared in a 20-page 1953 Academy Awards section, produced by the entire editorial staff working through the night.

I felt privileged Lowell asked me to contribute. Focused on box-office receipts, my story appeared on Page 8. Thanks to studio press releases, I wrote it in record time.

The Greatest Show on Earth, Cecil B. DeMille's Oscar winner, cost $4 million to produce and grossed $13 million for Paramount, top money-winner in 1952 as well as best picture. MGM's *Quo Vadis* ranked second at the box office with $10.5 million. Production cost was estimated at $6 million.

That and more facts and figures weren't exactly vital information for readers, but it satisfied Lowell, and that's what mattered to me.

The glamorous 17th annual event was held at Hollywood's ornate and spacious Pantages Theater. It marked the first time Oscar nominees in New York witnessed the West Coast show on television.

Readers praised the annual Academy Award sections undertaken by a relatively small staff that never left the office. Only Redelings and a few others received invitations to the gala events.

After covering the shows, Lowell rushed back to the office pumped up, ready to write. He removed his tux coat and bow tie, rolled up his sleeves and went to work. Those were the only times I ever saw Lowell formally dressed.

In 1961, Elizabeth Taylor surprised film experts by winning the best-actress Oscar for her performance as a prostitute in the MGM movie *Butterfield 8.*

For the Citizen-News, it was an unexpected opportunity to shine. Photos of the beautiful actress and interesting stories about her appeared throughout the issue. One article was particularly noteworthy because of a line that caught the editor's eye, unfortunately after the newspaper was published.

"Miss Taylor," it stated, "won the Oscar for her *hole* in *Butterfield 8.*

It's unlikely that typo was intentional, but it generated chuckles from a few cynical newsmen. It was the responsibility of copy readers to catch such mistakes, and I suspect Lowell had a few choice words for the desk chief in charge that night. Fortunately, I wasn't involved.

If Elizabeth Taylor, her agent or anyone at MGM contacted the paper to complain, I wasn't aware of it.

Chapter 14

System Fails, Gamble Pays Off

Normally a busy intersection in Van Nuys, the street corner was deserted at 3 a.m., when Charlene and I sat on a sidewalk folding 300 copies of the Los Angeles Times, which would fill most of my Plymouth for delivery.

A weekday, the newspaper weighed about half as much as Sunday's edition, but long before the final toss, my throwing arm was always sore.

Charlene, who accompanied me only once, slept in a back corner while I hurled papers out the passenger window, completing the route in ample time to report for work at the Citizen-News.

Six weeks into the job, I had saved enough money for a weekend getaway to Las Vegas, which was just beginning to attract visitors in the summer of 1953. As I recall, only six major hotels were open on the Strip, the Flamingo, Sands, Desert Inn, Thunderbird, El Rancho Vegas and the Sahara, where singer Peggy Lee was appearing in the main showroom.

To this day, the memory of what follows remains vividly painful. Only after many sleepless nights did I decide to write about this shameful incident.

Charlene, who had arranged for Patty to stay with her parents, was excited about getting away for the first time since my discharge, and so was I, each for a different reason.

Having heard about a progressive betting system to play the roulette wheel, I had practiced for weeks, using a deck of cards, pad and pencil. Not intended to cash in big, the system seemed logical and worked well at home.

Its objective was to complete betting cycles, starting with two chips wagered on either black or red or odd or even, which paid nearly 2 to 1. If successful, the bet would be repeated. If again successful, a new cycle would be started with two more chips. The gambler, however, must be willing to risk a sizeable investment for a small return should there be a prolonged losing streak.

I didn't attempt to explain any of this to Charlene, who waited in a hot car in the Sahara Hotel parking lot while I supposedly made reservations for Peggy Lee's show, after which we would find an inexpensive motel and check in.

Predictably, the roulette wheel immediately turned ugly for me and didn't improve. My meager bankroll soon was gone, leaving me with an empty wallet, no show reservations and no place to spend the night.

"Were you able to make the reservations, honey?" Charlene asked as I opened the car door to step inside. "You were gone quite awhile. It really got hot."

I can't remember how I broke the depressing news. I can only remember her tears, followed by unrelenting anger and a litany of questions for which I had no plausible answers.

Still a copyboy with a fading future in journalism, and suddenly a fractured marriage, I was faced with finding lodging for the night without a dollar in my pocket. I'm sure that was Charlene's primary question.

"Don't worry, dear," I probably responded. "It'll work out."

Thankfully, I had jotted down the name of a publicist at the Flamingo Hotel, which was thriving under the umbrella of reputed mobsters. I had planned to contact him in hopes he might comp a show. Instead, I decided to ask for a room.

"He's not here," a burly, sweaty-faced man in a tight-fitting tux said. "Whatta you need, kid?"

Embellishing my position at the Citizen-News, I told him I had come to write an article on Las Vegas, had encountered bad luck at the tables and hoped I might get a room for the night.

"Sorry. We're booked up for the weekend."

Charlene doesn't handle adversity well, never has, and at that instant, appeared on the brink of unleashing another flood of tears.

Eyeing my wife with a hint of sympathy, the man pondered, then added, "I can get you in the motel across the street."

"Oh, that's fine," I replied with as much restraint as I could muster. "I appreciate it."

The truth? I was desperate and I'm sure he knew it.

The five-hour ride home the next morning, coasting on downhill stretches to conserve gas, was interminably long and almost entirely void of conversation.

"I'll make it up to you honey," I promised. "I'm sorry."

Charlene didn't reply. She didn't even glance at me. I knew she was fighting more tears. I considered turning on the radio but decided to continue driving in silence.

If only I could have turned back the clock.

HOLDING HER favorite pink blanket, Patty stood inside her crib, not uttering a sound. Sometimes she would stand outside the crib, holding it, a signal she was ready for her nap. After entering the world crying incessantly the first month, she rarely shed tears and made few demands. Not a perfect baby, Patty was close to perfect. At least, that was our biased opinion.

Thus, my wife believed she could trust me to watch her through the night and feed her in the morning while she worked at Eastman Kodak in Hollywood. The timing was good. Shortly after Charlene came home, I left for the Citizen-News.

It wasn't an ideal arrangement, but we needed more money than I was bringing home as a copyboy, and I no longer delivered the Los Angeles Times. After almost a year without a raise and no indication when or if I would be promoted to a desk job, I began to consider other options.

Lying in bed a few feet from the crib, I opened an eye to see my daughter staring at me. I knew the look. She was hungry. Reluctantly, I opened the other eye, stirred a bit...then tossed Patty a graham cracker I had left on the night stand.

When her mother arrived home a short time later, found me asleep and Patty lying in her crib nibbling the remains of the cracker, it wasn't a happy scene.

I apologized and promised to do better, even though I knew this arrangement couldn't continue much longer. I was growing impatient waiting for a promotion.

It was late summer of 1953 when Jewett offered me a job cleaning pools.

"If you decide to leave the paper," he said, "I can pay you one-hundred dollars a week to start."

No question he, Evelyn and other friends in the apartment complex were aware of our financial struggle, but the offer was not a charitable gesture. Jewett and Dick McCrillis needed another serviceman and both knew I was qualified.

In previous years, I occasionally helped Jewett with acid washes, filter tank replacements and routine service. I also was knowledgeable about the business, having researched it for an article I submitted to Sunset Magazine. A rejection letter, informing me a staff writer currently was working on a similar piece, encouraged me to submit future ideas, but I never did.

Jewett's job offer came when I was most receptive. I rationalized that it would be only temporary but knew I was facing a critical decision.

A $60 boost in my weekly income was attractive to Charlene, but she liked her job at Eastman and didn't want me working for my school buddies. She left the decision to me.

"I know the money is tempting," my father said when I asked his advice, "but do you want to be cleaning swimming pools the rest of your life? Give it more time."

At 49, dad was in extremely poor health and undoubtedly knew he wouldn't be with us many more years. Looking back on his life, he had regrets and hoped I would make better decisions. I valued his opinions and decided to take his advice.

I rejected Jewett's offer.

I HADN'T been in the managing editor's office since Har Palmer hired me more than a year earlier. Now, I was applying for an editorial vacancy, and I had more reason than before to be terrified.

"As you know, John Hall will be leaving soon, and we're going to need another assistant sports editor," Palmer said. "I know you're a big sports fan. Covering the Hollywood Legion and

Olympic Auditorium fights each week is a major part of the job. Do you know anything about boxing?"

As a kid, I listened to an announcer describe Joe Louis' dramatic knockouts on radio and knew that my dad, like millions of others, thought the Brown Bomber was the greatest fighter to lace on gloves.

I knew that Jim Jeffries, a heavyweight champion at the turn of the century, had a barn somewhere in the Valley because my father once took me there to see the fights when I was a youngster.

I also knew that Bobby (Cisco) Andrade had made a name for himself as an amateur boxer at Fort Ord when I was stationed there, and that he currently was fighting locally as a professional.

Other than that, I knew nothing about boxing and had little interest in it. So I said, with as much conviction as I could muster, "It's one of my favorite sports."

I stopped filing paste pots in September of 1953, when John Hall accepted an offer to write a column for the Los Angeles Mirror-News, an afternoon tabloid owned by The Times.

And Bob Panella inherited a new assistant, me.

Totally unqualified, I was second in charge of a department that included a Pasadena-based columnist, fish and game editor, prep writer and racetrack handicapper, all part-timers. Panella covered UCLA sports, composed a daily high-pressure column on deadline and laid out the section.

A creative, prolific writer with a breezy, hip style, John Hall assisted on the desk and touched as many bases as possible.

The Southland was a sports mecca—two Pacific Coast League ball clubs, the Hollywood Stars and Los Angeles Angels, the Rams of the National Football League, small college sports, horse and auto racing, pro golf, bowling, wrestling, track and field and boxing. Even tennis promoters like Jack Kramer, fighting for recognition in those early days, occasionally got a plug.

I knew I could never match John's abilities as a writer or editor. Panella probably knew it too.

Chapter 15

Survival

About 10 years my senior, Bob Panella was in his mid-30s when Har Palmer dumped me in his lap. As a copyboy, I performed my duties but seldom exchanged a word with Panella when I filled his paste pot and picked up copy. He was too busy to look up.

A relatively small man with a pronounced lifelong limp, Panella wore black horn-rimmed glasses below wiry bristles of salt-and-pepper hair. He tolerated a domineering wife who didn't share his addiction to sports, and he had little quality time for a young son who was closer to his mother.

Normal desk work was scheduled to give the editor Saturdays and Sundays off and his assistant a weekday off plus Sunday. That meant each was required to produce the section by himself one day a week. But with me on board, Panella came in Saturday mornings as well.

My job started at 6 a.m. when I stripped the wires of overnight sports copy and photos for Panella to go through when he arrived half an hour later. He would select the photos and stories for that day, assign headlines and captions and dummy the section.

Initially, he was patient with me. He processed most of the stories and wrote captions before starting his column. He seldom completed it before the 10 o'clock deadline. I worked mainly on

95

fillers, many of which weren't used.

Possessing only a general interest in sports, unaccustomed to watching the clock tick and unfamiliar with the headline jargon of that era (Angels Cop, Nab, Snatch, Grab, Rip, Edge, etc.), I worked at a snail's pace, submitting heads Panella usually rewrote.

Sam Balter, a popular local sportscaster who subscribed to the paper and knew Panella personally, once mailed him a Citizen-News sports page. At least five shorts bearing the verb *Cop* in the headline were circled in red, accompanied by a sarcastic comment. My boss tossed it at me.

"Get with it," he snapped disgustedly.

Once his column was tubed to composing, Panella's routine almost never changed. He had coffee and doughnuts in the employee lunch room. He visited the john with the Mirror-News sports section, returned to the desk, opened his mail and proofread his column.

Previously, that ended Panella's morning shift. He would be out the door, headed for a ballgame, interview, luncheon or wherever, leaving my predecessor, John Hall, to oversee the composing room operation. After I arrived, Bob stayed until the section was put to bed, with me at his side observing.

Reading type backward and upside down opposite the compositor, Panella would spot typos as readily as if on a printed page. To speed up the process, he would take the line of lead to a typesetter to fix, wait for it and replace the corrected line. Being a union shop, editorial people were not allowed to touch type, a rule Panella ignored.

I eyed a 14-point headline. It looked like the Russian alphabet.

CHARLENE, STILL employed at Eastman Kodak, was off Saturdays, when I covered the Hollywood Legion fights. Since I had a pair of tickets, I suggested we spend a Saturday night together for a change. "We can make it sort of a social thing," I said. "The writers and others meet for drinks afterward in the press room."

I knew boxing wasn't high on Charlene's agenda, in fact not even listed. But she agreed to go. We arranged for a sitter and left early since I had to cover the full card.

Seated next to me in the front row with her legs under the

Charlene and Jack at ringside.

ring apron, Charlene squirmed when two black heavyweights squared off in the first preliminary match. In seconds, they were on the ropes directly above her, pummeling each other in a furious exchange that dotted the apron with blood.

Holding a large program in front of her face, she grimaced in horror.

"I'll never come again," she shrieked when the four-rounder ended, both fighters exhausted but still on their feet. "Why did you bring me?"

A fair question. I knew better but certainly didn't expect to christen her with a blood bath. I wanted Charlene to meet John Hall and the other writers, publicist Don Fraser and others I had come to know.

The beat was still new to me, and my inadequate coverage was adding to Panella's dissatisfaction with his so-called assistant editor. I had all day Sundays to compose roundups that included Saturday's results. I had no excuses for turning in unacceptable stories on Mondays.

Fights at the Olympic, however, were held Thursday nights, after which I wrote hasty stories in the press room before heading home. When Panella finished editing them on Friday, they were readable, considerably shorter.

It was clear my boss was growing weary of rewriting heads and fixing my stories. Worse, he was tired of making up the section six days a week. Panella's patience had come to an end.

"I can't carry you any longer," he said. "You'll be on your own Saturday. If you screw it up, I'm sorry, but I'll have to let you go."

After six weeks on the job and showing little progress as a

makeup editor, I saw it coming. Still, Panella's words struck me like a bolt of lightning.

I might have squeezed by on my writing, thanks to Don Fraser, my first boxing contact. He took me under his wing, fed me information for those weekend roundups and introduced me to fighters, managers and ring officials. But he couldn't help me on the desk. No one could.

Saturday. Three more days…

Working across from Panella the next two mornings was stressful. Both of us were aware of the approaching deadline when I had to produce or else. We never mentioned it. In a way, they were rehearsals for my solo performance Saturday. I tried to imagine myself doing what my boss was doing. And I watched the clock more intently.

I lay awake at night worrying. Was this it? Had I made the wrong decision when I rejected Jewett's job offer to clean swimming pools?

Saturday didn't go smoothly although I managed to produce the two-page section and barely made the deadline. Sunday lasted forever. I was optimistic, not confident, when Panella arrived Monday morning to give me his verdict.

Less than complimentary, he said I had used an incorrect word in a 48-point headline, *faze* instead of *phase.* I argued the point, even phoned the UCLA journalism department for an opinion, which I thought was inconclusive.

Panella insisted I was wrong. Maybe I was. But I wasn't fired. My boss apparently decided he had invested too much time and work training me to repeat the agony with another rookie.

Fraser was happy I had survived. He was looking forward to a good working relationship to assure a steady flow of his boxing publicity in our sports section.

Don was editor of a popular Los Angeles area publication, *KO Magazine*, and at 26 an astute boxing authority when we met. After compiling a perfect amateur record in the Army, five straight losses, he retired as a boxer but was hooked on the sport. It became his lifetime passion.

Wildly creative and a capable writer, Don fit in perfectly at the Legion. He quickly garnered the respect and trust of the press and those with whom he worked. I was impressed by his boxing knowledge, instant recall of facts and figures and leaned heavily on him in my job.

Of Scottish descent, Don was a practical joker with a dry wit, always ready with a sarcastic sting when warranted. We got along well from the start and our bond only strengthened as time passed.

When the Legion closed in 1959, Fraser became PR director at the Olympic Auditorium in Los Angeles and eight years later was hired by multimillionaire Jack Kent Cooke to head boxing and public relations at the relatively new Inglewood Forum.

In ensuing years, he was appointed to a two-year term as executive officer of the California State Athletic Commission and later promoted boxing at several Southland venues. In 2005, Fraser was installed in the capacity of promoter and matchmaker in the International Boxing Hall of Fame.

From left, boxing writer John Hall, Jack, and publicist Don Fraser.

A day at the races with friends Don and Ruth Fraser.

While Manager Red Tracton, not shown, rambles on about his featherweight champion Bobby Chacon, left, at a press conference, Ruth Fraser, Charlene and Jack appear less than interested.

Charlene and Don's wife Ruth, a striking redhead with a bubbly personality, also hit it off immediately. The four of us and our families became lifelong friends.

John Hall also proved a strong crutch to lean on. I hoped I might learn from him, follow in his footsteps and in time, gain a small measure of Bob Panella's approval.

A story John once told me about nearly having a date with Marilyn Monroe always intrigued me. I should have been so blessed. While researching this book, I contacted him to refresh my memory.

"I still call it a *date*," he insisted. "My big night with Marilyn was Nov. 20, 1952. Panella was off somewhere as usual; so on the way to covering the Art Aragon-Bobcat Bob Terrance fight at Hollywood Legion Stadium, I stopped by the Brown Derby to represent the Citizen at Look Magazine's annual party to unveil its 1952 All-American Football Team.

"By chance, Marilyn and I both got there early and sat next to each other in an otherwise still empty room at the back bar. We had a glass of champagne. She was still just getting started at that point, having bits in *All About Eve* and *Asphalt Jungle*. I told her how hot she looked in both movies. She obviously could never resist any sort of compliment. She gave me the smile.

"We talked about John Houston and George Sanders. Soon the room began to fill and she moved around to do her thing as the token guest bimbo of the evening. I had to leave early to get to the Legion, so I went out the back door to the valet parking booth.

"Suddenly I noticed she'd come out behind me. While we were waiting for our cars to come up, she asked why I was leaving so early. I told her I was heading for the Legion to cover the Aragon fight.

"'Oooh,' she said. 'I've always wanted to see the Golden Boy fight.' Lightning bolt! 'Really,' I said like Cary Grant. 'I've got an extra ticket—first row ringside. Why don't you come with me?'

"'I'd love to,' she said. 'But I've got something to do first. Can I meet you there?'

"'Terrific,' I said as I handed her the ticket. Her car came up first and she waved with a smile as she drove off. Of course, she never showed up at the Legion. But I still consider it a *date*.

"Later, I figured she was 26 at the time. I was 24. I think she got 'detained' in a meeting with Elia Kazan. Or maybe it was DiMag. She married Joe less than two years later on Jan. 14, 1954.

"I never ever saw Marilyn again in person," John concluded, "although I've always been one of the foremost experts on her life and times and movies and death by accidental overdose."

The Golden Boy, whose professional record was 90 wins, 26

losses and six draws, stopped the Bobcat in nine rounds.

Except for Marilyn and a few other celebrities, the golden era at the Legion had pretty well run its course for attracting Hollywood stars by the time I started covering boxing.

I would have liked rubbing shoulders with such Legion ring-siders as George Raft, Al Jolson, Lupe Velez, the Ritz Brothers and, in John's words, "every young starlet breathing."

The sensational tap dancer and actress Ann Miller was a regular at the larger Olympic Auditorium at 18th Street and Grand Avenue in Los Angeles, as was blond bombshell Mamie Van Doren (when her name was Joan Olandar), who seldom missed an Aragon fight.

I met the Golden Boy long before covering him in the ring.

Working part-time as a gas station attendant, I was told to return a customer's car to his nearby home after it was serviced.

"He'll drive you back," my boss said. "Don't pick a fight with him. He's a tough guy."

My boss cracked a thin smile. I had no idea what he meant, but assumed he was joking and didn't pursue the subject.

Entering the customer's driveway in Toluca Lake, near North Hollywood, I saw an opened garage with large boxing posters of Aragon in a boxing stance, advertising his fights, tacked on walls.

Only a few years older, Art greeted me at the front door licking his greasy fingers. He thanked me for delivering his car and drove me back to the station. I don't remember what we talked about, but I had no interest in boxing or him.

I never expected to be at ringside a few years later watching him in action. His courageous, often bloody and exciting fights packed Southland stadiums for almost two decades. Art was never a legitimate title contender despite his bid for a world championship in 1951, when he lost to lightweight king Jimmy Carter. A natural welterweight, Aragon blamed the defeat on dieting to make 135 pounds.

To say Art was quotable is to say watermelon is juicy.

"I'm the only fighter who ever had to be carried *into* the ring," he once said. The quote was widely used by sportswriters and published in his obituary.

Brash, flamboyant, good-looking and controversial in and out of the ring, Aragon commanded large purses for big-money matches, lived the life of a celebrity and mingled with them as well. He played golf with Bob Hope, flirted with Marilyn, had a widely publicized romantic fling with Mamie Van Doren and numbered actor William Holden—filmdom's original Golden Boy—among his friends.

Following retirement from boxing, he remained in the spotlight as a prominent bail bondsman and kept in touch with me and other writers for a plug now and then.

Welterweight Art Aragon, the California Golden Boy.

Ladies loved his charm, romantic overtures, wit and often outlandish behavior. His third or fourth wife—I lost count—was a wealthy Jewish woman who shared her hillside estate in the San Fernando Valley with her Mexican-American husband. To no one's surprise, Art agreed to embrace his wife's Jewish faith. After all, she was rich.

Charlene and I were among several hundred guests who gathered to witness the outdoor Bar-Mitzvah ceremony on a sunny summer afternoon, to be followed by a lavish, catered party. Seated next to us were Don and Ruth Fraser.

As the solemn ritual progressed, with Aragon at the rabbi's side, a majority of those present prayed aloud in Hebrew. Don, wearing a yarmulke, riveted his eyes to the religious manual in his hand and mumbled along incoherently. Embarrassed, Ruth poked her elbow into Don's ribs, to no avail. He ignored his wife and continued mumbling.

When it came time for Aragon to speak, a rare occasion for the

103

Golden Boy's seriousness, he expressed wonderment about many things. He wondered about the magnificent Jewish traditions, its storied history and about Moses. The rabbi seemed proud and genuinely touched.

"And I wonder," Aragon continued, pausing dramatically as if mulling a profound thought, "as I look around at all of you... I wonder who's going to *pay* for all of this."

Devout Jews seemed stunned. The rest of us nearly burst with laughter. Even Don Fraser couldn't contain himself.

I LEARNED to read type upside down, Charlene recovered from her blood bath, periodically returned to ringside...and another child began to stir in her body.

Chapter 16

A Pivotal Year

With the promotion to the sports desk, my weekly salary increased to $50, the amount I earned at Dime-a-Line News more than a year earlier. Fortunately, Charlene was still bringing home a paycheck from Eastman Kodak, so we were managing to pay the bills with little to spare.

One afternoon I was summoned to the office of T. Harwood Young, the advertising chief downstairs—Johnny Badovinac's boss. Having had no contact with that department since leaving it, I couldn't imagine what Mr. Young wanted.

I was pleasantly surprised.

"I think you might be eligible for the government's on-the-job training program," he said. "If you qualify, you will receive weekly supplements to your income. As your Citizen-News salary increases, government subsidies will decrease and finally end at a specific figure."

Not only had the U.S. Army launched my journalistic career, the GI Bill was coming to my rescue when I needed it most. Totally unexpected, it was a godsend. My application was quickly approved, boosting my weekly pay to $85. It was sufficient, I told Charlene, to buy a house with almost no money down, also through the GI Bill.

She was ecstatic. We began house-hunting and found a new development only a few miles north of the apartments.

An attractive two-bedroom house, on a quiet street just off Terra Bella Avenue, was priced at $12,500, with manageable monthly payments, affordable with our combined income. However, Charlene's job would be ending soon.

"We'll worry about that when the time comes," I told her. "The point is we qualify now."

Charlene likely would have argued against such an impetuous decision were it not a home being discussed. With another baby due, we absolutely needed more room. She had been counting the days when we could leave the apartment.

As insignificant as $500 might sound, the down payment wasn't immediately available. I don't believe I considered trying my luck at a poker table again, but if I did, I certainly didn't suggest it to my wife.

Somehow we scrounged the money, arranged a loan and moved in early in 1954. For my wife, owning a home was the fulfillment of her lifelong dream.

THE CITIZEN-NEWS sports section was in need of a column to replace the one written by John Hall. Eventually, I supplied it each Saturday.

Labeled *Jack in the Box*, my column included a thumbnail photo of me. One Saturday, I replaced the head shot with one showing a bandaged index finger.

Written in jest, the column targeted comedian Bill Cosby, a former basketball star at Temple University. He was among a group of actors who teamed against sportswriters, including me, in an exhibition game at the Sports Arena.

During a fast break up court, Cosby had the ball and was driving hard when he brushed against me. I went sprawling. No foul was called and apparently few noticed. All eyes were on the actor. I never heard from Cosby or his reps and never received a letter from anyone who might have read that column.

My stab at humor flopped. It left me with nothing more than a sprained finger and bruised ego. When I started the column, I received sporadic mail—almost none complimentary.

One critic suggested I find a new job after I misused the word *prostrate.* I had spelled it *prostate.* The letter writer provided a definition of each word, generously laced with sarcasm. It was humbling.

The most important lesson I learned about writing for a newspaper began with an early morning weekday phone call. It woke me from a sound sleep.

"The judge asked me to call," his secretary said. "He wants to see you as soon as you come in."

"It's actually my day off," I replied, "but I can come in if he wants me to."

After checking with Judge Palmer, she relayed his response: "He said tomorrow will be OK."

Why would the publisher want to see me? I should have at least asked what it concerned. Instead, I ended the call abruptly with some inane reply such as "Fine, then I'll see him tomorrow."

Tomorrow? Those 24 hours were the longest I can remember. I never had been in Judge Palmer's office and rarely saw him.

I thought of recent articles I had written and blunders I had made, none seemingly serious enough to warrant the publisher's attention. Charlene quizzed me, but I didn't have a clue about what prompted this summons. Primarily, I again worried about being handed a pink slip.

I slept fitfully that night, tossing in bed, my mind spinning.

The following day, I arrived at the paper earlier than usual. The secretary ushered me into the publisher's spacious office, where Judge Palmer sat behind a large mahogany desk. Several brochures and my column lay in front of him.

Obviously aware of my nervousness, the judge said nothing to ease my discomfort. He simply offered me a chair, then immediately got to the point.

"Do you know anyone in Eloy, Arizona?"

Initially, I could think of no one. Then it came to me.

"There's a boxer, Willie Vaughn, who used to live in Eloy," I said. "He's going to fight at the Legion, an important match for him."

"Yes," he said matter-of-factly. "I read your column. Have you ever been to Eloy, Arizona?"

"No sir."

He handed me the brochures containing vast information about Eloy, a small desert community not far from Phoenix. I examined them briefly. The scenic photos were attractive.

"Your column describes this town quite differently," the judge said, "pretty much of a dump—no running water, shacks, outhouses…"

"That's how Willie's manager, Charlie Gregoli, described it," I replied. "He was just trying to point out how Willie had come from a poor family, an impoverished neighborhood, and was making a name for himself in boxing."

"Maybe I missed it, Jack. I didn't find the manager's name or any reference to him in your column."

"He's the one who gave me the story, Judge."

"Then he's the one you should have quoted. I want a retraction in your next column. I want that column along with a letter of apology mailed to the Eloy Chamber of Commerce. Is that understood?"

"Yes sir."

I wasted no time contacting Charlie Gregoli, a loud, gravel-voiced Italian in his 50s who looked like an overweight truck driver.

"What was all that crap about Eloy, Arizona?" I asked.

Acknowledging he might have exaggerated slightly, Gregoli insisted most of what he had told me was true.

"Hey, Willie came from the slums. I don't care what the Chamber of Commerce says. He had a tough life. He's hungry and he's gonna whip Green. You pick him in the paper, and you'll be the only writer in L.A to have the winner. I'm tellin' ya, he's never been in better shape."

A murderous puncher, Charlie Green was a prohibitive favorite to score an early knockout. Other boxing writers didn't pay much attention to Gregoli, who found me more susceptible to his ramblings. For some reason, despite nearly getting fired because of him, I boldly predicted an upset.

It turned out Gregoli was right about me being the only newspaperman to pick his fighter, also about the outcome. Vaughn weaved, bobbed and danced for 12 dull rounds, won a decision and was crowned the California middleweight champion April 24, 1954.

And Eloy had a hometown hero.

Since I knew the judge would read my "skin back"—as retractions sometimes were called—I labored diligently to compose a sincere apology for my "misconception" of Eloy, placing most of the blame on Charlie Gregoli.

Boxing dominated my responsibilities away from the office, but I also was assigned USC football and covered all of the Trojans' home games at the Los Angeles Coliseum.

Bob Panella, a UCLA alumnus, took the Bruins. Both of us had season football tickets to USC, UCLA and the Rams, plus press box credentials and choice parking passes. I attended most home games, two, sometimes three each weekend.

One Friday, when Panella passed up a USC night game, he gave me his press box ticket and parking pass. I invited my dad. He was thrilled.

The evening began at Julie's restaurant a few blocks from the Coliseum, favored by the sports crowd. The vacant world middleweight championship was up for grabs that night, Oct. 21, 1953.

A scheduled 15 rounder, bookmakers made knockout specialist Randy Turpin, the former world champ and current European middleweight king from England, a heavy favorite against light-hitting Carl (Bobo) Olson from California.

The fight, nationally televised from New York, drew a large number of sportswriters to the restaurant for dinner. Immediately after, most if not all would hustle over to the Coliseum for the football game.

The "smart money" was on Turpin to stop Olson early. When I drew Round 15 in a one-dollar pool at the dinner table, I tried to persuade my dad to trade his early-round draw for my number.

"Don't try to con your father," he said, laughing. "No way this fight's going 15 rounds."

For one of the few times in memory, I got the last laugh on dad. Olson danced and bobbed his way to a 15-round decision and became world middleweight champion. And I pocketed the pool money.

The press parking area was within a few yards from the stadium entrance, but it was a nice evening and I thought the short walk from the restaurant across grass would be good for dad. It wasn't.

Weak and short of breath, he stopped midway and leaned against a large tree. I thought he might be having a heart attack.

"Dad! Are you all right?"

"I'm OK," he said after a short rest. "Let's go. We don't want to miss the kickoff."

A huge sports fan, dad couldn't have been more pleased his son had landed what he considered a "dream job." It was a night he had looked forward to for weeks.

Long lines into the Coliseum were moving slowly when we arrived. We quickly passed through a press gate, entered a small lobby and stepped into the elevator, joining a few other scribes.

At the top, the doors slid open to the spacious enclosed press box. My father emerged. First out, he stepped gingerly, fearful he might lose his balance.

"It's like he's walking on eggs," one of the young occupants behind us whispered to a companion, a comment my dad no doubt also overheard.

Settled in front of a large open window looking down onto the field, we had time before the kickoff to scan the slick color program and other press material. As the game progressed, play-by-play sheets and statistics were distributed by the PR staff. Soft drinks, burgers, hotdogs, ice cream, snacks, etc., were readily available.

Watching my father's reaction to all of this, I knew he was impressed. I couldn't help but smile. It was a highlight in his life.

I kept a close eye on dad, who seemed to have recovered almost miraculously. He borrowed my binoculars from time to time and became engrossed in the game.

When it ended, we waited in the press box as the crowd thinned, then took our time getting back to the car. He was fine.

About six months later, a Catholic priest was summoned to hear my father's last confession at the Burbank home of my aunt and uncle, where he was staying. They chatted at length, laughing occasionally as dad unloaded a few tall tales.

Two other vivid memories still bring a smile as I recall his last days.

"Could we turn on the Kentucky Derby?" he asked. "It's almost time."

Helped from his bed to an easy chair in the living room, dad saw his last Run for the Roses on the first Saturday of May, 1954.

About a week later, when I visited him in the hospital, he seemed to know that night would be his last.

"What time is it?" he asked.

"Almost 6," I said, glancing at my watch.

"Turn on Bob Kelly, KMPC."

If he could help it, dad never missed Kelly, the voice of the Los Angeles Rams and most controversial sportscaster in Los Angeles.

A commercial about Lucky Lager beer came on.

"It's Lucky when you live in California," the announcer proclaimed.

Almost inaudibly, my father mumbled, "It's lucky when you *live*."

My eyes welled up. I knew and he knew it was our last visit.

Dad died during the night. He was 50.

Only 24, I wished I had spent more time with dad over the years. I looked back on the happy times we shared together, wrestling on the front lawn, playing shuffleboard, billiards, pinochle.... I was crushed.

For my mother, dad's departure was a blessing. He had been seriously ill for at least two years and unable to work much at the Shamrock.

Suddenly a widow at 45, mom looked at a bleak future without the man she had lived with for 25 mostly difficult years.

"I don't know what I'm going to do, Jack," she cried.

During dad's illness, mom relied heavily on the hired bartender, Glenn Walton, to help run the saloon. They got along well, joked with each other and became good friends.

Less than a year after my father died, she married Glenn in Las Vegas. Their impetuous elopement was not unlike that of Glenn's younger brother Dave Walton who had married my sister four years earlier.

Jack's sister Bonnie Walton, married at 16, celebrates with grandkids after receiving her high school diploma at age 54.

Bonnie immediately accepted her brother-in-law as her new stepfather. However, I could never bring myself to address Glenn as dad and for many years strongly resented him. He was a good man who looked up to my father and often told me he could never fill his shoes. Glenn loved mom and cared for her to the end.

They were married 50 years when both died within a few months of each other. My mother was 94, Glenn 82.

ONE SUNDAY, during halftime at a Rams game, my attention was drawn to a familiar face directly below my press box seat. Dick Long, the Hollywood actor I had served with in PIO at Camp Irwin, was waving to me.

"Jack, can I talk to you a minute?" he hollered.

"Be right down."

A press box door provided access to stadium seats. Not having seen Dick since our Army days together, I asked about his movie career and we exchanged more small talk.

"Are you here with anyone?"

"My wife," he said, "a few rows down. She's got a problem getting through this crowd. Would it be possible for us to take the press box elevator down after the game?"

"Sure," I replied. "Be here right after it ends. I'll let you in. Is she sick?"

"She lost a leg a while back, but she's doing OK."

How do you reply to something like that? I wondered why she was sitting near the top row of that enormous stadium. I wanted to know a lot more, but the game was ready to resume.

"It's tough, but she's handling it," he added. "She's got a lot of spunk."

I met Dick's wife, actress Suzan Ball, in the press box after the game and the three of us rode the elevator down together. She turned a lot of heads. She was beautiful.

Second cousin of the legendary comedienne Lucille Ball, she was proclaimed by columnist Hedda Hopper one of the "most important new stars of 1953."

During a dance number while filming *East of Sumatra* that year, she suffered a leg injury that resulted in tumors and ultimate amputation. Dick and Suzan became engaged in December of '53, a month before her surgery, and married April 4, 1954, in

Santa Barbara. The actress continued to work with an artificial limb as the cancer spread to her lungs. She died Aug. 5, 1955, six months after her 21st birthday.

Dick and I saw more of each other during the years that followed, after I had taken up golf. He appreciated my articles about the Hollywood Hackers, a group of actors who played regularly around the Southland.

Dick once invited me to Torrey Pines, near San Diego, for one of their tournaments. The only thing memorable about that junket was the beautiful course overlooking the Pacific Ocean. My game was embarrassing.

In 1957, Dick married Mara Corday, a stunning dark-haired pin-up queen and showgirl who starred in a number of movies before taking an early retirement to care for her three children.

Meanwhile, Dick's acting career flourished after he switched from the big screen to television, including a recurring role in the TV western *Big Valley*. At the height of his career, Dick Long suffered several heart attacks. He died at 47.

AS CHARLENE'S "due" date drew closer, I kept urging her to quit her job.

"Just two more weeks," she finally agreed, "and I'll have enough points to get a camera."

She worked longer than I wanted but got her camera and resigned from Eastman Kodak for a short R&R before delivering our second child.

It was early evening when we left for the hospital. Charlene's labor pains were not unbearable, so I stopped for gas rather than risk driving on an empty tank.

Suddenly, Charlene panicked.

"Hurry," she cried. "It's getting worse. Oh, hurry…"

Now *I* panicked.

"You said I had time to…"

"Hurry!" she screamed.

I hurried. I'm not sure the station attendant did.

Upon arriving, my wife immediately was wheeled into a prepping room. Less than an hour later, Linda Sue popped out like a champagne cork.

"I don't even feel like I had a baby," Charlene said, her face beaming as she cradled our new daughter in her arms.

Two weeks after God took dad, He gave us another beautiful daughter in return. The date was June 5, 1954.

Life goes on. Nice.

Chapter 17

Sinatra, Friends and Family

By 1955, I had settled into a comfortable routine at the paper, no longer worried about losing my job. I was learning the ropes, so to speak, at ringside.

The Southern California Boxing Writers' Assn. was a close-knit group that rotated the presidency each year. Since I automatically became a member, the gavel eventually was handed to me.

Besides John Hall (L.A. Mirror-News), the group consisted of Cal Whorton (L.A. Times), Morton Moss and later Sammy Schnitzer (L.A. Examiner), George Main (L.A. Herald-Express), Johnny Allen (L.A. Daily News), Rudy Garcia (La Opinion) and publicist Don Fraser.

Unlike stereotype reporters who compete for exclusive stories, our small fraternity shared information, drank and dined together on fight nights and held annual awards banquets.

We sold tickets, promoted it all year long and kept award-winners secret until unveiling them the night of the event. We honored boxers, managers, promoters, fights and fighters of the year and a few other categories.

Held the first year at the Hollywood Athletic Club, the event became increasingly more popular with bookings at the Palladium, Statler-Hilton Hotel in Los Angeles, an intimate Sunset Strip nightclub called the Crescendo and other upscale venues.

Boxing writers go formal at their annual awards banquet. Standing from left, Rudy Garcia (La Opinion), Jack (Hollywood Citizen-News), Sammy Schnitzer (L.A. Examiner), Johnny Allen (L.A. Daily News), Don Fraser (boxing publicist), Cal Whorton (L.A. Times); kneeling on left, John Hall (LA. Mirror-News), George Main (L.A. Herald-Express).

We had prominent entertainers, streamlined our agenda and presented elaborate trophies.

One year 13 former world champions gathered on stage for a rare photo. Among them was bantamweight Alphonse Halimi, who flew to Los Angeles from France especially for the occasion.

A French Algerian champ, Halimi first came to L.A. in 1957 and defended successfully against Mexico's Raton Macias via a 15-round decision before a mob at Wrigley Field. Two years later, he was beaten by another Mexican, Jose Becerra, in the first sports event ever staged at the then new Sports Arena July 9, 1959. The following year Halimi again lost to Becerra at the Coliseum—all big-time promotions.

Also among the ex-champs in that photo was Jack Root, the world's first light-heavyweight king who began his professional boxing career in 1897, won the 175-pound title in a 10-round decision over Kid McCoy April 22, 1903, and lost it to George Gardner less than three months later.

Being voted Fighter of the Year or having participated in

116

Fight of the Year was the goal of nearly every boxer who entered a Southland ring. We scribes, of course, promoted the event to the hilt, building suspense throughout the year until winners were announced on "Oscar Night."

A name from my past, Bobby (Cisco) Andrade, was our Fighter of the Year in 1954, and in 1955 he won a prestigious lifetime achievement award.

Lightweight title contender Bobby (Cisco) Andrade and Jack, born the same day of the same year, celebrate together. One cake is decorated as a front-page newspaper, the other a boxing ring.

An amateur boxer who made headlines in the Fort Ord Panorama when I was stationed there, Andrade settled in Compton, California, following his Army discharge. He turned professional about the same time I joined the Citizen-News sports desk. We soon discovered we had much more in common.

Born on the same day of the same year, we married about the same time, both fathered four children virtually the same ages and once celebrated our birthdays together at a gala party hosted by Andrade's manager and wife.

I wrote so many columns about Cisco's steady rise in the

rankings to eventually become a world lightweight title contender, Bob Panella ordered me to pick some other fighter to promote.

A handsome, likeable and polished boxer with an impressive knockout record, Andrade remained undefeated after 28 pro matches from 1952 through 1954. In 1955, after two straight losses, he won seven more in a row.

Next up for Andrade was California's Golden Boy, Art Aragon. It had all the ingredients for a classic battle and tremendous gate. Sports pages bannered the announcement.

Then Frank Sinatra got involved. More headlines and a quickly called press conference I'll never forget.

I was running a bit late when I rolled into the Legion parking area behind a large sedan. I parked next to it.

Ol' Blue Eyes stepped out with his entourage. Sinatra was in a jovial mood, joking about something as he moved briskly through the front door and into the pressroom where reporters waited. I followed them.

Never enamored with the mainline press corps, Sinatra was comfortable with sportswriters and liked associating with the fight mob and its assortment of strange characters.

The informal conference was brief, not particularly newsy, but Frank's presence and his light-hearted mood gave reporters plenty to write about.

Early in his singing career, Sinatra made friends with a well-known boxing trainer named Al Silvani who later became his bodyguard and personal companion. Not yet a superstar, the skinny young vocalist told Silvani he wanted to box professionally and wanted him to be his trainer.

Silvani saw the determination in Sinatra's face, believed he had potential as a boxer, but strongly advised him against lacing on gloves.

"One shot in your Adam's apple kid," the trainer said, "you can forget about a singing career."

It took some persuading, but Silvani ultimately convinced Frank the closest he should ever get to a boxing ring was a front-row seat. Sinatra pursued his passion for the sport. In 1956 he hooked up with a roly-poly Italian friend named Ralph Gambina to co-manage Andrade for his Aug. 29 match with Aragon.

Young Frank Sinatra with aspirations of boxing professionally is dissuaded by trainer Al Silvani.

As a huge Wrigley Field crowd waited impatiently for the fight to begin following a lengthy delay, a tense drama was unfolding in Cisco's dressing room. Gambina strenuously objected to what he considered excessive collodion, a thick protective dressing plastered over Aragon's eyes.

"There will be no fight," Gambina insisted if the patches were not removed.

While fans stomped their feet in the stands and shouted for action, Gambina held firm as did Aragon's handlers who refused to remove any of the substance.

Then Frank arrived in Cisco's dressing room. He looked at Ralph with an expression only he could convey and said, "There *will be* a fight. C'mon, Ralph, all our friends are at ringside waiting. Let's get going."

No argument. End of stalemate. Frank, Cisco, Ralph and the

trainers exited the dressing room and headed toward the ring amid thunderous cheers from fans.

A gutsy welterweight who had a few pounds on Cisco, the Golden Boy registered a thrilling ninth-round knockout in a sensational match that saw both fighters on the canvas more than once.

For Frank Sinatra, the loss was disappointing, of course, but for Gambina, it was a major setback in his relentless pursuit of a world title fight for Cisco whose only shot came about four years later.

On Oct. 28, 1960, Joe Brown—a 34-year-old veteran nicknamed Old Bones—retained his 135-pound title with a 15-round decision. Cisco, meanwhile, had defeated three other world champions, Lauro Salas twice, Jimmy Carter and Wallace (Bud) Smith, but not when it counted.

All were non-title fights.

CHARLENE CONTINUED to accompany me now and then to the Legion on Saturday nights, recoiling in her ringside seat with every blow. But she was adjusting to a life she never could have imagined, making new friends, attending social events and joining me on out-of-town assignments when possible.

Particularly attractive were invitations to Gilman Hot Springs, a short drive from Los Angeles, where boxers sometimes trained for major bouts. Former champs Ken Norton, Sugar Ray Robinson and many others often stayed weeks preparing for their matches. Press invitations included complimentary golf, meals at a classy on-site restaurant, unlimited drinks and full use of resort facilities.

One of our most memorable junkets there was shared with our friends Johnny Allen, the Daily News writer, and his wife Annie.

Early in his career, Johnny Allen adopted that pen name because John Tschantre presented a challenge for editors to spell and readers to remember. Ten years or so my senior, he became my mentor when I was struggling to keep my job. Charlene immediately connected with Annie, a warm, generous woman who loved life and lived it to its fullest.

Johnny, conversely, was a conservative money-pinching newspaperman who ordered martinis with olives on the side because they took up too much room in his cocktail glass.

We often recalled the night the four of us raided a watermelon patch off the highway near Gilman Hot Springs following dinner and too many cocktails.

With my wife at the wheel and the three of us behind the car cradling melons, we spotted approaching headlights in the distance and a trailing cloud of dust.

Panic-stricken, Charlene drove ahead as we lumbered after the car, yelling for her to stop. Finally, we reached the opened trunk, tossed the melons inside, breathlessly piled into the rolling vehicle and made a clean getaway.

Annie was the daughter of an inventor who made a small fortune designing a water heater valve or something. She shared a sizeable inheritance with her siblings when her father died years after we had met each other. Even then, Johnny grumbled when his wife spent lavishly.

Annie loved to ski but seldom went because John objected to the cost. After she came into her money, she invited Charlene and me to join her for a day trip despite Johnny's grumbling.

As Annie and I waited on a mountainous run, getting up nerve to push off, we were visibly shocked when a male skier dashed between us, hurtling down the hill.

We couldn't believe our eyes. The man was nude. We laughed for years about that.

We had a barrel of fun with the Allens and Don and Ruth Fraser whenever we got together, which was often. Our best memory as a group was the week in Hawaii.

Annie insisted on picking up several large dinner tabs. As always, she also picked up leftover tidbits from her plates, wrapped them in napkins and placed them inside her purse.

Anyone observing her must have thought she was eccentric. Annie couldn't care less. She needed to eat something light every two hours because of a stomach disorder. To remind her, she wore a wristwatch that buzzed at the designated time.

Not only did his wife's ritual embarrass Johnny, her buzzing time piece usually triggered a sarcastic comment the rest of us ignored.

When our plane touched down in Los Angeles and rolled to a stop, Annie heaved a weary sigh. At that precise moment her watch buzzed, sparking a burst of laughter from the three of us.

121

"For God's sake, Annie," Johnny barked. "Can't you turn that thing off?"

The truth was Johnny loved his wife dearly. He was shattered when Annie died unexpectedly on an operating table while undergoing what was thought to be minor, routine surgery.

She left us in her early fifties. Way too soon. We missed her.

I ALWAYS felt life runs in cycles. After struggling for so long to make ends meet, we started perking up when I began earning extra money.

Besides my regular salary at the paper, United Press paid me $30 a week to phone in results from ringside, and a boxing magazine sent me monthly checks for features I enjoyed writing.

Now I felt I had really hit pay dirt. I was offered $50 a week to write seven or eight paragraphs about any collegiate football star I chose. Never mind that my article would be published on a gambling card that cost a minimum of one dollar.

On the back of the card, 20 college games scheduled that week were listed with point spreads and payoff amounts.

"There's nothing illegal about selling information," the man who contacted me said. "I don't care what you write. If you're concerned, don't use a byline."

What a windfall, I thought—fifty bucks for an hour's work.

For my first feature, I dug up a few statistics about Charlie (Choo-Choo) Justice, an All-American tailback from North Carolina. My next article featured J.C. Caroline, another Hall of Famer from Illinois. I borrowed metal cuts of the players from Citizen-News files to illustrate the stories and banked $100.

Before I could start a third article, I underwent emergency surgery, a hemorrhoidectomy, a few days before Sept. 21, 1955.

That was the date Rocky Marciano knocked out light-heavyweight king Archie Moore to retain his heavyweight crown. I watched the fight on TV from a hospital bed, not realizing I had dodged another bullet.

I later learned that bunko officers, who had been working undercover, raided the Hollywood office of the card-gambling ring. They made several arrests and shut down the operation. Betting cards, none bearing my name, were confiscated.

Fortunately, Bob Panella never knew about my involvement or

that I had borrowed metal cuts from the files which I returned.

Again, God's timing was perfect.

A MONTH later, Oct. 24, Charlene gave birth to Barbara Jean.

It was a complicated delivery performed by a physician we met at the hospital who told us our family doctor had been called away on an emergency.

As I sat in the waiting room for an interminable time, chain smoked and moved from chair to chair, I worried.

Finally, the doctor appeared.

"You have a beautiful little girl," he said with a thin smile. "We had a little problem during delivery, but your wife and baby are just fine."

Using medical terms, he explained that Charlene had lost an abnormal amount of blood but there was no cause for alarm. I *was* alarmed and wanted more details, which he provided.

"She's doing fine," he repeated. "You can see her in a few minutes."

After that experience, Charlene was not eager to endure another pregnancy, even though we both wanted a son.

In those days, the Catholic Church strictly prohibited the use of contraceptives under the threat of ex-communication. So we practiced the rhythm system, but obviously "danced" to the wrong beat. On Dec. 12, 1956, less than 14 months after Barbara was born, John Michael joined the family.

The Vatican never wavered in its stand on birth control. Absolution in the confessional seemed to depend on the priest seated on the other side of the screen.

We had no more children.

Chapter 18

Comps and More Part-Time Work

Bob Panella's daily mail consisted mostly of photos, news releases and items for his column, only a small number of which found its way into print. It also included invitations addressed to him personally or to the "sports editor."

When an event conflicted with a commitment or didn't interest him, he would pass the invitation to me. For the first few years as Bob's assistant, I tagged along like his shadow, sitting at his elbow at luncheons, dinners, meeting people and contributing little to the conversation.

One morning, Panella tossed an unopened envelope across the desk. It was addressed to me, sent by Walt Disney—an invitation for two to a press preview of Disneyland before its grand opening July 17, 1955. Panella, of course, received an identical envelope, as did hundreds of others.

Seemingly every newspaper in the Southland was represented that night, along with numerous radio and TV people.

Exclusively for the media and guests, the party was the largest, most festive I ever attended. Costumed Disney characters pranced about as we enjoyed thrill rides, marvelous exhibits, street entertainment, open bars, a variety of food stations and escorted tours of the sprawling 160-acre Magic Kingdom. It reportedly cost $17 million to build by opening day.

Charlene cuddles with Donald at Disneyland.

Sleepy little Anaheim surrounded by vast acres of orange groves before Walt Disney came along had undergone a remarkable transformation. The once obscure Orange County city became world-famous.

Over the next decade, the park underwent constant changes as rides, exhibits and attractions were added and replaced. The creative *Small World* was one of my favorites. It disappeared in 1966.

Almost 20 years later, I interviewed Jay Livingston and Ray Evans at the Beverly Hills home of fellow composer Richard Sherman, who composed the music and lyrics for that attraction. His song, *It's a Small World (after all)*, became an enormous hit. People who track record sales say they sold more than 250 million copies of their music.

By its second year of operation, Disneyland turned a profit. Obtaining complimentary press tickets for families required nothing more than a phone call.

Our four children became well acquainted with the Kingdom, where we once "lost" Barbara, a shy, stubbornly independent 5-year-old who had a habit of wandering off to inspect anything of interest.

Rushing to catch a nearly full parking lot tram after a long, exhausting day, our family found seats, but not together. When we arrived at our car and stepped off the tram, Barbara was not among us.

Unable to locate her after a short time, we contacted security, which conducted an organized search of the park.

Charlene and I tried to have positive thoughts, but the longer we waited in that small security room the more we worried. And we prayed.

Finally, word came. She had been found in the parking lot and was being brought to the front gate, where we went to meet her.

Tears rolling down her cheeks, the white tops of her saddle shoes smudged from placing one foot atop the other while resting on the sun-baked asphalt, she had little to say.

"I either got on the attached tram or sat on the other side," she said years later when trying to recall the incident. "I think someone in the parking lot asked me if I was lost and brought me back to the front gate. How long did I wander around? In the eyes of a 5-year-old, it seemed like hours."

Despite a tight family budget in those early years, the kids enjoyed summers. Like Disneyland, visits to Knott's Berry Farm, Pacific Ocean Park amusement center, Griffith Park Zoo and other nearby attractions were easily arranged. If comps were unobtainable, it was possible to gain reduced rates with the promise of a little publicity.

For instance, one summer the kids enjoyed a week of swimming, fishing, miniature golf and other activities at Lake Isabella in Central California at a fraction of the regular cost.

On that occasion, it was Linda who gave us a scare.

About 5 at the time, she waded too far from shore, stepped into a hole and was gulping water when Patty, playing on the beach, spotted her and began to laugh.

"Look at Linda," she said, not realizing she might be drowning.

In a matter of seconds, I had her safely on the sand and thereafter kept a closer watch on all four of the children. Charlene took the girls for swimming lessons when we got home, a top priority after our scare.

When Roy Harris prepared for a 1958 title fight against heavyweight champion Floyd Patterson at a plush out-of-town resort, Don Fraser invited our family for several days while I covered the challenger's training routine on site.

A big underdog, Harris was virtually unknown outside his backwoods Texas town of Cut and Shoot. Fraser took care of that in a hurry. His publicity releases, my stories and others gave the title bout credibility. Initially thought to be an unworthy opponent, Harris surprised experts by lasting12 rounds before being stopped.

Charlene often accompanied me to Las Vegas when I covered fights there. One time, the kids joined us for several days.

They played on hotel elevators, swam in the pool and ran up a big tab at a Strip dinner show. I assumed that was complimented along with everything else. I was shocked when the waiter handed me the check. Short on money, I ended up mailing the hotel payments after we all returned home.

After that embarrassment, Charlene always snooped at the reservation sheet as we entered Vegas showrooms and waited to be seated.

"Is it in red?" she once asked an impeccably dressed maitre'd.

He glanced at the list, looked up and smiled broadly.

"As red as your dress."

Always escorted to a choice table, we typically saw two Strip shows each night, including a dinner show, sometimes a third. Charlene's first trip to Las Vegas, although never erased from her memory, became less painful with the passing of time. And yes, she finally saw Peggy Lee on stage.

But it was Bobby Vinton who thrilled her more. Facing a blinding spotlight in front of our booth during his performance one evening, Vinton serenaded Charlene and kissed her hand. Decades later, we revisited the singer backstage following his engagement in Sun City West, where I retired. Reminded of that special Las Vegas moment, Vinton again planted a kiss on Charlene's hand. Nice.

Roses are red, violets are blue, sugar is sweet...

Ah, those romantic moments of yesteryear. For Charlene, there were many.

THE OCCASION was an overnight press junket to the Bermuda Dunes Country Club in Palm Desert, California, where Bob Hope hosted the media to promote his new Chrysler Golf Classic.

A chartered plane brought reporters, gorgeous models, movie stars and other celebrities to the desert playground to eat, drink, socialize and play golf. Those who did brought clubs. As I had not yet taken up the sport, I brought Charlene and my video camera.

Spotting Argentine actor Fernando Lamas at a cocktail party, I asked if he would mind being filmed with my wife.

"Not at all," he said, "but let's include some others."

Involved in a messy divorce with actress Arlene Dahl, Lamas was playing it safe, even in those days. William Holden volunteered to make it a threesome.

Standing between the handsome actors, Charlene beamed as I recorded the moment.

Afterward, publicist Stan Wood joined us. As we sipped cocktails and chatted with Holden at the edge of the dance floor, Stan saw his wife Maryanne and beckoned her.

"I want you to meet William Holden," he said as she approached carrying a full glass of wine.

Flustered, intoxicated or just plain clumsy, Maryanne stepped close to Holden, extended her hand and dumped the entire contents of her drink on the front of the actor's white dinner jacket, drenching it with red wine.

Maryanne immediately apologized. Stan was mortified. We all were shocked. Holden attempted to downplay the incident observed by everyone nearby.

"Well," the actor said with a forced smile, "I better go to my room and change. Excuse me."

And he left.

The story spread and didn't die quickly. Maryanne suffered through months of embarrassment when "reminded" of it.

Another memory linked to the annual tournament involved my granddaughter Theresa Mann, who was one of three Hope Chrysler Classic girls in the 1996 event.

Selected each year from many entrants, the girls—officially called tournament ambassadors—wander through the crowds, smile and look gorgeous.

Theresa sent Charlene and me pair of tickets and a VIP parking pass for the weekend of the five-day event. Unfortunately, the attendant didn't accept the VIP pass. He directed us to a huge dusty field where fans parked their cars and took bus-like shuttles to the tournament entrance.

When we saw Theresa, I kidded her about the invalid pass.

**Jack's and Charlene's granddaughter Theresa Mann, center, joins
the other Chrysler Classic ambassadors at the 1996 Bob Hope golf
tournament in Palm Desert, California.**

It didn't take long for her to provide another for Sunday's final
round.

"You won't have a problem with this one, Grandpa. I don't
know why they wouldn't take the other one."

As Charlene and I were preparing to leave the parking area
that Saturday I set my trifocals on the narrow rear panel of our car
while I changed out of my golf shoes for the drive to our hotel.

Several miles later as the sun was setting, I removed my dark
glasses, reached into a shirt pocket for my trifocals, and...

"Oh, no," I exclaimed. "I left my damned glasses on the bumper of the car when I changed shoes. They're long gone."

"Maybe they're still there," Charlene replied. "Why don't you
pull over and look?"

"Not a chance. There were several thousand cars parked there.
With all those mounds to go over, there's no way they wouldn't
have fallen off. They probably got crushed in the dirt."

Charlene was too nervous to drive to a restaurant that evening, so we walked to one. She read the menu to me and I sulked.
Not only did I desperately need my glasses, they were relatively
new and expensive.

The following morning we stopped for Mass en route to the golf course.

"Dear God," I silently prayed, "I know this request would be pretty low on your priority list, but if You could see your way clear to help me find those glasses, I sure would appreciate it."

Being an eternal optimist and never underestimating the power of prayer (even for selfish reasons), I elected not to use the VIP parking pass.

"I thought Theresa gave you another one," Charlene said as we funneled through a mass of vehicles toward the general parking area."

"She did but, well, I want to check on those glasses."

If Charlene responded, I don't remember. Knowing her, an eternal pessimist, I'm sure she thought it was a waste of time.

Finally at the gate, I paid the stone-faced attendant and was handed a ticket.

"Just follow the car in front of you," he said, waving me on like a sweaty traffic cop who hated his job.

"I know this is asking too much," I said, "but did anyone happen to find..."

Before I finished my long story, the driver behind me hit his horn. The attendant eyed me incredulously.

"Glasses? Are you crazy? You're holding up the line. Get going."

"Sorry. I just thought..."

I pulled forward to close a long gap in the line, turned down a designated lane and rolled over several mounds. I parked somewhere in left field. We exited near a waiting shuttle and in minutes were at the course entrance.

Suddenly, I realized I had left my camera in the car.

"Wait here, honey. I'm going back. I want to get more shots of Theresa."

Charlene was exasperated. But she waited.

Returning to my car on foot, I was hailed by a young man driving an empty shuttle. He offered me a ride. I climbed aboard.

"I'll wait and take you back," he said as I stepped out.

"That's okay. I can walk."

He insisted. I thanked him, quickly retrieved my camera, climbed back on the shuttle and took one more shot at a miracle.

"I was here yesterday, parked way over there somewhere," I told him, pointing to the general area. "Did anyone happen to turn in..."

"You know," he said after pondering a bit, "my supervisor mentioned some glasses someone turned in last night. Just a minute."

Using his cell phone, the shuttle driver exchanged a few words with his supervisor, then turned to me."

"Were they in a brown case?"

"Why, yes. They were. Trifocals."

The driver relayed my response and ended the call.

"He'll be right over with them."

"*Really*," I said as if truly shocked. "What are the odds?"

Somehow, I wasn't surprised.

ONE EVENING in the mid-1950s, local sportscaster Mark Scott, whom I had never met, took his assigned seat next to Charlene and me at a Hollywood press dinner.

Scott broadcast Hollywood Stars ballgames in the Pacific Coast League and had a 15-minute weeknight sports program on radio station KFWB, three blocks from the Citizen-News.

He was among a dozen or so prominent sportscasters in the L.A. area who competed for jobs. Competition was fierce, but at that moment, Mark Scott was exceptionally busy.

"I don't know if you heard," Mark said, "but Irv Kaze is the new public relations director for the Hollywood Stars."

I hadn't heard, nor did I know Irv Kaze had been Scott's writer at KFWB.

"I'm looking for a replacement," Mark said, "someone who could work a few hours each afternoon to write my show. Do you know anyone who might be interested?"

"Not offhand," I replied.

The words had scarcely left my lips when I felt a sharp kick under the table.

"Well," I quickly added, exchanging a meaningful look with my stone-faced wife, "I might be interested."

Less than a week later, I was writing Mark's sports show.

Chapter 19

The Olympic

Long before I first set foot inside the massive 10,400-seat Olympic Auditorium, the arena had compiled an impressive history.

It opened Aug. 25, 1925, to radiant Hollywood film stars, prominent citizens in tuxedos and fans closely identified with the rough and tough heavyweight king at the time, Jack Dempsey. The Manassa Mauler shoveled the first pile of dirt for the ground-breaking ceremony.

Weekly boxing matches were staged Tuesday nights through the 1940s but had shifted to Thursdays by the time I arrived in 1953.

Hot-blooded crowds showed up early at the entrance and spilled out into the street. They funneled through the main entrance, congregated in the marble-floored hallway that circled the arena and chomped on cigars. Many made bets, almost all talked boxing.

As a rookie on the beat, I stood back, listened and took notes as John Hall, Johnny Allen, George Main and the other writers chatted with managers, trainers, referees, ex-pugs, gamblers, anyone spewing out information possibly worthy of print.

The ritual never varied from week to week, big crowds or small. The most colorful characters were those that lived and breathed the sport, night and day with virtually no other interests.

They clustered in the hallway behind the lower level seats. They told tall stories promoting their stables of boxers and bitched about bad decisions. They sought headlines, but settled for at least a mention in the sports pages. Sometimes they just rambled.

"You know how I got this?" asked referee Mushy Callahan, an ex-fighter with a nose that spread to his cheeks. "A horse stepped on it. I'm not kidding."

Not to be outdone in story-telling, referee and ex-title contender George Latka with a similar flattened beak and scar tissue over his eyes recalled a traffic altercation with an irate driver.

"He was furious," George said. "He jumped out of his car and was ready to throw a punch when I told him to back off. 'Take a look at this face,' I said. 'Does it occur to you how I got a face like this?'"

The man's eyes raked Latka's wiry, rock-hard frame.

"He thought about that a moment," George continued, "got back into his car and drove off."

Harry Kabakoff, a short, rotund manager always good for a laugh, chimed in.

Dedicated to his stable of boxers, Harry treated them like family. He represented mostly Mexicans, which didn't pose a communication problem, since he spoke fluent Spanish.

Harry's real name was Melville Himmelfarb.

"I took the name of my favorite uncle," he told me, which in itself, needed further explanation. I explored the subject briefly, then dropped it.

Kabakoff's prize pupil was bantamweight title contender Jesus Pimentel. They were so close Harry always spoke of Jesus as if they were inseparable.

I asked Harry to confirm a rumor that Pimentel had made wedding plans for a certain date.

Kabakoff did a double take, his eyes widening, as if news to him.

"We can't get married then," he said. "We got a big fight that night."

An incurable publicity hound that often passed along tips to reporters, Kabakoff usually followed his hush-hush news with an admonition, "...but don't quote me."

Once, John Hall not only quoted Kabakoff about an especially controversial topic, but completed his lengthy quote with the manager's four favorite words, "but don't quote me." Period. End quote.

The column item generated some laughs, and Kabakoff got his name in the Los Angeles Times. He was happy.

Covering Olympic boxing left me with many indelible memories. One still haunts me.

When I arrived for the fights one Thursday night, Joe Stanley was waiting for me at the entrance. My column a few days earlier featured bantamweight world title contender Billy (Sweetpea) Peacock, managed by Stanley. They were like father and son.

Low-key, mild-mannered, Joe thanked me for the column and extended his hand. When I grasped it, I found a folded $20 bill in his palm. Christmas gifts were one thing. Taking cash was not only embarrassing; it could cost me my job.

Joe insisted. I took it.

Less than 12 hours later, I reported for work at the Citizen-News, stepped into the wire room and ripped off a story from the City News Service.

It was brief. A man had taken a taxi from the Olympic to the train yards after the fights, the story said, paid the fare, got out and stepped toward the tracks. At the last moment, he threw himself in front of a slow-moving freight train. He was identified as Joe Stanley.

There was considerable speculation about what led to Joe's suicide. No one I talked to knew for certain. Some said he had tax liabilities, but Don Fraser said "it was because his girlfriend dumped him."

Peacock was devastated, his ring career shattered. Over the next three years the once near champion suffered 18 straight defeats before retiring.

THE NIGHT of April 30, 1964, was unforgettable. A wild, sell-out crowd of hot-blooded Mexicans suddenly hushed awaiting a decision in the ring.

Hiroyuki Ebiharra, a flyweight champion from Japan, had traded blows with Mexico's Efren Torres for 15 rounds, a furious match that could have gone either way. I scored it for Ebiharra by a single point.

The decision was slow in coming. Finally, the referee appeared in the center of the ring. He grabbed the microphone and read the officials' scorecards. To no one's surprise, the verdict was split.

The protest began even before the referee raised the winner's hand. As if anticipating the crowd's reaction, the official seemed concerned about his safety. I felt like I was sitting on a time bomb.

Finally, the dreaded announcement.: "The winner, Hiroyuki Ebiharra."

His words were lost as fans erupted. At first, paper cups flew down from the balcony, then other objects. Those seated below quickly retreated to the covered hallway to observe the mounting violence.

In a matter of seconds, I was under the apron, on the phone to United Press reporting the opening salvo of a full-scale Olympic riot.

The unoccupied ring became littered with debris. Seats ripped from the balcony floor were hurled below. Small fires broke out. Water from wall-mounted hoses flooded floors. Don Fraser locked himself in his office.

A one-gallon mustard jar, thrown from the balcony, suddenly exploded on the ring apron inches from my face. As I drew my hand across my eyes, shards of glass produced streaks of ketchup-like blood. My sport jacket was ruined.

Scooting deeper under the apron, I continued dictating a story to the wire service that made front-page headlines the following morning.

I remained on the phone under the apron as the riot escalated, then gradually subsided as police and fire trucks began to arrive.

Hanging up the phone and emerging from under the ring, I walked up the aisle with my face caked in mustard and blood. Fans lingering in the hallway seemed amused.

I recall no serious injuries being reported, but the building had extensive damage.

United Press paid for a new sport jacket, a small price for exclusive coverage.

AILEEN EATON, the grand dame of Southern California boxing, was a major presence in Los Angeles for almost half a century.

Olympic boxing and wrestling promoter from 1942 until 1980, she later served on the California State Athletic Commission, which controlled the sport.

135

MAIN EVENT - JULY 28, 1977
ALBERTO SANDOVAL vs. ALBERTO MORALES

CARLOS PALOMINO
WELTERWEIGHT CHAMPION

DANNY LOPEZ
FEATHERWEIGHT CHAMPION

ALBERTO SANDOVAL
"SUPERFLY"

Souvenir of Aileen Eaton's 35th Anniversary
of Boxing Promotion At The Olympic

Olympic boxing promoter Aileen Eaton celebrates a milestone with welterweight champion Carlos Palomino, featherweight king Danny Lopez and super flyweight Alberto Sandoval.

Aileen once estimated she had seen more than 10,000 professional fights and staged more than 100 world championship matches. When the Olympic was too small for a major show, she took them outdoors. In 1963 Aileen promoted an unprecedented three title bouts the same evening at Dodger Stadium.

Born in Vancouver, Canada, one of three children, Aileen and her family moved to Los Angeles when she was a teen. She graduated from Los Angeles High School and shortly thereafter married Martin LeBell, an osteopath.

Eager for a career, she studied law for two years at Southwestern Law School, but quit when one of her sons became ill. Her husband died in 1941 following a swimming accident, and she went back to work.

While employed as a private secretary for Frank A. Garbutt, president of the L.A. Athletic Club, which owned the Olympic, the ambitious young woman was sent to the boxing and wrestling arena to determine why the club was losing money and not paying its bills.

She quickly discovered irregularities in the bookkeeping and recommended hiring Alvah (Cal) Eaton, a boxing commission inspector, as the new promoter. She also became instantly captivated by the sport.

Six years later, after Cal Eaton divorced his first wife, the couple married.

Although the weekly boxing cards were labeled "Cal Eaton promotions," his wife took charge of every detail. When Cal died in 1966, she made it official.

Sportscaster Jim Healy, a former Citizen-News sportswriter who announced the Olympic cards on TV from 1970 to 1978, recalled on-camera interviews he conducted with young boxers who were under Aileen's thumb.

"You've heard of questions being written beforehand," he said. "Well, she used to write the answers. I had copies of the scripts and I would devise questions to fit. These poor boxers would try to memorize the answers before we went on, and they were petrified. That's how scared of her they were."

Times columnist Jim Murray, paying a 1980 tribute to her fighting spirit after she underwent heart surgery, wrote: "Red-haired, blue-eyed, pound for pound, she was as tough as any welterweight who ever came down the aisle."

Harry Kabakoff, asked to describe Aileen in her prime, replied, "One afternoon you can find her with five hardened managers, screaming, yelling, talking man-talk. Two hours later she's having cocktails at the governor's mansion—all charm."

A shrewd businesswoman who recognized the value of good publicity, Aileen catered to the media, particularly those of us who occupied the same reserved ringside seats every Thursday. Whether the vast arena was bulging with fans or virtually empty, she could open any Friday sports section in the city and always find the Olympic boxing results.

At Christmastime Aileen spent freely on parties at major hotels and country clubs and gifts for a long list of writers and columnists. She was especially generous to the beat reporters (suits, topcoats, silver coffee table accessories, glassware, gifts for wives, etc., purchased and delivered by Fraser). Occasionally, she invited writers to her Beverly Hills home directly across the street from attorney Paul Caruso, her close friend who managed Art Aragon.

When Don and I ran out of money in Paris, our final stop on

a 1966 European tour we took with our wives, he wired Aileen for loans. She promptly sent each of us $100. Upon our return, I handed her my check, which she immediately tore up. Believing she also had refused repayment from Don, I commented about her generosity.

"Good for you," he replied resentfully. "She took the hundred out of my paycheck."

Aileen also came to my rescue on another occasion.

Late one night, an hour after the last fight had ended, I was hunched over the typewriter in Don's second-floor office, laboring over a routine story. Fans had cleared the building and the other writers also had gone.

"Turn off the lights when you go," Don reminded me as he, too, left.

"I'm almost finished," I mumbled, embarrassed to be grinding over a story that would be buried on a back page the next day.

Always last to start writing after calling in results to the wire service, I usually was last to arrive at the Brown Derby or elsewhere for a snack and nightcap after the fights. If Aileen didn't join us, Don did and, of course, signed the check.

It was past midnight when I finally finished writing. I flicked off the lights, exited the office and started down the dimly lighted hallway. Descending the stairway, I stepped to the front doors and saw two were chained together, secured by a padlock.

Assuming another exit had been left open, I began circling the semi-dark hallway checking doors, looking for a clean-up crew, a janitor...anyone.

Eerie lighting cast weird shadows on walls, particularly on large murals of great champions and other ring idols in menacing boxing poses. They seemed to look down on me like ghosts from the past, poised to float off the wall. A mind can conjure up strange thoughts at such times.

With every step on the marble floor producing an echo in an otherwise dead silence, I became uneasy, walked more softly, heard nothing. It soon became obvious I was the only living soul in the tomb-like auditorium with 10,400 empty seats and no way out.

Although fairly certain Aileen would be home asleep at that hour, I could think of no option and picked up the phone.

Whatever explanation I gave for what my colleagues later would tease me about, it was embarrassing to admit my predicament. I apologized for waking her.

"I'll call Mike to unlock the front door," she said. "He'll be right there."

Mike LeBell, Aileen's oldest of two sons who worked the Olympic box office (Gene, his brother, was a prominent pro wrestler) soon arrived with the key to set me free.

"We used to keep police dogs locked inside overnight to guard against break-ins," Mike said. "Good thing they weren't here tonight."

Yes. A very good thing.

I thanked him, walked around the building where my car was the only one remaining in the huge parking lot, stepped inside and drove home.

Having called Charlene from the Olympic, I wasn't surprised to find her asleep when I wearily eased into the sack.

Even in retirement, Aileen's passion for the sport never diminished.

"I don't think there was a night we didn't talk on the phone two or three times about boxing," said Don Chargin, the Olympic matchmaker for 18 years. "Since she got out of boxing, nobody has really tried to develop talent the way she did. There's been nobody like her, and I don't think there ever will be."

After a series of illnesses, Aileen Eaton died at 78. Her obituary, published under my byline in The Times, appeared Nov. 9, 1987.

Chapter 20

Radio and Television

Hurrying down the concrete steps outside the post office on Wilcox Street, a stone's throw from the Citizen-News, Milt Rosner came face-to-face with me, his former Camp Irwin sergeant, as I headed up with something to mail.

As surprised to run into me as I was to bump into him, we greeted each other with huge smiles. It had been about six years since we parted ways at the Presidio of San Francisco and hadn't kept in touch.

"Jack," he blurted out, stopping in mid-step.

Never having called him by his first name and probably not even remembering it at that instant, I replied, "Lieutenant...what a surprise!"

"Milt."

We exchanged some meaningless conversation after which Rosner suggested I apply for a job at the Los Angeles Times.

"I like it here in Hollywood," I said. "I live in the Valley. It's only about a 20- minute drive to the office."

"Another 10 minutes down the freeway," he replied with a shrug.

The truth was I never considered applying at The Times, one of the nation's largest and most respected newspapers, because I felt I wasn't qualified to work there.

Following his tour of Army duty, Rosner returned to his Beverly Hills literary agency to represent writers who mostly worked in television.

"Why don't you write a western?" he said. "They're easy. The money's great."

"I don't know anything about writing for TV," I told him.

"It's not difficult, just a different style. Think about it and give me a call."

He handed me his business card, then glanced at his watch.

"I've gotta run. Call me."

With that he was in motion, bounding down the remaining steps. The lieutenant hadn't changed. Always in a rush, his mind racing, he still found time to offer advice and extend a helping hand.

A western? I certainly watched enough on TV.

I put the project on a back burner and promised myself I would give it a try when I had time.

Meanwhile, I was pocketing an extra $50 a week after a $15 raise from sportscaster Mark Scott for writing his show. Not bad for about two hours work. If there were phone interviews, it would take less time.

Mark had little trouble getting local people to interview, but he wasn't well known nationally. Sometimes he had to improvise.

Unable to connect with Archie Moore before his nationally televised fight with heavyweight champion Rocky Marciano, Scott paid a black janitor to impersonate the light-heavyweight king in a live phone interview.

A day or so later Scott handed me written answers to a few questions he had planned to ask Marciano's manager, Al Weill, on the air. When the interview fell through, Scott asked me to fill in for Weill.

I told Mark I wasn't comfortable doing that. To him, it was no different than recreating baseball games on radio. Sportscasters employed all types of sound effects and invented plenty of creative incidents such as a dog running wild on the field to fill time when teletype reports were delayed.

Scott was an extremely persuasive person. Besides, he was my boss. I did it. Don Fraser, for one, recognized my voice immediately. I wondered how many other listeners did. My young high-pitched voice was not even close to Al Weill's. I was relieved no one else mentioned that fiasco.

When Scott landed a local weekly television show at KCOP, I helped produce it along with Tom Gries, who worked as a reporter for a Chicago newspaper before arriving in Hollywood in 1947.

A competent writer with lofty ambitions, Gries and I worked together for about six months on Mark's show which included film clips and commentary.

It was my first television job. Tom, a former World War II marine, was eight years older and a strong influence on my life. He, too, was inexperienced but learned fast. One night he substituted for Mark on camera. When possible, he sat with the director in the control room, absorbing as much knowledge as possible.

Gries went on to a successful career in the industry as a talent agent, publicist, TV script writer and story aide for producer/director Stanley Kramer. Tom focused on becoming a respected film director and achieved his goal.

He received an Emmy in 1963 for directing the TV series *East Side/West Side* and directed a number of highly acclaimed movies, including *Muhammad Ali: The Greatest,* and *Helter Skelter,* a TV documentary of the grisly murders committed by Charles Manson and his followers.

After our brief association ended, I lost track of Tom until we happened to pull up side-by-side one sunny afternoon at a Beverly Hills traffic signal. He was behind the wheel of a shiny Rolls-Royce convertible with the top down.

We exchanged a few words before the light turned green.

"Give me a call," he shouted as he drove away. "I'm in the book."

It was the last time I saw Tom. I'll always remember that unlikely meeting and his beaming face. I later read he suffered a fatal heart attack while playing tennis in Pacific Palisades. He was 55.

I don't recall why I stopped working for Mark, but I do remember having a difficult time collecting $100 he promised me for a special one-time show dealing with the New Year's Rose Bowl game. He finally paid me after I pestered him on the phone for weeks.

After Scott and I parted company, Bill Brundige hired me to write his nightly radio show at KHJ, where he was sports director. Busy with other commitments, Bill wanted me to serve as his backup on the air, a wonderful opportunity.

At the time, Jim Healy occasionally subbed on the air for Bob Kelly at KMPC. After Kelly died, Healy quickly joined elite L.A. sportscasters with a style patterned after newscaster Walter Winchell's clickety-click ticker-tape gossip.

Healy's broadcasts of behind-the-scenes scoops and recorded interviews, spiced with weird sound effects, were hilarious.

But I was no Jim Healy. I reluctantly agreed to a recorded audition, but with my tenor voice and inexperience in front of a mike, I was a complete failure.

It's a wonder Brundige didn't look elsewhere for a writer. Even my scripts didn't capture his style. He often rewrote items when time permitted; when it didn't, he ad-libbed.

Brundige had good sources, including Brooklyn Dodgers executives who strolled along station hallways with him when they came to town. Their conversation almost always centered around the team's proposed move to Los Angeles, the hottest topic in all of sports for months.

Typical was Bill's introductory line for a major news item: "I learned exclusively just an hour ago that..." even though the wire services probably carried a version of that "exclusive" an hour earlier.

Dodger owner Walter O'Malley announced Oct. 8, 1957, that after 68 seasons in Brooklyn, the club would relocate. On April 18, 1958, the Los Angeles Dodgers played their first game at the L.A. Coliseum, winning 6-5 over the Giants, who had moved from New York to San Francisco about the same time. The Coliseum crowd was reported as 78,672.

That historic game was followed by hot rumors, predictions and lingering controversy surrounding O'Malley's deal with the city of Los Angeles to build a ballpark in Chavez Ravine. The media ate it up.

Brundige got more than his share of scoops but lost his show and his writer as well. Bill, I believe, remained employed at KHJ. Despite the loss of income, I wasn't greatly upset. I needed a break, but it didn't last.

Bob Panella also was moonlighting at CBS, writing Tom Harmon's nationally broadcast show that was carried locally on KNX five nights a week. One night, Bob couldn't be at the studio. He asked me to sub for him.

I was delighted.

A relatively easy format to script, the show consisted mostly of straight sports news rewritten from the wires, a short editorial, taped interviews and a humorous tag if needed to fill the time slot. Of course, I faced another deadline.

As I sat at the typewriter, I think I was shaking.

I got through it, however, and had other opportunities to fill in for Bob. Writing for Harmon was quite different, starting with filling out a CBS tax withholding form. I was amazed when I received my first paycheck from the network. It was quadruple what Scott and Brundige paid me out of their pockets.

No wonder Panella could afford to invest in expensive residential property above the Hollywood Freeway and make payments on the sleek sports car he drove.

I was substituting for Bob the night Harmon interviewed driver Billy Vukovich, who was seeking his third straight victory in the 1955 Indianapolis 500-mile auto race.

In the early days of that annual classic, gas tanks exploded on impact and wheels spun off cars, flying into the stands. Drivers often were killed or seriously injured in spectacular accidents.

Harmon asked Vukovich about the dangerous aspects of flying around the track in bumper-to-bumper traffic at 200 miles an hour.

"The only thing I fear," he said, "is fire. But I try to stay focused on the race and never think about that."

Early the morning of the event, I stepped into the Citizen-News wire room to strip the teletype machine.

A bulletin clicked out an Indianapolis dateline. It was followed by a one-line news item stating that an unidentified car was burning in the middle of the Indy racetrack. Seconds later, the car was identified as Billy Vukovich's. He died at the scene.

Very sad.

I continued working at CBS off and on, writing for Harmon and several other sportscasters the network had under contract. Among them were Tom Hanlon, Roy Storey and Tom Kelly, all specialists with unique styles.

Even though Panella and I were newspapermen, we had a legitimate reason to attend weekly sportscasters' luncheons and looked forward to them.

In 1958, we attended a *special* luncheon at the famous Hollywood Brown Derby restaurant on Vine Street. It was hosted by Bob Cobb, the wealthy restaurant owner and president of the Hollywood Stars baseball club.

That event was the birth of the Southern California Sports Broadcasters Association, which celebrated its golden anniversary in 2008.

Surviving members continue to look back on that historical day when Harmon, the legendary Heisman Trophy winner from Michigan, was elected president and mapped ambitious plans for the future.

Panella and I and maybe one or two others in the print media had little input in the broadcasters' concerns. Nonetheless, we were listed among the 35 chartered members.

A full page ad in its annual awards magazine proudly recalls that June 6, 1958, meeting.

"Harmon was becoming weary of standing in the back of the dressing rooms, tape recorder in hand, waiting for the newspaper guys to complete their interviews," the magazine states. "Harmon, along with other prominent sportscasters and commentators, agreed that an association was needed to fortify the image of the electronic media and he asked for the support of the Dodgers and Rams. It worked.

"Harmon, with Dodger help, forced baseball to open its World Series and All-Star dressing rooms to the electronic media. The Rams and NFL Commissioner Pete Rozelle quickly responded... During the week of Super Bowl I, the NFL's 'press' conferences were finally opened to sportscasters."

Also in attendance that day was a sportscaster from Illinois with a fistful of impressive credentials, Francis Dayle Hearn.

Hearn, who preferred to be called Chick, joined the CBS stable and immediately was showcased in a new 15-minute sports program. I was asked to assist him.

Hearn's quick mind and rapid-fire staccato delivery made him an instant hit among basketball fanatics.

As the Los Angeles Lakers' play-by-play announcer, Hearn introduced fans to such colorful phrases as "slam dunk, air ball, no harm, no foul." He set a record for consecutive broadcasts with 3,338 games.

After six weeks of being handed nightly radio scripts, Hearn informed me he no longer needed anyone to put words in his mouth.

We went our separate ways, Chick eventually to NBC to escape Harmon's shadow at CBS and me to KTLA to help Harmon produce a new television show.

Tom did a lot of traveling and frequently called on his friend Bill Symes, a likeable, easygoing owner of a Cadillac dealership, to sub for him.

Symes was not a professional sportscaster but a capable substitute who relied on me for help. Together, we managed to avoid any disasters. To show his gratitude, Bill sold me a used 1956 Coupe de Ville at a good discount.

On Aug. 14, 1958, a wire service bulletin reported that UCLA football coach Henry (Red) Sanders had been found dead, the victim of an apparent heart attack.

During a commercial break, I handed Bill the wire copy, which he read verbatim without comment. Details relating to the circumstances surrounding Sanders' death were sketchy and suggestive, triggering rumors among insiders that the hot-blooded 53-year-old Southerner had died in the arms of a prostitute.

The media never pursued the story, and Red was laid to rest, ensuring his unblemished legacy as one of college football's greatest coaches.

An enduring story about Red still brings a laugh from younger people who may not remember Sanders.

It was said that when one of his players fouled up in practice and was nearly in tears, Red sympathetically threw his arm around the young boy's shoulder. The coach looked him in the eye and, in his Southern drawl, said, "Son, it ain't a mattah a life 'n' death. It's *moah impotant* than that!"

The youngster verily trembled.

Predictably, Harmon's TV show was short-lived. He had a long list of commitments and the local TV show apparently was not high on it. That historic Brown Derby meeting helped open

146

new doors for him and other sportscasters as well.

Usually, I can't recall what I eat from one day to the next. But as time passed, that Derby luncheon became increasingly more meaningful.

"I hope everyone likes their lunch," Bob Cobb told his guests as waiters delivered large salads to the tables. "It's my specialty."

As the story goes, Cobb was tired and hungry late one night in 1937. So he raided the massive icebox in the Derby kitchen, pulling out greens, avocado, tomatoes, chicken, hard-boiled eggs and Roquefort cheese. Sniffing cooked bacon being prepared for the next day, he grabbed a few strips of that, too. He tossed it all together in a bowl, served himself and a friend and they dug in.

That salad might've been remembered only as a scrumptious midnight snack, except the friend was Sid Grauman, one of Hollywood's top promoters. He was the man behind the elaborate Chinese Theatre, where celebrities are memorialized with their footprints and handprints in the courtyard's cement.

Grauman raved about the concoction and began ordering it regularly when dining at the Derby.

For lack of a better name, its creator simply called it a Cobb Salad.

Chapter 21

The Greatest

Still generating headlines after his light-heavyweight gold-medal performance in the 1960 Rome Olympics, Cassius Marcellus Clay, Jr., sat next to Charlene and me at a Hollywood restaurant.

Clay had won 12 professional bouts with nine knockouts before arriving in Los Angeles to fight George Logan at the L.A. Sports Arena.

A glib, brash, refreshingly articulate 20-year-old, the Louisville Lip as he was aptly nicknamed kept a small group of writers and guests entertained throughout dinner, particularly Charlene who found him charmingly attentive.

"When Clay first came to town," publicist Don Fraser said, "I picked up a badge and had a printer print the words *I'm the Greatest*. Later, others tried to take credit."

It didn't take long for sportscaster Howard Cosell to launch Clay into the national spotlight. Cosell sparred with him verbally in TV interviews, at weigh-ins, before and after his fights, whenever, wherever. Pure entertainment.

It was a platform Clay relished. He ridiculed opponents with his rhyming, often remarkably accurate, predictions of when *they* would fall, described his lightning-fast hit-and-move style as *floating like a butterfly, stinging like a bee* and proclaimed himself not only the greatest, but *the prettiest.*

For two decades, I conducted interviews, covered many of Clay's fights from ringside and brushed shoulders with him at social events. He took the name Muhammad Ali after he upset Sonny Liston to win the title in 1964. He also embraced the Black Muslim religion.

A three-time world champion, Ali's pro record of 56-5 was not the best among his heavyweight contemporaries, but most experts rank him as one of the three best of all time with Joe Louis and unbeaten Rocky Marciano.

Charlene and I never imagined that first meeting with young Cassius would become such a special night in our lives. We cherished that memory more as time passed and his fame mushroomed.

The night Clay destroyed George Logan at the Los Angeles Sports Arena on April 23, 1962, became special to me, too.

Cassius dazzled the huge crowd with his fancy footwork, bobbed and weaved out of harm's way, fired stinging machine-gun jabs and devastating rights before ending the mismatch in the fourth round.

Three weeks later, he knocked out Billy Daniels in New York then returned to Los Angeles in July to face Alejandro Lavorante, a lanky, hard-hitting Argentinean.

With 19 victories, 15 by knockout, and only three losses, Lavorante seemed a formidable opponent after an impressive performance against light-heavyweight king Archie Moore four months earlier in a non-title bout that lasted nearly 10 rounds.

Clay peppered his opponent with jabs and rapid-fire shots to the head before stopping Lavorante in the fifth round.

Despite suffering two consecutive knockouts, Lavorante climbed into the Olympic ring only two months after losing to Clay to face John Riggins, a mediocre Washington state heavyweight with a spotty record.

The 26-year-old Argentinean appeared sluggish, backpedaling defensively much of the time until the sixth round, when Riggins delivered a soft glancing blow to the head. The punch drove Lavorante against the ropes directly above me. His legs buckled as he slid to the canvas, unconscious.

While the referee counted him out, Lavorante remained

motionless. The ringside physician immediately jumped between the ropes, attempted unsuccessfully to revive him, then called for a stretcher.

As the large crowd hushed in disbelief, the young boxer was carried out of the ring and rushed to a hospital. He remained there in a coma until he was returned to his Argentina home weeks later.

Six months after being injured, Lavorante died without ever regaining consciousness.

I don't recall the official medical report of Lavorante's injury, but there was considerable talk that he probably had suffered brain damage in his loss to Clay, and possibly to Moore earlier that remained undetected during a routine medical examination before his fight against Riggins.

Less than a year later, March 21, 1963, I witnessed another boxing fatality at Dodger Stadium when featherweight champion Davey Moore struck the back of his head on the lower ring rope after being floored by Sugar Ramos in their title fight. Moore died at the hospital during the night.

Jack interviews Sugar Ray Robinson, left, and Davey Moore. Robinson, a five-time world middleweight champion who also held the welterweight title, was stopped only once during his 25-year professional career, by world light-heavy king Joey Maxim. Moore suffered fatal injuries in the ring in his 1963 world featherweight title defense against Sugar Ramos.

While Moore lay near death, a popular sportscaster, Hank Weaver, was critically injured in an auto accident after leaving the ballpark.

He suffered brain injuries that left him unresponsive for almost a year before he also died.

BOXING THRIVED in the 1950s and '60s when smaller clubs emerged from time to time, including the famous Moulin Rouge nightclub in Hollywood. It staged 20 shows in 1963.

Joe Louis was listed as a promoter but two brothers, Leo and Walter Minskoff, were his financial backers. Later, the brothers operated a more successful club in Santa Monica.

Following Louis' retirement from the ring, the Brown Bomber remained a highly visible public figure, particularly in boxing circles. In his new role as a promoter, the media welcomed him with major coverage.

Fifteen Moulin Rouge shows were locally televised by KCOP, but attendance was sparse and weekly gross gate figures barely exceeded $4,000. A unique experiment to boost attendance by offering gourmet dining at ringside generated a lot of publicity but few paying customers. Soon it was abandoned. It's easy to understand a ringsider might not have wanted to mix blood with his rare steak.

One evening after the fights, Joe invited Charlene and me along with a few others to his Hollywood home he shared with his third wife, Martha Jefferson. She was a sharp attorney he married in 1959.

Typical of the press' post-fight gatherings at bars and restaurants, drinks flowed freely at Joe's home long past midnight. Among Louis' friends were several young Black Muslims who cast flirtatious glances at my wife. When one approached her, I interceded. The moment became uncomfortable after words were exchanged, so we left.

Joe's reign as a promoter was short lived. Still saddled with money problems stemming from massive debts incurred during his ring days, Louis lived mainly off the charity from family, friends and perhaps from golf winnings.

A near-scratch golfer, Joe gladly accepted offers for "friendly" wagers from country-club members who could tell their grandkids about the times they played with the famous ex-champion.

A series of physical and mental health issues plagued Louis during the next decade. One of his final tributes was a glitzy event staged by Caesars Palace in Las Vegas, where Louis was employed as a greeter.

Joe died from a heart attack in 1981 at his Las Vegas home at age 67.

It was a sad farewell to one of boxing's greatest. Among Louis' statistics are two records that may never be broken, 25 consecutive title defenses and 12 consecutive years as a world champion. He had only one loss in his first 62 professional fights.

In the process, he transcended the evils of racial discrimination and intolerance and became a role model for millions.

Another legendary champion, Rocky Marciano never fought in Southern California, but I had the pleasure of meeting him after his retirement one evening in a Los Angeles hotel room. It was a fleeting few minutes during which the Rock posed for a photo with comedian Red Skelton, sportscaster Chick Hearn and me.

Rocky Marciano, the only undefeated world heavyweight champion, from left, Los Angeles Lakers broadcaster Chick Hearn, Jack and comedian Red Skelton at a Los Angeles hotel.

Born and raised in Brockton, Massachusetts, Marciano strayed from East Coast rings only once when he knocked out Don Cockell in San Francisco. It was the champ's next to last bout. I wish I had seen him from ringside instead of on television.

Nicknamed the Brockton Blockbuster, Marciano was a stocky, ferocious 185-pounder. He didn't employ the classic boxing skills of Ali or Louis, but his relentless hammering at close range accounted for 43 knockouts among his 49 pro victories. Only six opponents went the distance.

The only unbeaten heavyweight champion in boxing history, Marciano established himself as a legitimate title contender when he knocked out an aging Louis in 1952, and 11 months later won the crown from Jersey Joe Walcott. After defeating Louis, Marciano reportedly wept in his hero's dressing room.

"I thought it was a mistake when Joe Louis tried a comeback," Marciano told the New York Times when he retired April 27, 1956. "No man can say what he will do in the future, but, barring poverty, the ring has seen the last of me...."

Some say Marciano retired prematurely. He was 32. That's debatable. Clearly, he left the world much too early. He died in a private plane crash near Des Moines, Iowa, Aug. 31, 1969, the day before his 46th birthday.

Another great and colorful champion was Archie Moore, who failed three times to win the heavyweight championship.

The world light-heavy king fought gallantly against Louis, Ali and Floyd Patterson, but was stopped by each. Nonetheless, from 1936 to 1963, Moore won 191 of 225 professional fights, 137 by knockout, and made headlines outside the ring as well as in it.

Archie didn't need a publicist; he promoted himself. Before virtually every title defense, Moore ballooned up well over the 175-pound limit. As weigh-in dates approached, the media speculated about his secret weight-loss program, how a weakened champion might perform and if the fight might be declared a non-title match should he fail to make the weight.

Often amazed when he stepped on the scale to register 175 pounds exactly, reporters badgered the champ to disclose his reducing secret. He never did until the night he dined with Charlene and me at a restaurant.

"Come on, Archie," I said, "give me an exclusive."

Beaming light-heavyweight champ Archie Moore discloses his secret.

He smiled, cut a piece of steak and placed it in his mouth.

As he chewed and chewed and chewed, he pondered my request, then casually plucked the bulk of meat from his mouth and placed it on his plate.

"I just swallow the juices," he said, "never the meat."

I doubt Charlene appreciated my exclusive.

Of the hundreds of boxers I covered, Archie Moore was the only one ever to admit to me he sometimes made pre-fight agreements with unscrupulous managers, never to intentionally lose but to delay the inevitable until his opponent got in a few good licks and fans got their money's worth.

Not often, but occasionally Archie got more than he bargained for.

Chapter 22

Moving Up

As a new decade was dawning, life suddenly became happily complicated with new opportunities, increased income and a move to Reseda, where we found what Charlene called her "dream home."

The house was two years old and in pristine condition with four bedrooms, two baths, a large kitchen, attached garage, a rock fireplace and a spacious walled-in backyard.

Located on a quiet tree-lined street a few blocks west of a large park and the Reseda High School, the home would remain our family residence for 32 years. Our cost in December of 1959 was $23,500 with monthly payments of $132.

I took Milt Rosner's advice, applied for a job in sports at the Los Angeles Times in 1960 and was hired as a part-timer. I worked mostly on weekends editing copy and writing headlines.

When time permitted, I holed up in the rear bedroom of our new home late at night to grind out story ideas for TV westerns.

Our 4-year-old son John slept six feet from me despite the noisy typewriter and swirling smoke from my Lucky Strike and Camel cigarettes. Over time the desk lamp shade turned yellow.

Like millions of others, I ignored medical warnings that linked smoking to cancer, but John never complained. It took me

20 years to stop, but our son never started. I often wondered if that smoke-filled bedroom was a deterrent.

I sent Rosner a steady flow of story ideas, kept close contact with him on the phone and received nothing but rejections from story editors.

Almost a year later without a nibble, I was ready to abandon ship, but Rosner's encouragement kept me trying. I stayed on that treadmill of working mornings at the Citizen-News, Thursday and Saturday nights at the Olympic and Legion along with a couple of shifts each week at the Times.

Nighttime meant struggles to create an acceptable giddy-up, gun-slinging story for television. Instead of submitting outlines to various shows as I had been doing, I decided to focus on a 30-minute series titled *"Lawman,"* starring John Russell and Peter Brown.

I tried never to miss an episode and became so familiar with the series, I was certain one of my ideas would connect. Finally, one did.

"Warner Brothers wants to buy your story for *Lawman*, Rosner said over the phone. "I'm negotiating with the producer on a contract. We haven't reached an agreement yet, but I wanted you to know."

Negotiating? I had so many rejection slips from Warners' television division, I had lost count. What was there to negotiate? The Writers Guild of America governs payments to writers who sign studio contracts. I told Rosner I had no problem accepting the minimum, whatever it was.

"They want to buy your *story*," he said, "for two-hundred dollars. They want to assign an established writer to do the script. You can write the script. It's not that difficult."

Milt's words sounded familiar. Of course, he was right. I had pounded the typewriter for too many months, burning cigarettes into early morning hours in my son's tiny bedroom to settle for $200.

A few days later my persistent agent called again.

"You will be getting the guild minimum for a half-hour teleplay," he said, "a total of twelve-hundred dollars. I'm sending you a contract. Look it over, sign it and send it back."

Guild contracts divided minimum payments for story, first

draft and final draft, bearing such labels as "Story by…," "Written by…" and "Teleplay by…." In many cases, more than one writer shared credit for a script and, therefore, for years to come, residuals would be divided accordingly.

Should my final draft, for example, not meet the producer's expectations and require considerable work by another writer, I would still receive $1,200 but lose many times that amount in residuals and find future assignments in television more difficult. Multiple writers' names on a script sent up red flags.

When credits were disputed, the guild assigned three disinterested writers to read all stages of development and make a determination, which would be binding. Names of the writers involved in the dispute were withheld.

My *Lawman* story, *The Witness*, was about a revengeful traveling cartoonist whose sketch of a murder suspect nearly sends an innocent man to the gallows. The outline was well defined and I anticipated no problem writing the shooting script. But it was my first.

After returning the contract, I met with Coles Trapnell, the series line producer. We discussed the project, then I went home and immediately started the teleplay.

Creating scenes, writing dialogue, suggesting camera angles and text to describe action by actors was a format totally foreign to me. I had been submitting only outlines for stories, but I did have sample scripts to study.

It was understandable Rosner had difficulty persuading the producer to gamble on a newcomer. But Milt had built a solid reputation as a literary agent, had good contacts and was liked.

I completed the first draft quickly, delivered it and waited days for the phone to ring. The longer I waited the less confident I became. I reread the copy I had retained, searching for mistakes, poor dialogue, anything I could have improved.

Finally, the producer's secretary called.

"Mister Trapnell likes your script," she said. "Can you come in tomorrow to discuss it with him?"

"Of course I will be there tomorrow," I said.

My relief was almost indescribable. I couldn't wait to tell Charlene.

The final draft necessitated, in my mind, little more than

polishing, and I soon received the last payment totaling $1,200. I immediately began thinking about other series ideas before *The Witness* was scheduled for filming.

Then, Milt Rosner delivered some devastating news. Coles Trapnell had been replaced by a producer with his own stable of writers. My script and others ready for filming were shelved.

Yes, I had padded my bank account but suddenly was weary of writing for television that wrought so many disappointments. I stopped sending Rosner story ideas.

After a short time, I was surprised not to hear from him. Literary agents are never *devastated* by setbacks for their clients.

I learned why when his wife called the paper. She informed me that Milt had been suffering severe migraine headaches for some time. She said doctors confirmed he had an inoperable brain tumor.

Chapter 23

Ten Years Later

The year 1962 began with exciting news.

Warner Brothers television division had reinstated Coles Trapnell to produce several more *Lawman* episodes. One was *The Witness*.

He had pulled the final draft of my script dated August 31, 1961, from a shelf, dusted it off and scheduled a filming date.

The bold-face word "FINAL" on the cover of my teleplay followed a long process of changes. All but six of 37 pages were revised by Trapnell or a staff writer, many dated Jan. 25, 1962, my 32nd birthday.

A page labeled "revised" could mean a word or line change, deletion or addition of a scene or a complete rewrite. My keepsake at home looks like a rainbow with its white (original), blue (first revision), pink (second revision) and green (third revision) replacement pages.

It was disappointing to find so few of my original words in the shooting script when filming began the last week of January. Nonetheless, I showed up on the set, stood in the background and quietly observed like a curious spectator.

When an actor sought my advice about how he should play a scene, crew members took note of my presence and my cover was blown.

More important than that momentary ego boost, I retained full writing credit. Consequently, I never shared residual income that far exceeded my original payment. I received rerun checks periodically for many years. After my TV writing career was all but forgotten, a residual check for $302.50 arrived from the Writers Guild in January of 2010, almost 48 years after *The Witness* aired.

Six months after the episode was filmed my family gathered in front of the TV. They saw my name flash on the screen for five seconds and probably wished I had written something other than a half-hour giddy-up.

Family life was good. The girls and John were attending St. Catherine of Siena Catholic elementary school about two miles from the house. Charlene was a devoted mother, chauffeuring the kids, volunteering in a parish food program for the poor and assuming many of my parental responsibilities. Still, I tried to be home for dinners and spend quality time with the family when I could.

John Michael Hawn II, as he labeled his grammar school papers, helps dad celebrate at his parents' 50th wedding anniversary party in 2001.

Love birds Jack and Charlene celebrating something... or not.

Jack's and Charlene's daughters, from left, Barbara Alonzo, Linda Pierce, Patty Mann.

Our ambitious home improvement plans, merely pillow talk when we moved to Reseda two years earlier, had materialized from freelance writing.

We added a spacious family room with sliding glass doors, full-length, mechanically operated drapes, built-in bar and a bathroom accessible from John's bedroom. A large swimming pool was under construction.

Bob Panella had been having health problems for some time and unable to work steady. A city side editor with a sports background filled in for him at the Citizen-News, and I subbed for Bob writing Tom Harmon's scripts.

I got to know Tom better but was never close. He wasn't inclined to engage in small talk, at least not with me. One evening he lingered in the studio after signing off the air to chat with his director, Len Corbosiero, his engineer and me. It was a rare occasion.

He told a fascinating World War II story about the time in 1943 when he got caught in a tropical storm flying over the South American jungle. He bailed out of his P-38. Others aboard went down with the plane and were killed.

Tom said after his aircraft was reported missing a massive search was conducted to find him. Four days later, he stumbled into a clearing in Dutch Guiana. It is documented that he saved his silk parachute and later used the material for his wife's wedding dress, but Tom never mentioned that.

A handsome, natty dresser with his impressive athletic physique, Tom was a model of success. Women were attracted to him, especially female athletes. I can't speak generally about Harmon's social life, but I recall tennis star Gorgeous Gussie Moran, as she was known, leaving the studio arm-in-arm with Tom one night after his show. I also observed Harmon socializing with a few women golfers on the pro tour.

One day Charlene and I were invited to the Beverly Hills home Tom had just purchased. An older house, it needed work, like the large swimming pool with a layer of stained tile. The interior was beautifully furnished, equipped like a model home. Our complete tour included a glimpse of Tom's bedroom closet filled with expensive suits and sport coats.

Tom's wife Elyse Knox, a former fashion designer, actress and daughter of onetime Secretary of the Navy William Franklin Knox, was a gracious hostess. We also met the couple's three young children, Kristin, Kelly and Mark.

Initially following in his dad's cleat marks, young Mark became a star quarterback at UCLA before embarking on an acting career. He ultimately gained starring roles in film and television.

What had been an exciting beginning of 1962 suddenly turned black March 7, when I heard part of a news item on my car radio.

While driving home from the Citizen-News early in the afternoon, a monotonous trip on the Hollywood Freeway, my mind was elsewhere. The radio might as well have been turned off until I heard "...The victim was identified as Jack R. Lewis of Burbank."

Jack Lewis? My uncle?

I turned up the volume, tried other stations, but learned nothing more; I could only imagine what had happened.

Arriving home, I phoned the paper to confirm my fears. The story had been carried by the City News Service, and the city desk had received several calls.

While attempting an emergency landing, Jack's single-engine aircraft clipped high voltage wires over the communities of Saugus and Newhall, sending the two-seater into a rugged mountainside where it exploded. His body was never recovered.

Long before Jack and aunt Maurine hosted our wedding reception, I had become close to my uncle. During World War II, he was a Navy Air Corps crew member. On July 7, 1945, his light bomber was shot down in Tokyo Bay. Only four of 13 aboard survived the crash; the rest were captured by the Japanese.

"When I came to, I was underwater still in the plane," Jack later wrote in a report to the Navy. "I made my way to the surface."

The life raft had split and sunk, so he grabbed a tire and plane strut, he said, when he realized he had lost feeling in his right leg and arm. After he was captured, he struggled to walk, and when his legs gave out, the Japanese soldiers beat him. He was fed dry biscuits and no water.

Brutally tortured until he was liberated Aug. 18, 1945, Jack returned home to heal his mind and body. It took years before he was able to fully regain his carefree adventurous spirit. He bought a motorcycle and an old Navy airplane, a Vultee trainer with a canopy over the cockpit. He restored the plane and flew

163

over the Valley whenever he found time.

A few days before Jack was killed, he promised to take me for a joy ride. I penciled in a possible date and was looking forward to it.

Bad news persisted.

Bob Panella's prolonged absence sparked rumors at the paper about his mysterious illness. Ultimately I learned he had been diagnosed with leukemia some time earlier and that the cancer was in its advanced stages.

On March 25, only 18 days after Jack was killed, Bob died. He was 39, a year older than my uncle.

Sadly but not unexpectedly, Milt Rosner, my former Army boss, agent and friend, succumbed to a brain tumor about the same time.

It was a spring I'll never forget, especially the night I heard Charlene yelling for me.

With four youngsters under the age of 10 engaging in various degrees of havoc from time to time, yelling wasn't unusual. So, I assumed the problem could wait until I got out of the bathroom on the other side of the house. When Charlene yelled again, I realized it was something serious.

Rushing through the kitchen, I crossed the living room and opened the door to John's room. Smoke rolled out, window curtains were burning and flames were licking the wood paneling, spreading into the adjoining bathroom.

"Get the kids out of the house," I told my wife. "I'll call the fire department."

Using a backyard garden hose, I was able to put out the fire before it spread into the family room, but smoke was filling the house by the time fire engines arrived. It was nearly dark.

I was unable to locate Charlene and feared she might have reentered the house after taking the kids next door.

One of the firemen climbed into the bedroom through the window and I entered the family room from the patio. Crawling on our hands and knees through smoky darkness, we searched for my wife until certain she wasn't inside.

Minutes later, she appeared from next door. Her eyebrows had been singed while fighting the fire with a hose on the side of the house.

John, in tears, confessed he had been lighting matches under his bed, which set the mattress on fire. He then left the room, shutting the door behind him.

His bedroom was a total loss. The adjoining bathroom walls were blackened. Smoke damage throughout the house was extensive. Our insurance company covered everything, cleaning bills for clothes, curtains and drapes, replacements for ruined dolls and other items, even nightly restaurant expenses for about two weeks.

In short time, the bedroom was rebuilt, walls painted, clothes cleaned and new dolls.

For our 6-year-old son, the near disaster was traumatic. To this day, he remains sensitive about that horrible night and probably wishes I hadn't included it here. In fairness to him, I must say he learned a valuable lesson and never again gave his parents any serious problems.

Before that year was over, Tom Harmon hired a permanent writer who could travel with him around the country and assist him with remote broadcasts of his show. Among Tom's assignments was the Sugar Bowl in Florida and San Francisco 49er games.

While Tom searched for my replacement, I wrote him a formal letter applying for the job. No sooner had I mailed it, I regretted doing so. It wasn't as if I couldn't have merely spoken to him.

Tom never replied to my letter or ever mentioned it. I was embarrassed when I later ran into him at a local golf tournament. He hired Bob Seizer, a former Mirror-News sportswriter.

Eleven years my senior, Harmon died of a heart attack March 15, 1990. He was 70.

My moonlighting days ended with a last hurrah, when I did a favor for a newspaper colleague, Alan Mallamud. He wrote a nightly sports show for the Dodgers' legendary broadcaster, Vince Scully. Alan nearly begged me to fill in for him Christmas Day.

"It'll only take a couple of hours," he pleaded.

My family wasn't pleased, but Alan was right. It was a snap. I merely clipped the sports wire, weeded out the top stories and gave them to Scully to read on the air. He thanked me, wished me a Merry Christmas and handed me a $100 bill for an hour of my time.

Although 1962 started and ended well, the year left sad memories were it not for what transpired after meeting with Har Palmer, the Citizen-News managing editor.

Seated in his office to discuss my future, I was reminded of the day 10 years earlier when Har offered me a job as copyboy at $40 a week.

"I understand you're working part-time at the Los Angeles Times," he said, "in the sports department."

I never tried to conceal that and wasn't surprised he knew. I'm sure he was aware I needed the extra income and didn't object as long as it didn't interfere with my job. Now it mattered.

"It wouldn't look good having the Citizen-News sports editor working for another newspaper," Har said. "Of course, you will be getting a pay raise as the editor, so if you want the job, you'll have to quit the Times."

End of discussion.

Citizen-News sports editor Jack Hawn, right, and his assistant Bob Daniel, left, interview football coach John McKay and Athletic Director Jess Hill at a USC practice in the 1960s.

I immediately quit the Times and began expanding our sports coverage, particularly of high school and small-college athletics. One of my first changes was to move our department into what had been the morgue in the back room, an ideal location for a rowdy young staff.

So much had happened since that day 10 years earlier when Bill Kershaw set fire to Ralph Palmer's article in that very room. As far as I knew, it remained a lifelong secret.

Chapter 24

Perks, Golf and Champagne

United Press carried a few lines about my promotion, and it didn't take long for publicists all over the Southland to update their press lists. Soon I received annual passes and generous allotments of tickets, which I shared with our staff, school buddies and others.

My reign as sports editor lasted less than a year when the Citizen-News hired Maxwell Stiles to replace me. I was promoted to executive sports editor, with no guild provision for a pay raise.

Max was one of many talented journalists hired by other local newspapers when the Times-Mirror tabloid ceased publication in 1962. Mirror Sports Editor Sid Ziff and his protégé John Hall were among several picked up by the L.A. Times, the company's flagship publication.

Stiles, a harmless, gentle, ink-stained veteran, had a reputation as one of the country's top track and field authorities. Unaccustomed to working for a small newspaper, he often carried copies of his Citizen-News column with him to give to people he wrote about. After so many years, Max finally achieved his career-long ambition and enjoyed his status immensely.

Although Max now controlled season tickets, I continued to make major departmental decisions and was partially relieved of the work load. Consequently, I spent more time away from the office.

Among my perks was an annual golf pass for two valid at all Los Angeles City courses. I might never have used it were it not for Bob Panella's older brother Bill, an avid golfer who scored in the low 70s.

Bill was a single, happy-go-lucky, part-time mechanic who lived with his mother in Monterey Park. He seemed content to drift through life with little ambition, a complete opposite of his brother.

A likeable hanger-on, as my wife labeled him, Bill became my golf tutor, regular playing partner and buddy. He almost always was available for a free round on short notice. With his patience and encouragement, I soon became addicted to the game.

I accepted occasional invitations to pristine country-club courses and usually embarrassed myself but enjoyed playing.

I had covered a few professional tournaments played locally, including the Los Angeles Open. I saw how frustrating it could be for the pros when shots went awry and putts failed to drop.

L.A. Times sportswriters Shav Glick (golf and auto racing), left, and Mal Florence (Rams), right, join L.A. Mirror-News mail room foreman Lee Strelecki and Jack for media day at the Hesperia Invitational golf tourney in 1962.

I can think of no better example of frustration any pro ever experienced in competition than when Arnold Palmer played the second round of the L.A. Open in 1961. The site was Rancho Park, a public course I also played.

With a potential for eagle-3 at the par-5 No. 18, Arnie unloaded a booming drive. It sliced right, over a towering fence into the driving range. He reloaded, took another imposing swing and duplicated the shot. Attempting to correct his swing, Palmer hooked his third drive way left into the street. Incredibly, his fourth tee shot followed the same exasperating path.

Undaunted, Palmer finally found the middle of the fairway on his fifth try. He got down in three more shots for birdie, not counting his eight penalty strokes.

Asked later by a reporter how he happened to take a 12 on the hole, Palmer is said to have shrugged and replied, "I missed the putt for an 11."

Largely because of that horrendous exhibition, now immortalized with a plaque near the 18th tee, Palmer failed to make the cut in that January event. He went on to win six PGA tournaments that year after his banner season of 1960, when he won nine.

Perhaps driven by that embarrassing demonstration in 1961, Palmer captured the L.A. Open title three times in subsequent years, 1963, '66 and '67.

In 1965, members of the media previewed the La Costa Resort and Spa near Carlsbad, which became a longtime site of the Tournament of Champions. For those who brought their clubs, it was a rare treat; for non-golfers, a wild overnight party.

Wives and families of pros usually accompanied their husbands to La Costa, where they were treated royally, as were wives of the working press.

Every January, the previous year's top professional played a few holes with the press on media day at La Costa. I played with Hal Sutton, Al Geiberger, Scott Simpson and Johnny Miller four straight years, not necessarily in that order.

My most vivid memory was when Miller stood at the rear of a large green on a par-5 hole he had reached in two shots. He faked a yawn while waiting for me to hit out of a front bunker. Spraying sand, I sculled the ball out of the trap on my third try. It rolled to the back of the green, stopping a few feet past Miller.

As Johnny and a small circle of spectators waited for me to walk to my ball, seemingly a city block, I think I must have prayed to hit a good putt to end my misery.

The ball stopped inches from the cup to ensure an 8.

"Well," Johnny said, unimpressed as he bent over his ball, "let's see if I can make my first eagle of the year."

He tapped in for birdie-4.

Bill Panella was no pro but as long as I played with him, I never saw him drive four straight balls out of bounds. I never saw him reach a par-5 hole in two shots, either. But he knew how to play the game and was a good teacher.

Eventually I lost contact with Bill Panella, but I didn't lose a golf partner.

Bill Caplan, a publicist employed by Santa Monica boxing promoters Leo and Walter Minskoff, shared my complimentary pass for years.

Fierce competitors on the course, Caplan and I wagered a dime on every shot, argued about longest drives and usually ended up winning or losing 20 cents.

Bill also kept me well supplied with column items, as did Don Fraser.

As competing publicists, they clashed often. They even took a few swings at each other one night on a ring apron in front of a big boxing crowd that found the incident hilarious.

While Fraser generated more widespread publicity with his imaginative stunts, Caplan's creativity often was for laughs.

Don once gained national publicity when he persuaded former world lightweight champion Lauro (the Little Lion) Salas to stick his head into the mouth of a caged lion at an animal compound in Thousand Oaks, California. Wearing trunks and boxing gloves, Salas looked fearless in a variety of poses Associated Press moved on the sports wire.

Caplan had a great sense of humor and gave us a good sample of it when he joined us one night for a movie at the Hollywood Pantages Theater.

"Want anything from the snack bar?" he asked as he rose from his seat.

"Two cold martinis," I joked, "straight up."

Caplan grinned and headed back up the aisle. Ten minutes

later he returned carrying a tray with two chilled martinis, straight up, purchased at a nearby bar. How he smuggled them into the theater remains a mystery.

Charlene and I nearly doubled over with laughter.

With such a competitive L.A. sports market, publicists came in all shapes and sizes to promote their events. But when a phone caller asked for the Citizen-News skiing editor, I almost laughed aloud.

Skiing editor? Skiing?

I could have reminded him that snow almost never fell in our circulation area and if it did, our small section didn't have space for skiing. Instead, I simply replied, "That would be me, I guess."

"We're getting a group together for a trip to Reno," he said. "There's a big skiing tournament at Heavenly Valley and Red Skelton is opening his act at Harrah's at the same time. We're looking for press coverage in the L.A. area."

"I don't know," I stammered. "I'm married with four children, and..."

"Bring the whole family if you want," he interrupted. "Bill Harrah is picking up the tab for everything."

He couldn't be serious, I thought. He was. We brought Patty, while Charlene's mother cared for her three siblings. Writers, columnists, radio and TV people, wives, girlfriends and our daughter were flown to Reno. We were booked into luxurious rooms at Harrah's and issued badges as valuable as greenbacks everywhere, except in the casino.

Cabbies, bars, restaurants, even a skiing instructor who gave Patty a lesson, were reimbursed by Bill Harrah while the media got cramps signing tabs.

I covered my one and only professional skiing event, wrote a glowing review about comedian Red Skelton and ran up an obscene bar tab buying strangers drinks, particularly the final night of our stay.

Almost too embarrassed to face our publicity host on the flight home, I merely thanked him for a wonderful trip and forgot about Reno.

Two weeks later, the phone rang.

"We're going again," the same voice said. "Can you make it?"

I could think of no reason we couldn't, especially considering grandma's offer to care for all the kids this time. So, Charlene and I flew back to Reno with the same group of freeloaders.

As Yogi Berra once said, it was déjà vu all over again, another exhausting junket, except for my bad luck at the tables.

"You lost how much?" Charlene snapped. "I'm going to get some of that back."

An ultra-conservative gambler who almost never risked more than one coin at a time in slot machines while sipping exquisite complimentary Chardonnay, my wife left me at the bar. She strode to an unoccupied blackjack table and took a seat.

After a few minutes, I checked on her, still playing head-to-head with a young male dealer, who seemed to enjoy her company. He also found her luck unbelievable.

"How's she doing?" I asked.

"She hasn't lost."

"Really."

I watched her bet a silver dollar, win, bet another dollar, win, wager another, win….

"Bet more than a dollar, honey. You're on a streak. At least double up."

Charlene ignored me, bet another dollar.

Finally, I checked my watch. Time was fleeting.

"Dear," I reminded her, "we need to get a cab. It's time to go."

She stood, played another dollar and won.

"Dear…"

"Okay, okay," she replied, her tone rather harsh. "One more."

It was Charlene's wildest, most exciting and probably most profitable gambling session ever, though it's doubtful she won more than $30.

Not only did I appoint myself skiing editor of the Citizen-News, I also took a sudden interest in harness racing when Biff Lowry, a Western Harness Racing Assn. director, sent a letter containing a small check.

The letter explained that the check was the payoff for a $2 win ticket wagered on a horse "assigned" to me. It also stated that a $2 win ticket would be purchased on "my" horse for future races in which he was entered.

I don't know how horses "assigned" to other writers fared, but "mine" seemed to win consistently, with varying payoffs. Suddenly I was a huge sulky fan. So when Biff Lowry invited me to join a group of scribes for a week in DuQuoin, Illinois, to cover the prestigious Hambletonian, the Kentucky Derby of harness racing, I selfishly accepted, leaving Charlene with the kids.

I interviewed sulky drivers, wrote a few advances, covered the race and couldn't wait to rejoin my family.

When I arrived at Los Angeles International Airport, Charlene looked gorgeous in her colorful miniskirt and golden tan. The four kids looked disheveled.

"Mom got lost," one of the girls immediately informed me. "She took the wrong freeway."

"You look great, honey," I cooed, "really tan."

"All she did while you were gone," another tattled, "was float in the pool."

It was good to be home.

Thoroughbreds at Hollywood Park, Santa Anita and Del Mar also got my attention over the years, although I can't say I was a true fan. Without pari-mutuel betting, I probably wouldn't have visited the tracks as often as I did.

Occasionally, Charlene joined me, enjoyed a complimentary lunch in the Club House and placed a $2 show bet on a long shot. She actually got excited when it thundered down the stretch like the legendary Silky Sullivan, one of the most thrilling last-second winners ever.

Invited to the Hollywood Park Director's Lounge for lunch one afternoon, we stopped behind a Cadillac in the parking lot. A driver stepped out to remove two saw horses blocking his way.

"I think that's Cary Grant," I told Charlene.

"Oh, no," she insisted. "He wouldn't do that. Besides, there's a dent in his fender."

Fifteen minutes later, the handsome, charming actor, a Hollywood Park director, was introduced to us.

"Delighted," he said, or something like that.

Impeccably dressed and smiling as only Cary Grant could, he gently lifted my blushing wife's hand and kissed it.

I had a notion to ask about the dent in his fender, but thought better of it.

It seems off-beat organizations always had trips scheduled somewhere to promote something, such as the Sportsmen's Club. One January the promoter flew us to Clear Lake in northern California.

An icy rain ruined fishing and a fluttering snowfall made the golf course almost unplayable, but not quite. My fingers seemed frozen around the clubs, but Fred Claire and I sloshed on before finally abandoning the senseless challenge.

At the time, Fred wrote for a small newspaper in Whittier, California, the Daily News. It didn't take long for his career to explode. He spent 12 years as a newspaperman before joining the Dodgers as its public relations director. Eventually, Fred was appointed executive vice president.

After Clear Lake, the Sportsmen's Club decided Arizona was considerably less of a weather gamble and began booking junkets to Lake Havasu for fishing and other activities.

A lucky angler in our group once won $500. All I snagged that day was the ugly bait that resembled a half-smoked stogie with legs, fat, slimy Creepy Crawlers that squealed when you pierced them with a hook.

Charlene, our adventurous daughter Barbara and her best girl-friend Gina accompanied me to Havasu another time, when I covered an exciting hydroplane race, some of it from a helicopter.

Relatively new in those days, helicopters weren't for everyone, including my wife who remained on the ground while the three of us soared overhead. It was for the best. The pilot gave us a thrill ride, swooping low over the bouncing, speeding hydros as they circled the course, our cameras clicking.

Barbara recalled years later that she went on a bus, helicopter, boat and plane.

"It was the most exciting day of my life at the time," she said, then added with a grin, "except for getting lost at Disneyland."

Barbara took photos from the helicopter while I hung on with white knuckles during the aerial acrobatics. I still was more comfortable than during my first whirlybird ride over the Valencia Golf Course and Country Club.

Just before the course opened, the press previewed it from above. We got a glimpse of nearby Six Flags Magic Mountain theme park in the northwest corner of Santa Clarita Valley.

Flying low over lakes, pristine fairways and lush greens, the pilot pointed out ideal landing areas for tee shots, bunkers to avoid and other noteworthy information.

I listened, peered below, but also kept a wary eye on the controls. I was happy when we settled back onto terra firma.

Even though uncomfortable during that flight, I didn't considered it life-threatening, like, say, driving a race car around a dirt track at break-neck speed.

That, I told Ray Rosenbaum, I would never consider.

Ray headed Headlines, Ink, a public relations agency that listed bowlers, professional billiards players and race car drivers among its off-beat clients. He had come up with the ingenious idea of a stock-car race pitting members of the electronic media against sportswriters.

"I've got a few radio and TV guys signed up," he said, "but I need writers."

Not a chance, I told him.

"I'm not even comfortable driving the freeways. Forget it, Ray."

A successful, hard-working publicist I had helped in the past (even covered one of his boring billiards tournaments), Rosenbaum had a good sense of humor, was likeable and persuasive.

"It's a stock car. No one gets hurt driving a stock car," he said. "It's a month away. You can always cancel."

True. I reluctantly agreed.

The month passed quickly. I had forgotten about the race when Rosenbaum called to remind me it was scheduled for the coming Saturday.

"Saturday? This Saturday, September 12th?"

A far more important event would take place that day in 1964. Charlene's younger sister Mary West would exchange wedding vows with Edward Viau.

Perfect. I explained, apologized for having to cancel the race and again thanked God for rescuing me. But Rosenbaum wasn't through, nor, I guess, was God.

"It won't start until four o'clock," he said. "You would have plenty of time to make it after the wedding."

"I don't think so, Ray," I said with a tone of finality. "I'm sorry."

"I really need you," he pleaded. "Try to make it. I'll be looking for you."

After the ceremony, after the reception and after too many glasses of champagne, I sat behind the wheel of a badly dented stock car, still fuzzy from the overdose of false courage. The car's engine was running. An attendant strapped me in.

Charlene sat in the stands, probably not terribly concerned about my safety, having consumed a generous amount of the bubbly as well.

"Any advice?" I asked the attendant.

"Push the pedal to the floor and turn left."

Wonderful.

I don't remember how fast I drove, how many laps I covered or how far I was ahead of the second-place car when I crossed the finish line. I was told, however, I was the only newspaperman in the race and only three sportscasters were behind me.

I do, however, remember the beautiful young race queen who kissed my cheek, handed me a big trophy…and an opened bottle of champagne.

Chapter 25

Cops and The Fugitive

Long past midnight, the streets were practically deserted as I drove up Vine, crossed Hollywood Boulevard and continued slowly up the hill. It had been an exhausting week.

My friend Bob Myers who covered mostly professional golf for Associated Press apparently drew the short straw in his Los Angeles office. He was assigned to cover the United States wrestling trials at the Hollywood Legion Stadium for the 1964 Olympic Games.

Never having covered amateur wrestling and more interested in a Phoenix golf tournament the same week, Bob recommended me for the assignment.

"The money's good," he said. "You phone in the results and write a few short features about the main guys for their home-town papers."

"I don't know anything about amateur wrestling," I told him. "I don't even watch the pros. I hate wrestling."

"They have people who are experts. They'll help you. It'll be snap."

Enticed by a lot of money for a week's work that fit into my normal schedule, I accepted the offer.

After completing my morning routine at the paper and killing a few more hours, I drove to the Legion for the afternoon bouts and seldom left before midnight.

Watching bodies twist and turn on a mat while listening to agonizing grunts was dreadfully boring, almost hypnotic, at first. By mid-week, I was hooked and thought I had become an overnight expert in scoring amateur wrestling.

I even secretly began rooting for various athletes, particularly Dan Gable, who became a legendary athlete at Iowa State, won a 1972 Olympic gold medal and coached wrestling at the University of Iowa.

After six days and nights of double-duty and almost no contact with my family, I felt exhausted when I left the stadium following Saturday night's final competition.

I was almost in a daze when I heard a siren.

Checking my mirror, I saw an unmarked, nondescript sedan with a flashing red light atop its roof racing up the hill behind me. As I slowed, the car pulled alongside and forced me to the curb.

"Police. Get out and get your hands up."

The sedan stopped behind my car. Two men in sport coats and slacks jumped out, guns drawn, aimed at me.

I stepped out, hands raised, asked obvious questions and was told to shut up. They wouldn't say why I had been stopped or allow me to reach inside my coat for identification.

As the younger detective kept his revolver pointed at me, his partner opened the lid of my trunk, found it empty, then searched the interior, front and back.

A 1948 Cadillac with many thousands of miles on its odometer, it had well-worn leather seats with stitched seams. At one point, an exposed tip of a stiff wire snagged and badly ripped the sleeve of the detective's jacket.

Popping out of the car, he was red-faced furious.

"This is a new coat," he barked. "Get that damned seat sewed up."

The detectives finally allowed me to identify myself and explained that someone had just robbed the Palladium, a few blocks south on Sunset Boulevard. They said I matched a description of the thief and that my vehicle matched the description of the getaway car.

Offering no apologies, the detectives reentered their sedan and made a mid-block U-turn back toward Hollywood Boulevard. I continued up the hill toward the freeway.

First thing next morning, I stopped by the City Desk to report my brush with the law and learn more about the Palladium heist.

The editor was busy, not interested in my story and had seen nothing on the city news wire about a Palladium holdup.

I probably should have called the police station, but I wasn't a crime reporter. I wasn't even a city side reporter. At the moment, I needed to strip the sports wire and have the pile of copy ready before Bob Panella arrived.

I forgot about the incident and heard nothing more about the alleged robbery.

It had been about three years since I stopped writing for TV, but a couple of residual checks for reruns of *The Witness* renewed my interest.

One of my favorite shows was *The Fugitive*, the intriguing, long-running drama starring David Janssen as a doctor on the run, accused of murdering his wife. I began to lie awake in bed at night, plotting a story in my mind.

Soon, I was back pounding the typewriter, often past midnight, the ashtray overflowing as before. My son still slept undisturbed a few feet away.

In most cases producers wouldn't accept submissions from freelance writers. Since I no longer had an agent, I decided a shooting script might hook one more than an outline. Actually, how I would get the manuscript to the producer didn't concern me. I planned to address that problem when it was completed.

Meanwhile, expenses were increasing and bills were piling up. Topping the pile was a property tax invoice with a rapidly approaching deadline. I didn't have the money and didn't expect to have it in the immediate future.

But as my mother-in-law might have said, it arrived from heaven.

Following Coach Red Sanders' death, Tommy Prothro, a former member of his staff who led Oregon State to a berth in the 1965 Rose Bowl, returned to UCLA to head the football program. He immediately landed a local TV show.

Sportswriters who appeared on his nightly program received a new Suzuki motorcycle as a gift. Eventually I was invited.

When I made a guest appearance with other boxing writers

on Bud Abbott and Lou Costello's nationally televised show in the mid-'50s, the comedians presented us with autographed wristwatches.

But motorcycles? Wow!

My turn seemed perfectly timed to meet the tax-payment deadline, but I didn't expect a delay in delivery. Looking back, I can't imagine why I worried so much about a $300 tax bill. But I did.

Of course, the motorcycle arrived in time to sell it uncrated at a bargain price, avoiding a late-payment penalty.

That financial burden lifted like a Band-Aid heals a broken arm, I still needed extra income to meet expenses and pay bills.

The Frank Bull Advertising Agency in Hollywood needed temporary part-time help. I didn't know Frank personally, but knew he moonlighted as the public address announcer at Los Angeles Rams games at the Coliseum. I figured he owed me one.

When I was in high school, Frank Bull hosted a popular teen gossip program on radio. I was shocked and embarrassed one evening when I heard Frank talk about me and a couple of my friends dating the same girl. I don't know who sent Bull the juicy item, but he had fun with it at my expense. My buddies ribbed me for days.

I didn't mention that program when I applied for a job at Frank's agency, but would have had I been hired by him instead of someone else. I went to work immediately grinding out publicity releases about fundraising events sponsored by the L.A. Times.

Glenn Davis, the 1946 Heisman Trophy winner known as Mister Outside when he teamed in the Army backfield with Doc Blanchard (Mister Inside), was the Times' director of special events.

I didn't see much of Frank Bull and never saw Davis. I worked alongside a veteran sportswriter, Hugh Penney, an incurable chain smoker.

As he bent over his typewriter, cigarettes dangled precariously from his lips and rising smoke caused him to squint. Hot ashes burned holes in his ties. None of that bothered Hugh. One day I accompanied him to a nearby market where he bought six cartons of cigarettes. I bought two packs.

A recovering alcoholic, Hugh couldn't quit smoking. He died

of lung cancer not long after we shared that brief time together. Although I never forgot his addiction, it didn't stop mine. I continued to smoke up to two packs a day.

My job at the Bull agency helped pay bills as I optimistically looked forward to a bonanza once I sold my *Fugitive* script. It was nearly completed, but I still didn't have an agent to peddle it.

Charlene and boxing referee George Latka, who unwittingly helped Jack change careers.

Among our close boxing friends were referee George Latka and his wife Kay, who invited Charlene and me to a 1965 Christmas party at their North Hollywood home. Reminiscing about his college days at San Jose State, George mentioned a classmate he had kept in touch with over the years, Bill Gordon.

"Bill's a big boxing fan," George said. "He's an associate producer of a TV series."

"Which one?" I asked.

"The Fugitive."

"Really," I replied or some similar restraint. "What a coincidence...."

It was another surprising development along my uncharted journey. But I didn't fall out of my chair. It simply was out of my control.

Thank God, I wouldn't need to find an agent.

Chapter 26

A Career Change

Before meeting William D. Gordon, my *Fugitive* script was in his hands at the beginning of 1966.

After months of work, I had trouble sleeping at night as time passed without any word from Twentieth Century Fox's TV division, which produced the series.

I reread a copy more than once and wished I hadn't rushed to complete it. My mind conjured up all sorts of implausible scenarios. For weeks, every time the phone rang, I hoped the caller was Bill Gordon.

Finally, my manuscript arrived in the mail, accompanied by a typical two-paragraph form letter rejecting my submission.

I was stunned. I don't remember whose signature was on that letter but it wasn't Bill Gordon's. Did he even read my manuscript? If so, couldn't he at least have softened the blow with a personal letter?

That would have ended my desire for a career in television had it not been for a casual conversation with George Latka. I guess I was too embarrassed about that rejection to bring it up. But George did.

"By the way," he said, "Bill liked your script. But he's not with *The Fugitive* anymore. He's producing *12 O'clock High* now. Why don't you give him a call?"

Wow! Another shock!

I had no trouble reaching Bill Gordon on the phone. He praised my work and apologized for not getting back to me. He said if I had any ideas for his series to send him an outline. Mostly, however, he wanted to talk boxing, which we did at length.

He watched the fights on TV and kept abreast of the local talent but seldom attended the Olympic or Hollywood Legion. I invited him to join me at ringside some night. He was thrilled but never did.

Six months later, the first draft of *The All-American*, a *12 O'clock High* episode bearing my name as writer, was distributed to the cast and crew. It was dated July 29, 1966, my mother's 57th birthday.

Inspired by the story Tom Harmon told that evening after his radio show about when he bailed out of his fighter plane during World War II, *The All-American* centered on a Heisman Trophy winner who became a B-17 pilot assigned to an American bomber unit in England.

The episode opened with the football hero's widely publicized arrival and footage of the plane's crash landing on the runway. As flames spread through the interior of the aircraft, the pilot and his crew were helped out in a dramatic rescue.

It was a spectacular teaser, one I wish I had written. Instead, Bill Gordon rewrote my script extensively, as he did most. Yet, he never shared screen credit.

An imposing figure well over 6-feet tall, Bill wore expensive Jodhpur boots below comfortable, loose-fitting, western-style clothes. He had the demeanor of a free-wheeler and disdained any form of censorship.

Holed up in his office with a good supply of expensive bourbon, door locked, Gordon often worked as long as 48 hours at a time to make his deadline. When totally exhausted, he slept briefly on his leather couch. He refused all calls, even from his often exasperated executive producer Quinn Martin.

I received $3,500 for *The All-American*, the first of only 13 episodes filmed in color. The money helped finance a 30-day summer trip to Europe with our friends Don and Ruth Fraser. Upon returning, I received a phone call from Gordon.

"I need a story consultant," he said. "Are you interested?"

I didn't give it a second thought. I accepted.

My new office near Santa Monica Boulevard was spacious and lonely. As story consultant, my job was to meet with writers with story ideas for the series. I wrote synopses for Bill but made no recommendations. I really wasn't qualified for the job. Pitching and listening to story ideas wasn't my long suit. I spent most of my solitude mulling ideas of my own.

I later regretted sending away one freelancer who became a staff writer on another show, was promoted to producer, then executive producer. He went on to create several new series and became a multimillionaire. He would have been a valuable contact for future assignments. He refused my calls.

Although my newspaper salary tripled, I missed sports, especially when Coach Vince Lombardi came to Los Angeles. He brought his Green Bay Packers to play Kansas City in the first Super Bowl game, Jan. 15, 1967, at the Coliseum.

I wangled a press invitation to a pre-game party where I met the legendary Lombardi but missed seeing the Packers win, 35-10.

Meanwhile, I struck up a friendship with the *12 O'clock High* technical advisor, Jim Doherty, a retired Army and Air Force sergeant who served during World War II.

A stubborn, likeable Irishman and high-handicap golfer, Jim loved sports. We found time many afternoons to play nine holes at a nearby course and over the next decade got together often, occasionally with our wives.

After several months on staff, I came up with another story, ran it past my boss and soon started work on a script titled *The Eleventh Commandment*.

Completed just before Christmas of 1966, retyped by a secretary and seemingly headed for production, my script suddenly became worthless. TV ratings for the once popular series based on a 1949 aerial war movie nose-dived like a plunging bomber. The network canceled the long-running drama.

The timing of my career change couldn't have been worse. I was unemployed along with the entire staff, including producer Bill Gordon. Fortunately, my contract with Quinn Martin Productions, negotiated by an agent who received 10 percent of my earnings, remained in effect for six months.

185

I went home and began focusing on ideas for other shows.

My first story conference was with the line producer of *The Fugitive* and his associate. Having rejected my earlier submission, they evidently had not been impressed by my position as Gordon's story consultant. I assumed my agent arranged the conference through their boss, Quinn Martin.

I walked in with a basic idea for an episode that needed major fleshing out. Both executives were cordial but not eager to begin plotting a story. They offered me a box of colored pills of some sort, which I declined, then an alcoholic drink, which I also declined. Each downed a few pills, presumably to sharpen their creative skills.

We began. Although the concept was mine, I contributed little to the story's development. At one point, they questioned my logic for an off-the-cuff suggestion I made dealing with a scene. Of course, they were right. I felt stupid.

Nonetheless, when the meeting ended we had a deal. I went home and began writing. The outline and every draft of the teleplay required considerable revising. Finally ready, a shooting date was scheduled.

My story centered around a clandestine reunion between Richard Kimble, the fugitive, and his sister, portrayed by an actress locked into the role, having appeared in previous episodes.

Incredibly, I struck out again.

"I'm sorry," the producer informed me over the phone, "the actress who plays Kimble's sister can't work now. She's eight months pregnant. We'll reschedule it as the first show next season."

Disappointing as that news was, I shrugged it off until a bombshell exploded several months later.

I never thought Lieutenant Philip Gerard's relentless four-year pursuit of the desperate fugitive would end with my script topping the list for the coming season. After 120 episodes, anther Quinn Martin series was history. Again poor ratings.

Although my work was trashed, I received the minimum payment, $3,500.

Martin's longest running series was *The F.B.I.*, starring Efrem Zimbalist, Jr. It lasted nine seasons, but was in its infancy when story editor Mark Rodgers handed me the framework for an episode based on an actual FBI case.

Typically, the assignment didn't run smoothly. Mark contributed significantly to the project, yet gave me full screen credit for *The Messenger*.

A talented dramatist who later became the series producer, Mark went on to other top productions. He remained friendly and a good contact, but I never worked for him again despite two or three other story conferences.

None of my ideas clicked.

When paychecks from QM Productions stopped, my agent's 10 percent also ceased. But he continued working hard to arrange conferences. One finally paid off with an assignment for an episode of *The Iron Horse*, a western.

Starring Dale Robertson, it was in its second and final season when I sold *Six Hours to Sky High*, one of 30 episodes aired. The plot intrigued the producer, but as usual, the script required excessive work. I volunteered to do whatever was needed despite a guild contract limiting rewrites to protect writers from studio demands.

I parted company with the producer and his editors amicably. Too bad the series didn't last. I'm sure I could have landed another assignment. But as things had been going, I was getting used to bum breaks.

When I learned that producer Sterling Silliphant would be holding a weekly seminar at his spacious Pasadena home, I contacted him and was among a small group of writers chosen to attend his classes.

One of television's most prolific dramatists in the 1960s, Silliphant's credits were extensive. They included work on *Naked City* and *Route 66*, two of that era's biggest hits. His long career spanned theatrical films and novels. He reportedly authored more than 30 books.

Unfortunately, Silliphant's success didn't rub off on me. His broad concepts of screenwriting failed to address the techniques of producing a shooting script, my glaring weakness.

I dreaded the long drive to Pasadena each week and stopped going when Silliphant postponed a couple of meetings because of other commitments. I learned they didn't last much longer.

For two years, I struggled to gain a foothold in the industry. I submitted outlines, series proposals and scripts for dozens of shows. Among them were *The Virginian, The Big Valley, Murder, She Wrote, Run for Your Life, Have Gun, Will Travel* and *The Virginian.*

Charlene, meanwhile, was raising the kids practically by herself. Between failures, we survived with timely residual and unemployment insurance checks. When it seemed I would never make another sale, the phone rang.

Bill Gordon had been hired and given a large budget to produce a series pilot called *The Professionals.* He asked me to write one of six 90-minute teleplays.

I was ecstatic (again).

It was a project that kept me isolated in John's bedroom for several months. I spent a week at the Van Nuys courthouse observing and interviewing a deputy district attorney to help me develop the central character for my story.

Unfortunately, none of the six pilot scripts was filmed. *The Professionals* ultimately became three separate series about doctors, cops and lawyers. Bill Gordon moved on to other projects.

For my work, I received the minimum pay, this time $4,500 which again kept the wolves away.

"It couldn't have come at a better time," I told Bill. "We were absolutely broke. Why is it when I get an unexpected assignment or I'm surprised with a residual in the mailbox I'm always desperate for money?"

"You know why," he said.

To my knowledge, Bill wasn't a religious person. But I understood his simple explanation and readily accepted it.

When the $4,500 was nearly gone, my agent relayed an offer from the *Gunsmoke* producer.

"They want to buy your outline," he said, "for three-hundred dollars."

"Three hundred? That's not even guild minimum for a story."

"They're calling it a *notion*, not a story," he replied. "It needs development, and three hundred is all they'll pay."

A notion? I was irate. I immediately contacted the Writers Guild to appeal my case. After a few weeks, the guild determined the outline qualified as a story. I thought I had won. I didn't. The studio withdrew its offer.

"They're going to pass," my agent said. "Sorry."

Sorry. That was it?

I had watched enough *Gunsmoke* episodes to know my outline was on target. It had the potential for a strong, above-average episode. I told my agent that and he agreed.

"I tried, Jack. That's all I can do."

That wasn't all I could do. I called the producer's office, determined to plead my case to whoever would listen. What was there to lose?

It was late afternoon on a Friday when the secretary had gone. The story editor Paul Savage was headed out the door when he took my call.

He admitted the outline was intriguing but pointed out the obvious, that *Gunsmoke* didn't employ novice writers. I admitted I had few credits but pointed out they were episodes for highly rated series. I simply asked for an opportunity. I offered to expand my outline with no commitment and if acceptable, I would sign a contract for the story only.

Savage pondered, then reluctantly agreed to a meeting with his producer. It began a long exasperating process that became my biggest challenge as a TV writer.

The first meeting went well. I took copious notes and returned a couple of weeks later with an outline I was certain would impress them.

"I'm sure glad you made that phone call," Savage beamed when he along with producer John Mantley and associate Joe Dackow praised my in-depth story for which I was paid $1,000.

Even then, it was questionable CBS would approve the episode. It was a controversial story that focused on loveable Doc Adams.

He is about to leave Dodge City on a stormy night to deliver a baby when he witnesses a murder. Marshal Dillon chases down the killer and critically wounds him practically at Doc's feet. The man surely will die if Doc doesn't remove the bullet. He works through the night, unable to get to the farmhouse to deliver the baby. It's still-born. Doc has saved the killer's life and now must give courtroom testimony that will send him to the gallows.

Mantley battled network executives for weeks before the story was approved. He gave me an unprecedented opportunity as a virtually unknown dramatist to write the shooting script. I couldn't wait to start work.

Working from such a detailed outline, I found it relatively easy to deliver a shooting script with dramatic scenes and believable dialogue.

It didn't take long to be summoned to a meeting. When I entered the office, I found Paul Savage waiting, no one else. He wasn't smiling.

"Have a seat, and we'll go over this," he said as he picked up my script.

My heart sank.

The story editor went through the manuscript page by page, noting penciled comments here and there by Producer John Mantley.

None was complimentary. I was disillusioned, embarrassed and immediately realized I had blown a career-changing opportunity.

I was paid the contracted figure, $3,500, but would have nothing to do with the final draft. Savage rewrote my work and listed himself as the sole writer. He gave me story credit.

Clearly, Savage made major changes, more professional perhaps, but not all for the better, in my opinion. Again I appealed to the guild. Thee anonymous writers compared the two scripts. At least two of them decided that my story concept and character developments bore sufficient evidence that entitled me to story credit and equal teleplay authorship with Savage.

Monetarily, it was a major victory, considering future residual income.

America's longest running television western, *Gunsmoke* appeared weekly on CBS from 1955 to 1975. It retained its worldwide popularity in reruns long after the series was canceled. Even in 2010, episodes showed up periodically on the tube.

But for me, it was a one-shot flop.

Mantley's associate, Joe Dackow was elevated to producer the following season. Despite my script problems, Joe liked me and apparently recognized my creative potential. He promised me more work.

It never happened. Dackow produced nine shows before I learned he had died of an undisclosed illness. It took at least a year before my episode, *The Reprisal*, was aired Feb. 10, 1969.

The previous year was painful in almost every respect. Residual checks arrived less frequently, unemployment insurance income dried up, I was experiencing writers' block and my marriage was suffering.

Eventually, our financial situation became critical. Not only were bills stacking up, the refrigerator and cupboards were becoming bare.

Charlene always let me solve our money problems, but it was obvious I had exhausted my options. She hadn't.

My wife went to her parents who were in no position to make loans to anyone. But Charlene's mother had a nest egg even her husband didn't know about. She loaned us $500.

Even then, we realized $500 wouldn't last long. Although Charlene had no nursing experience, she was able to find a job at a Jewish home for the aged, about six blocks from our house.

She cared for infirmed, difficult patients during a graveyard shift at a minimum wage. I slept through the night and labored unsuccessfully over a typewriter during the day when my wife tried to sleep. We attended to the kids as best we could.

And we argued constantly. When I couldn't come up with a plausible story idea while meditating on a lounge chair beside our pool, I sometimes would head over to the nearby course for a round of golf.

Charlene restrained herself for awhile, then insisted I stop wasting my time and get a real job.

I knew she was right.

Early in 1969, the Citizen-News rehired me as a night sports makeup editor, an ideal full-salaried job that required little work with no set hours. I worked alone, came into a deserted newsroom, breezed through the job and left.

My intention was to freelance during the day. But I had become disillusioned with television after so many disappointments. Usually, I just played golf.

After months of supporting the family, Charlene happily resumed her role as homemaker thanks to my steady paycheck.

We repaid Charlene's mother and I cast aside any further aspirations of becoming a TV writer. That was before my phone rang one day.

"Jack Webb just hired me to produce the *Adam-12* series," Jim Doherty said. "I figure between you and me we can write most of the shows this season."

It was another shocker. *Most of the shows*? I felt like I had hit a lottery jackpot.

My old buddy from *12 O'clock High* had written for Webb's previous mega hit *Dragnet* and now was in charge of his new half-hour series about two uniformed police officers on patrol. Episodes ranged from violent crimes to comedy.

My first script, *Exactly One-Hundred Yards,* focused on a grammar school kid. My second, *Once a Junkie,* was heavier. Both shows aired late in 1969.

My third teleplay was in the works, when my hot-tempered Irish buddy clashed with Webb, his executive producer. Predictably, Webb summarily fired Jim and hired a producer who brought his own stable of writers for the show.

Jack Webb was a powerful force in the industry. Doherty was blackballed. Without an agent and now another smudge on my TV credentials, I also was unable to land an assignment.

Thank God I still had my Citizen-News job.

Despite an enduring bitterness, Doherty had kind words for his old boss in a Times article I wrote following Jack Webb's death in 1982 from an apparent heart attack at age 62.

"I've heard people imply that Jack Webb was old-fashioned," Doherty said. "Maybe he couldn't adapt or make dirty movies. I admired him for that, but he adapted well enough to get a number of series on the air....

"One thing about Webb—you may have quit or might've been fired, but usually good people would be back. He never stayed mad at anybody. Maybe a couple of years later, he would call you and say, 'Hey, come down. I've got something for you.'"

Chapter 27

A Dodgers Road Trip

It was early summer, 1970, an awful night.

I was aboard the Dodgers' private plane, returning from a lengthy road trip to New York City, Philadelphia and Montreal, Canada. The aircraft bounced violently through the stormy skies somewhere over Nebraska. Suddenly, it pitched downward.

Second baseman Ted Sizemore, a couple of others and I were playing cards. *Swish!* They flew off the table. The pilot informed us over the intercom to prepare for an unscheduled landing at the Grand Island airport.

Moments later, the Boeing 720 Lockheed Electra touched down in heavy wind, rain and lightning strikes. It fishtailed on the slick runway and finally stopped. I heaved a heavy sigh as I'm sure everyone aboard did.

We were only 47 miles from Kearney. I had fleeting thoughts about my unknown birthplace and wished the circumstances were different. I thought one day I might visit Kearney. Mom spoke highly of the little town that became a sizeable city.

When weather permitted, we resumed our flight to L.A.

My first and only road trip with the Dodgers had not gone well from the start. During a refueling stop in St. Louis, I over-heard a comment from the pilot as I was re-boarding.

"I think it'll be okay," he told a ground crewman as both stood under the wing, peering up at something.

Fortunately, the pilot was right.

Four or five of us from the Los Angeles area newspapers accompanied the team on that trip. All except me were beat writers familiar with the routine. When we arrived in New York, Manager Walter Alston handed each of us an envelope.

An itinerary maybe? I opened it.

Wow! I pulled out six one-hundred-dollar bills. I knew the Dodgers paid expenses for writers to cover road trips but I didn't expect such a generous allotment for meals.

The first game with the Mets ended late at night. I don't remember if the Dodgers won, but I was relieved to get through that first story and send it off by Western Union. My paper would have it first thing the next morning.

I had become chummy with a writer from the Long Beach Independent who knew the ropes. After filing our stories, we decided we needed a nightcap to unwind, as writers sometimes like to believe. We downed more than one before leaving a bar near our hotel sometime after midnight.

As we walked along a deserted street, two young women came up from behind us. Provocatively dressed, they immediately propositioned us.

Before we could get rid of them, one rubbed up close to me and threw her arm across my shoulder. I didn't think about it at the time, but they weren't persistent. They stepped across the street and were gone.

Minutes later in my hotel room, I emptied my front pockets onto a dresser preparing to retire. I withdrew a money clip containing about $300. I reached for my wallet in my hip pocket.

It was gone and with it the rest of the Dodgers' meal allowance.

I was furious. I never felt my pocket being picked. I phoned my friend. Luckily, he hadn't been robbed.

"Come on," I told him. "Let's see if we can find them."

We quickly left our rooms, hailed a taxi and cruised the area. As we expected, the hookers were nowhere in sight.

My nightmare continued with filing a police report I'm sure the officer considered almost laughable although he restrained himself.

Unable to reach Charlene on the phone the following morning, I called George Main, a boxing writer friend from the Los Angeles Evening Herald Express. I told him what had occurred and asked him to phone my wife later in the day.

"I have to get on the team bus for the ballpark, George. Please ask her to call the bank right away and cancel my credit card. I'll call her later."

A typical sportswriter who found the incident humorous, George joked about my encounter with the street walkers, but promised he would relay the information. Whatever he said triggered an explosive overreaction by Charlene, followed by a tearful phone call to her parents.

Our miscommunication got worse.

As I stood in the Shea Stadium press box while the National Anthem boomed over the ballpark's loud speakers and a commercial airliner roared off from nearby LaGuardia Airport, I was summoned to the telephone by a public relations person.

"I think it's your wife," he said.

At the height of the noise, I understood nothing Charlene said. She was hysterical. I attempted, unsuccessfully, to calm her. I asked if she had canceled the credit card, but her reply was lost in the din of the ballpark.

"I'll call later, honey. Settle down. It's going to be okay. I love you…"

Returning to my seat, I tried to concentrate on the game. I thought it would never end. After we returned to the hotel, I called home and got no answer. Repeated calls also went unanswered. I assumed, correctly, she had taken the kids and was staying with her parents. I decided to let her calm down another day when the team would be in Philadelphia.

Charlene knew my itinerary and phoned the Bellevue-Stratford Hotel, where the Dodgers always stayed when they played the Phillies. I later learned a desk clerk had told her I was not registered.

Eventually we connected, not happily. During my 10-day absence, phone conversations with my wife seemed only to exacerbate the situation. Charlene's suspicious nature was reinforced when I arrived home, filed an insurance claim and spoke with an adjuster who seemed to share her distrust.

"Uh, huh," the agent replied dubiously, "and you weren't aware that your wallet was gone from your back pocket until you returned to your room alone and began preparing for bed?"

Although embarrassing, the phone interview was worth a $300 settlement, a considerable sum during those lean years, particularly then, when my future employment appeared in jeopardy.

The stolen credit card was never used, and Charlene eventually forgave me. Decades later, she still couldn't understand why my friend's pocket wasn't picked.

"If you had gone straight to the hotel after the game instead of into that bar," she often said, "you wouldn't have lost your wallet."

Returning to the sports desk after that road trip, I had more serious things to worry about, my job.

Six years after that nightmarish trip, the Bellvue-Stratford Hotel received worldwide notoriety when it hosted a statewide convention of the American Legion. Soon thereafter, a pneumonia-like disease killed 34 people and sickened 221 guests, the vast majority there for the convention.

I wondered if that clerk was still employed at the time. Why he couldn't find my name on the registration sheet when my wife called, I can't explain. I still blame him for causing me so much misery.

Part Three

THE TIMES

Chapter 28

The Tryout

After Judge Harlan Guyant Palmer died in 1956 and his son, Harlan Jr. became publisher, the Citizen-News underwent numerous changes.

The paper began to accept cigarette and liquor ads, circulation gradually dropped among longtime subscribers and I wondered how much longer I could count on a job there.

As a new decade approached in the late '60s, the newspaper was sold to a Beverly Hills real estate executive, David Hyler. He wrote a front-page trivia column about such exciting things as weekend joy rides up the coast with his wife.

By 1970, the paper had another owner as circulation and advertising plummeted along with its lofty reputation nurtured for so many years under the pious leadership of Judge Palmer.

Serious financial problems soon became evident to employees, despite management statements to the contrary. Editorial payroll checks began to arrive a day or two late, eventually not at all.

One day while covering a Dodger game in the press box, I sat next to John Weibusch, a nervous young L.A. Times beat writer who had a habit of chewing on Styrofoam cups. I told him about my tenuous situation at the Citizen-News.

"I heard Bill Shirley is looking for another copy editor," he said. "Why don't you give him a call?"

I thought about it. I had known Bill for years and he knew my work. After failing to receive a Citizen-News check for an entire week, I took my annual vacation, phoned Shirley and was granted a two-week tryout.

Early morning traffic was light when I drove into the Los Angeles civic center to meet with the sports editor.

I felt confident but nervous as I glanced at the cluster of government buildings I virtually ignored 10 years earlier, when I worked weekends. They seemed imposing that day.

Located a few blocks from City Hall, the court house and federal buildings, the newspaper covers a square block, stands tall and dominates the area.

Boasting "the largest metro in the USA" in 1990 with a daily circulation of 1.1 million, readership was considerably less that August morning in 1970 when I entered the Globe Lobby.

In the early '60s, I used the small back door, along with ink-stained pressmen and other weekenders. The narrow concrete walkway sometimes left blotches of ink on the soles of my shoes. When presses were rolling the noise was deafening.

Located on 2nd Street between Broadway and Spring, the rear of the building was a stark contrast from the attractive main entrance. Delivery trucks wheeled in and out with thousands of bundled newspapers headed for distribution.

The transplanted Redwood Restaurant, a favorite hangout for writers, was across the street. Squeezed among scrubby nondescript stores on the fringes of Skid Row, it was too classy for that block where the homeless wandered aimlessly, hungry and desperate.

Using the main entrance was a pleasant change for me.

"I have an appointment with the sports editor," I told the security guard seated in front of a bank of elevators.

"Third floor," he said matter-of-factly.

At that early hour, the sports department was virtually deserted. Cal Whorton, the paper's former boxing writer who knew me well, was too busy with the bulldog edition to look up. He, his desk assistant and a copy boy took little notice as I was greeted by Editor Bill Shirley.

Shirley paid little attention to me when I worked for him a decade earlier, except for one afternoon when I called his attention to a disturbing photograph in the first edition.

Outfielder Albie Pearson stood next to Los Angeles Angels owner Gene Autry at the end of a dugout. A cherubic little guy, Albie was the smallest man in the major leagues at 5 feet 5 ½ inches. The photograph, taken by an Associated Press photographer was a filler, nothing more.

"Take a look at this photo, Bill," I said while scanning the section looking for problems. "I don't know if you want to re-plate, but..."

Shirley looked.

"What's wrong with it?"

"Take another look."

He stared at it for a moment, then quickly reached for his phone, called the press room and stopped the run.

The photo showed part of a baseball bat that seemed to be leaning against Autry's crotch. Little Albie was grinning, his arm raised as if about to pinch his boss' cheek.

Not only did we replate, we recalled as many papers as possible from news racks. Shirley sent Autry a letter of apology. His response: "I'm flattered."

I doubt the editor remembered that when I began my tryout after which he would decide about permanent employment.

At the very least, I would be generously paid. Thanks to Otis Chandler, salaries at the Times, a non-union newspaper, compared favorably with those at the New York Times.

A fourth generation of family publishers, Otis assumed command of the Los Angeles metro in 1960 and remained publisher until 1980. Believing the newsroom was "the heartbeat of the business," he increased the size and pay of the reporting staff and expanded its national and international coverage. During the 1960s, The L.A. Times won four Pulitzer Prizes, more than its previous nine decades combined.

I had no thoughts of winning a Pulitzer down the line, but I began to feel better about the tryout as Bill explained the process.

"You will be editing copy and writing heads and captions for the bulldog edition to start with," he said. "I want you to edit heavily, particularly wire copy. That doesn't mean to gloss over staff stories and columns. Make whatever changes you consider necessary. That goes for everything except Jim Murray's column. If you find a typo, fix it, but don't mess with it. He's our *staar*."

An excellent administrator, copy editor and capable writer, Shirley ran his department like Captain Bligh commanded the Bounty, which, of course, is an exaggeration, but an irresistible simile, nonetheless.

On one occasion, Shirley stood directly behind me, looking over my shoulder as I labored over a piece of copy. After a moment, I dropped the pencil, rose and stepped to the coffee pot. Bill returned to his office.

A former semipro baseball player from Arkansas with a trim, athletic physique, Shirley retained a slight Southern drawl after years in Los Angeles. He exemplified the role of a well-dressed Times executive despite his lack of a college degree. Having moved up from a slot man, Bill relished his authoritative position.

He maintained rigid control. He pulled writers off beats, some temporarily, some permanently for being inaccurate, missing obvious angles, deadlines or when necessary to fill desk vacancies.

Constantly striving to improve the section, Shirley periodically posted memos when writers used words or phrases he disliked.

"Athletes are not heroes," one stated. "Firemen who pull people out of burning buildings are heroes. Policemen who save lives are heroes. Never call an athlete a hero."

Other memos: "Never refer to a record as a *new* record. That's redundant," and "It's a *coming* event, not *upcoming*."

A daily ritual occurred at 11:50 each weekday morning, when Shirley would step to the coat rack for his jacket and beckon one or two senior staffers who happened to be in the office at that hour.

"Well, shall we do it?"

They dropped what they were doing, donned their sport coats and headed for the elevator to the prestigious Picasso Room on the top floor to enjoy a free lunch.

I ate in the cafeteria on the 10th floor, which accommodated several hundred people. A skeleton staff remained on duty long past midnight and weekends to serve a variety of relatively good meals.

After initially working days during my tryout, I was assigned to the night shift under the watchful eye of the assistant editor,

Chuck Garrity. He was an outstanding slot man from the Denver Post responsible for producing the morning editions.

Garrity was everything Bill Shirley wasn't, gregarious, fun-loving, leader of the pack. Good guy, sometimes bad guy, cruelly insensitive when slashing a writer's story, occasionally killing it.

An incompetent woman hockey writer in the eyes of the entire staff, new to the beat, stood over Garrity as he edited one of her early features. Finally, watching it being hacked up and virtually destroyed, she erupted.

"*What are you doing*?" she blurted out, almost in tears.

"Sit down and be quiet," Garrity said, "or I'll kill the whole thing."

She sat down. Hockey clearly wasn't her strong suit and she was soon replaced.

STARTING TIME was 4 p.m. when Garrity handed out assignments, some less desirable than others, and released the day crew at his discretion. Because of time restraints, he decided when and where everyone would have dinner. One night it was a short cafeteria break, another a leisure meal at a nearby restaurant. He decided who might go home early, who would stay late to handle incoming copy.

I got along well with Garrity and felt even more confident about being hired after working with him a week or so without fouling up, or so I thought.

When the two weeks were nearly over, Shirley opened his door one afternoon after I had arrived for work. He called me into his office. Judging from his cool manner and tone of his voice, I wasn't being summoned for anything good.

In a matter of seconds, my mind raced with thoughts about mistakes I might have made, a wrong score in a headline, an inaccurate caption, sloppy editing…

Garrity was present. A heavily edited copy of a Rams story written by Bob Oates, a nationally known and highly respected National Football League authority, lay on Bill's desk.

"Have a seat," Shirley said as he picked up Oates' story. "Bob wasn't happy about your editing. Let's go over it."

Attempting to explain every change I had made, I was relieved when Garrity backed me up, having approved the copy before

203

it was shipped to composing the night before. But considering Shirley and Garrity were not always on the same page about a number of issues, I felt uneasy when the meeting ended.

Oates was a veteran sportswriter even then. He had worked at the Examiner and Herald Examiner before starting a lengthy career at the Times and went on to become a member of the original pro football Hall of Fame selection panel. He covered 39 consecutive Super Bowls.

And he often dined with Shirley in the Picasso room.

Why had Garrity tossed me Oates' story to edit? If he didn't approve of my changes, why would he have sent it to composing? Had I blown the job?

The meeting resolved nothing. I worked that night with the confidence of a rookie pitcher whose wild throw filled the bases with no one out in the bottom of the ninth.

After a few more days under the microscope and sleepless nights, I finally got the word, in writing. A brief memo on the bulletin board simply welcomed me to the staff. I remember thinking it strange that no one informed me personally, but seeing it in writing was a great relief.

It wasn't until I contacted Garrity while researching this book that I learned it wasn't Bill Shirley who had hired me.

"Shirley headed off on assignment or vacation, I can't recall which, and left me in charge," Garrity recalled almost 30 years after he resigned from the Times to accept an offer to help start a National Football League magazine.

"Leonard Riblett, the assistant managing editor, told me I had to hire someone. *Now.* Well, about 10 different guys had come in and tried out and none of them could handle all the things you could. So, I recommended you. And it was done.

"I found out much later over a beer with Riblett, that if I hadn't hired you, they were going to freeze the staff and we couldn't have hired anyone. Shirley, being Shirley, never said thanks, of course."

I became a permanent Times employee Aug. 16, 1970. Almost the same day the Hollywood Citizen-News ceased publication.

In retrospect, I'm not certain Bill Shirley would have hired me had the decision been his.

When Bob Oates died in 2009 at age 93, Times columnist Steve Harvey penned a few words worth repeating here.

"He told me once with a smile that when he had proposed to his wife as a young man, he made it clear that he would never work a day in his life," Harvey recalled. "Instead, he told her he was going to be a newspaperman. And indeed he was—from the time he went to work at a Yankton, S.D., daily in college until the last piece he wrote for the Times in 2007, 75 years later."

Chapter 29

The Star

Ifirst met him in 1961, when he arrived at the Times with a background that included writing and editing for Sports Illustrated and Time magazines, general assignment and rewriting positions with the Los Angeles Examiner and earlier stints with the New Haven (Conn.) Reporter.

In his first Times column, Jim Murray fired a heavy salvo at L.A. readers, an overview of his major likes and dislikes, laced with a unique style that became his trademark.

"I hope Steve Bilko has lost weight," he wrote. "The last time I saw him in the Coliseum, the front of him got to the batter's box full seconds before the rest of him."

Instantly recognizable, Murray's style didn't always produce laughs or even a chuckle, such as his famous closing line in a column leading up to an Indianapolis "500" race, "Gentlemen, start your coffins."

It infuriated race sponsors and, no doubt, thousands of fans as well. But it hit home as a grim reminder of the carnage that event left on Indy tracks during those early years.

I'll never forget Billy Vukovich's fiery death in 1955.

Also unforgettable was the horrific multi-car accident at the beginning of another race in that era when car wheels and other parts flew into the stands, killing and injuring spectators.

Murray also enraged Notre Dame fans, probably a few church-goes as well, when he compared USC's upset win one year to Christians eating the lions.

I wish Jim had been alive to cover Rachel Alexandria's victory in the 2009 Preakness Stakes, the second leg of horse racing's Triple Crown. The first filly to win that jewel since 1924, Rachel Alexandria might have been compared to another filly Jim wrote about in the 1984 Kentucky Derby.

Murray described the winner like this:

"A great gorgeous spotted lady, with these long shapely legs that looked as if they belonged to a Bolshoi dancer, humiliated the best 3-year-old boy horses in the country at the Kentucky Derby Saturday. She was never headed. She ran them into the ground with contemptuous ease...."

"They said a filly couldn't win this race, that the ones who had—2 in 113 years—were flukes...."

"You think of all the disaster areas in sports. You think of the 2-yard-line of the Chicago Bears, you think of the ropes in a Dempsey fight, the top of the key with Magic Johnson coming down court with the ball, the pitcher's mound with the bases loaded and Aaron up—and they all look like a picnic in the park compared to the homestretch at Churchill Downs...."

"Winning Colors, an Amazonian filly with a stride as long as Rhode Island, came into this pastoral setting Saturday with her ears pricking, full of run, looking for horses. If she knew what she was getting into, she didn't show it. She dug in and invited the boys to come, catch me if you can—like an Ali inviting a George Foreman or Sonny Liston to come mix it up...."

Murray's style was unmatchable, yet, incredibly, a small West Coast newspaper once published Jim's column bylined by one of its writers. The plagiarism was easily detected and reported to The Times.

Asked if he wanted to press charges, Murray declined, saying, "He's young and he made a mistake. He apologized. I think he learned his lesson."

An article by Dave Kindred, published Aug. 31, 1998, in *The Sporting News* further describes Murray's uniqueness.

"Every sportswriter in the last 30 years has gone to the typing machine to do what we called 'a Murray column,'" Kindred wrote. "We all failed. An editor gently explained these failures to Mike Littwin, then new to the Los Angeles Times and in thrall to the newspaper's star."

"I had Jim Murray disease bad," Littwin was quoted. "So one day an editor put his hand on my shoulder and said, 'Son, you should try to be somebody else. Only Jim Murray can be Jim Murray.'"

Kindred continued.

"Anybody can write a one-liner. Only Jim Murray, soft, quiet and brilliant, could write 50 laugh lines and make them sing harmony."

"If there were a Bartlett's quotations of sports writing," Littwin says, "three-quarters of the book would be Murray lines."

Only Murray could say of Cincinnati, "Nothing to do there in the summer but listen to the tar bubble." Walter Alston came from a farm town so small "the trains stopped only if they hit a cow." Mike Tyson had a way back: "Become a vegetarian." (A reference to the chunk of ear Iron Mike chewed off opponent Evander Holyfield.)

Perhaps Jim's most remarkable achievement as a writer occurred at the height of his career, when he suddenly went blind yet managed to produce his columns through the eyes of John Scheibe, a copyboy assigned by Bill Shirley to assist him.

According to a published report and as I remember it, Murray's optical problems began in January of 1979, when he was preparing to cover Super Bowl XIII. He underwent emergency surgery for a detached retina in his left eye, but that procedure, as well as follow-up operations, was unsuccessful. Meanwhile, he had developed a cataract in his right eye.

As the vision in his "good" eye deteriorated and while awaiting risky cataract surgery, Murray faced the possibility of permanent blindness at age 59. The copyboy, meanwhile, drove Jim to games and interviews, read him box scores, described action from press boxes and accompanied him to locker rooms.

Years later, Sheibe's hardcover book, "*On the Road With Jim Murray: Baseball and the Summer of '79,* told the fascinating story that ended happily for "America's Best Sportswriter," as he was named 14 times by the National Assn. of Sportscasters and Sportswriters.

Murray's column appeared on Page 1 of the section five days a week and was syndicated in more than 200 newspapers. His awards include a Pulitzer Prize for Commentary in 1990 and a Times Mirror Lifetime Achievement Award in 1998 after 37 years with the L.A. paper.

Commenting about winning the Pulitzer, Jim wrote: "This is going to make it a little easier on the guy who writes my obit...I always thought you had to bring down a government to win this. All I ever did was quote Tommy Lasorda accurately."

Despite his fame, Jim had no ego, shunned public appearances and was most comfortable around fellow journalists and athletes he came to know.

The following is an excerpt from his column about the legendary jockey Bill Shoemaker:

"The only line of communication between a horse and rider is in the hands and Shoemaker's touch has been likened by track experts to 'the wing of a dove.' It's an attribute a rider is born with and is to racing what Sam Sneed's swing is to golf or Warren Spahn's motion to baseball. There is almost nothing that can go wrong with it and Shoemaker should be riding as long as he is breathing."

"Booting home 4,000 winners after only 12 years on the track is an astounding accomplishment when you consider it took John Longden and (Eddie) Arcaro a quarter-of-a-century to achieve it."

Shoemaker went on to win 8,833 races before retiring from riding and becoming a trainer. In 1991, at age 60, he suffered a near-fatal auto accident that paralyzed him from the neck down, yet he continued to train horses for six more years. He died in 2003 at 72.

I don't recall Murray writing about Shoemaker's ability to strike a golf ball, but I know first-hand his game was impressive. I once followed Shoe in a pro-am tourney and saw the 4-foot, 11-inch 95-pounder consistently drive the ball 200 or more yards off the tee. I wasn't surprised.

Murray would have liked emulating that smooth, effortless swing. Jim loved the game, but had an embarrassingly high handicap. An honorary member of the Riviera Country Club in Pacific Palisades, Murray couldn't begin to handle that tough layout.

Several years after I retired, I ran into Jim at the Nabisco Dinah Shore golf tournament at Rancho Mirage in Palm Desert. He told me a joke he recently had heard about a golfer who died "prematurely," went to heaven and was sent back to earth with a new identity of his choice.

"After giving it a lot of thought," Jim continued, "the guy decided to go back as a lesbian. When asked why, he said, 'so I can play around with the girls and hit from the ladies' tees.'"

I seriously doubt I would have committed that one to memory had it not been for Jim's following comment.

"You know," he added with a smile, "they let me hit from the ladies' tees now."

As far as I know, Bill Shirley always hit from the white tees and usually shot in the 80s but seemed prouder of setting speed records.

"Ah finished 18 holes in three hours and five minutes," he might brag to staff members upon arriving in the office after a morning round, never mentioning his score.

Murray's final column, Aug. 16, 1998, captured the moment after a racehorse named Free House won at Del Mar in San Diego:

"He's not a What's-His-Name anymore. He's a Who's Who.... The bridesmaid finally caught the bouquet. The best friend got the girl in the Warner Brothers movie for a change. The sidekick saves the fort."

The day after writing those words, Murray died of a heart attack in his home at age 78. Thanks to his Pulitzer, the author of his obituary no doubt found it a bit easier to compose, as Jim jokingly had predicted.

It's understandable Bill Shirley ordered me not to mess with his column. I wouldn't have dared.

Chapter 30

Captain Bligh and His Crew

The weekly posting of the department's work schedule usually generated plenty of grumbling, but to Bill Shirley's credit, he tried to accommodate those with special requests.

A complicated, time-consuming project, completing the schedule was one of Shirley's major accomplishments each week, shuffling names and assignments in an effort to cover all bases with a productive lineup. Once posted, however, he was reluctant to make capricious changes.

A night assignment might immediately be followed by an early morning shift; two successive off days were rare; occasionally someone might work a full week or longer without a break, and writers sometimes filled desk vacancies.

Chuck Garrity worked the slot most nights, a high-pressure job his relievers didn't covet. Chuck usually sailed through his shifts with few ripples, leaving ample time for a bit of boyish frivolity, except on Saturday nights, crunch time.

A special breed of gray-haired incurable sports fanatics included Harley (Ace) Tinkham, Malcolm Florence, Dan Hafner and several others who contributed to one of the best sports sections in the country.

Tinkham had the uncanny ability to recall scores of Notre Dame-USC football games through the years as effortlessly as reciting the alphabet. His recollection of track and field records was phenomenal. Others had similar capabilities and were called upon to provide instant answers to phone questions when the copyboy was too busy to look them up.

Sports dominated their lives. If they had other interests, I wasn't aware of it on the job or when I joined them for golf. Conversations ranged from griping about Shirley's latest memo to the PGA's hottest rookie, the fight, the game, the controversial play, whatever. Not that I didn't participate in the chit-chat. I enjoyed sports, but it didn't absorb me.

While seated at the desk one Saturday afternoon, my attention was drawn to the television set where a group had gathered during a lull to watch Stanford quarterback Jim Plunkett hit receivers in a dazzling passing performance.

"P-l-u-n-k-e-t-t," they chanted in unison as he connected on play after play. "P-l-u-n-k-e-t-t..."

Forget Shirley's memo. At that moment, Jim Plunkett was their hero and their adrenaline was pumping. It was no surprise when he won the Heisman Trophy.

Florence, a prolific writer assigned to various beats over the years, not only was in demand on the Times speaking circuit but also kept the night crew entertained. With his warped sense of humor, he concocted devilish pranks at the expense of his colleagues.

At least once, however, he was on the receiving end.

Having taped a college football game, Mal turned on his TV, set the VCR controls and got comfortable in his Tarzana living room. The phone rang. It was Harley Tinkham calling from the paper. His message was succinct:

"Stanford 28, Trojans 27."

Click.

I don't profess to remember the actual teams and scores, but I do recall it being one of the few times anyone got the better of Mal Florence. He was furious, of course, and soon retaliated.

Avrum Dansky was of a different mold, lanky, non-demonstrative, not inclined to idle conversation, but like the rest, irretrievably submerged in the world of sports.

A statistical genius, Dansky was responsible for what probably was the most widely read page in the section. Like a bookish accountant who reveled in his chosen field, Avrum made few mistakes, had a remarkable memory for facts and figures and took great pride in his work.

Night after night he quietly went about his routine, checking accuracy of team standings, scores and other statistics, gleaning two-line trivia notes from wire stories and filling pages with an array of six-point type.

One busy Saturday night in the composing room, a printer was rushing to make deadline for the makeover edition.

He locked up a chase of agate type on the flat metal surface of a heavy table called a turtle and rolled it to a press. In his haste, he had not lowered the surface of the press to slide the chase onto it. Garrity spotted it.

"By the time I yelled," he recalled, "he had given it a shove. When it didn't work, he really laid into it. Of course, the chase hit and flew back. Half the type fell to the floor, and all hell broke loose because we had some late prep or JC type in there."

Already past deadline, it was a disaster. I wondered how Garrity was going to handle that situation, no game results, no standings, nothing. Phones, no doubt, would be ringing off their hooks the next morning.

After presses began rolling and copies of the paper were delivered to our department an hour later, I immediately turned to the back of our section. There it was, Dansky's page intact with a line stating *"results incomplete."*

Garrity had found the agate page mat used in the previous edition and substituted that for the one dumped on the composing room floor.

Dansky, unfazed, never looking up from his typewriter, already was hard at work to make the deadline for the final.

"As usual," Garrity said, "Dansky was able to get everything back together before the last edition. But we had missed the areas where the JCs were located."

If it wasn't one problem, it was another, night after night.

Ross Newhan had more than his share of problems covering ball games.

When taking dictation from him on the phone one night, I relayed a message from Garrity who again was in composing.

"He's screaming on the squawk box for your lead, Ross. He wants it *now*."

Typically, Newhan had sent a running account of the game as it was being played. Already in type, the story needed a one- or two-graph wooden lead, hopefully with the final score. If the game ran late, the incomplete story would be rewritten for the final edition.

Beat writers, such as Newhan, almost prayed for low-scoring quick games and fast getaways from the ballpark.

Chuck Garrity seldom fudged on deadlines. Being late, even a couple of minutes, was a serious matter and sometimes had to be explained the next day.

"One more out and it's over," Ross pleaded with me.

"Give me the damn lead, Ross. It's already late."

"Tell Garrity he'll have it…"

Suddenly, in mid-sentence, Newhan exploded.

"*Shit!*" he screamed. "It's gone. I can never get a f'n break."

I couldn't resist telling Garrity how Ross reacted when the home run tied the game and sent it into extra innings. That story quickly spread through the department. Whenever Newhan came into the office, he would be greeted with a question he quickly got tired of hearing.

"Hi, Ross. Had any breaks lately?"

Initially, Newhan shrugged it off with a grin. Then he got a bit testy, which only prolonged the ribbing.

Sometime later, I edited a game story that featured a hard-luck Angels' pitcher who finally got enough team support to post a win. His name was Gary Ross. I wrote a six-column head and tubed the story to Garrity in composing.

Suddenly I heard a burst of laughter over the squawk box.

My headline: "Ross Finally Gets a Break, Hurls 3-Hit Shutout…"

It was one of many inside jokes never shared with Times readers.

During one baseball season, Shirley decided against running box scores to conserve space. It didn't take many angry phone calls or letters to restore them. But subtle changes seemed to go unnoticed by readers.

One was when Willie Stargell, a star first baseman and outfielder for the Pittsburgh Pirates, inexplicably became Wilver Stargell in the Times sports section.

214

The name change came after Managing Editor Frank Haven phoned the office one night between editions. He was upset, reportedly calling from a bar.

"His name is *Wilver*," Haven barked. "It is not Willie. I don't care what other papers call him. In the Los Angeles Times, he will be *Wilver* Stargell. Is that clear?"

It was. Thereafter, for as long as I can remember, the alert desk almost never allowed the name *Willie* Stargell to get into print. It was always a high-priority fix.

Years later, Garrity asked me if that was the night Haven smashed his car into the retaining wall coming off the Pasadena freeway.

"Maybe," I replied.

After working mostly nights for more than a year, I was assigned to assist Editor Jim Kuentz producing Sunday's early edition. It was a convenient pairing, since Jim and I lived near each other and shared driving.

A large, unhappy teddy bear of a man with a seriously ill wife at home and a job he didn't like, Kuentz heaved weary sighs as the shift droned on. He complained a lot and couldn't wait to retire.

Nonetheless, he was a good editor and excellent mentor. When he left, I replaced him. Bill Shirley assigned Frank Finch as my assistant.

Frank wasn't happy and I was apprehensive.

Relegated to boring desk work after almost four decades of covering Pacific Coast League baseball, the Rams, Dodgers and boxing, Frank went from the major leagues of editing to the minors.

I wouldn't say I was intimidated by Frank, 20 years my senior, but at the outset of our working relationship, I treated him with kid gloves. And I valued his opinions.

Like others who lost their beats and bylines to talented upstarts, Finch often reported to work surly and indifferent. A heavy drinker who wore a metal brace on his lower leg, Finch could get argumentative in public at the least provocation.

When Charlene and I shared a table with Frank at Lawry's "Beef Bowl" one night, he ordered a bottle of rare wine to go with our complimentary prime rib dinners.

215

"That's a one-hundred-dollar bottle of wine, sir," the waiter stammered.

"I can read," Frank replied, eyeing the wine list. "Now go get it."

The "Beef Bowl" was a big deal for the invited media as well as Lawry's famous restaurant, which picked up the tab for two private parties held days apart just before the Rose Bowl game each year.

The team representing the Big-10 conference in the New Year's Day classic "competed" against the Pacific Coast team, usually USC or UCLA, to determine which squad would consume the most prime rib. The restaurant kept track of the pounds ordered, and the media gave the event extensive coverage the next day.

It would be unfair to criticize Frank Finch for taking advantage of Lawry's generosity. Few members of the media restrained themselves. Eventually the "Beef Bowl" was discontinued.

In my 21 years at the paper, I ate in the Picasso Room only once, in 1976. I sat next to Finch at his retirement party. He was 65 then, facing what seemed a bleak future. But he was sadly aware that his heyday was far behind him. He was tired of working in my shadow.

Frank became misty-eyed when he gave his farewell speech, a few words that barely touched on his career. For a time, he was observed sitting alone in the reading room opposite the cafeteria, engrossed in a paperback novel. Eventually Frank found a job with a deposition firm, where he worked 14 years.

A loner who always vacationed by himself riding trains and busses in Mexico and elsewhere, Finch took his last one in May of 1992, when he learned he had leukemia. It was a 2,500-mile automobile trip through the western United States.

He died three months later, Aug. 7, at the age of 81.

Finch never talked to me about having a family. I was surprised when I read that he left a wife of 62 years, a daughter, granddaughter and great-granddaughter.

As an assistant, Finch was tough to replace. I marveled at his creative headlines that at times seemed automatic. He could process stories and captions almost as fast as I could pile up the copy, but sometimes I needed additional help when nearing a Friday night deadline.

When necessary, Shirley told me to distribute copy to editors working on home editions.

Sunday's early edition had limited circulation. It consisted of oversized photos, timeless rambling features, press releases and other fillers, along with staff-written columns, golf, bowling, fishing, auto racing, boxing....

Garrity replaced most of it with hard news. If space was tight he trimmed columns, sometimes killed them. On rare occasions, I would flip through the makeover edition unable to find my boxing column. All I could do was sulk. I understood the drill and never complained.

To produce Sunday's final required so many copy editors on Saturday nights it often was difficult to find a vacant seat. Besides a full copy desk, editors were scattered around the room, particularly during football season.

I didn't like passing out stories on the rim. I know editors resented it, even if they sat idle from time to time.

The most memorable reaction was when I placed a story with a headline order in front of Charlie Park, another demoted writer so bitter he sometimes worked the entire shift without speaking.

Before I could step away, Charlie wordlessly took his pencil and slowly pushed the copy across the desk until it hung over the edge. He paused, then gave it a final nudge, sending it to the floor like a floating autumn leaf. Eyeing me defiantly, Charlie then resumed what he had been doing, sometimes nothing.

The incident sparked laughs from those who witnessed it, but I didn't appreciate the humor and never again asked Charlie to write a headline.

Park, who covered Pacific Coast League baseball for the Mirror-News before joining the Times, once was the center of a major dispute when he robbed Oakland pitcher Sam (Toothpick) Jones of a no-hitter.

As I remember it, Charlie was the official scorekeeper that day. He ruled a ninth-inning grounder that an infielder couldn't handle a hit instead of an error. According to other press box reporters, it was an incorrect call that deprived Jones of recording a no-hitter. The controversy lingered in the press, subjecting Charlie to a ton of abuse from irate fans.

John Hall, my predecessor at the Hollywood Citizen-News, worked with Park at the Mirror and recalled that incident.

"Park was such a great guy, but he never got with it at the

Times," Hall said. "It was Zim (Paul Zimmerman, who preceded Shirley as editor) and Chuck Curtis (also a former editor) who took Charlie off the USC football beat in 1964 and put me on it while sticking him on the desk.

"I thought for awhile Charlie was mad at me, but he was mad at everybody at the Times, (including) Shirley who he worked for when Shirley was the slot man."

I never got to know Charlie Park on the job. After he retired and spent time at his cabin in Wrightwood, California, where he was a neighbor of my good friend Johnny Allen, I saw another side of Park.

John Hall was right. He was "a great guy."

I enjoyed producing that early edition.

I worked independently in a corner somewhere and took pride in creating an attractive cover. It was gratifying when Garrity kept a photo or feature I had selected for the entire run.

Press agents knew their releases stood a good chance of being used. They showed up personally each week with stories and photos to publicize their events.

And, yes, there were payoffs—booze, gift baskets and press junkets. When a longtime PR friend offered me free use of a motor home for two weeks, I almost gasped.

"I don't think I can accept that," I told him. "I could get into trouble with Shirley."

"If you don't take it, someone on another paper will," he said. "It's not a big deal. Shirley takes what he can get."

I had no plans for my two-week summer vacation. The offer was enticing. I thought about it and decided to risk it. I accepted.

I had never driven even a small pickup when I climbed behind the wheel of a compact 27-footer with Charlene at my side.

We headed north up the scenic but dangerous U.S. Highway 1. I think Charlene closed her eyes on every hairpin turn as we retraced the route of our honeymoon more than two decades earlier.

Highlights included a wild tow-truck ride to Monterey when the RV failed to start after being parked overnight in a Big Sur camping grounds and our visit to My Attic while the motor home was being repaired.

As we sat at the bar sipping drinks, I recalled that day in 1948 when I shared a beer with the overweight PIO corporal who re-layed a message from Colonel Flemings that made me tremble.

Charlene and I enjoyed a few hours there, I believe, before a driver from the repair shop, dressed like a chauffer, stuck his head in the door.

"Mister and Misses Hawn. Your car is here."

A few heads turned. We felt like celebrities.

After two weeks on the road in that small RV, I was happy to get home, but it left indelible memories about our scenic getaway that made up for the botched honeymoon.

It was campground barbeques one night, classy restaurants the next, visits to Hearst Castle and the Santa Cruz amusement park, a round of golf on a seaside course, romantic overnight parking on a Carmel beach...

Even more than that, it was one of our best vacations.

Refreshed but not eager to return to work, I arrived just in time for an important general staff meeting in Bill Shirley's office.

He read from a printed memo distributed throughout editorial. Effective immediately, employees no longer could accept gifts of any type from promoters or press agents.

A jaw-dropping shocker.

"Even Christmas gifts?" someone asked.

"Even Christmas gifts," Shirley replied matter-of-factly.

Shirley seemed to accept the new policy without blinking an eye, but he was one of the first offenders, according to Times photographer Ben Olender.

Photographers worked out of their own department and covered events as they saw fit. Sometimes, Shirley or Garrity opted for Associated Press photos rather than staff shots, which infuriated Olender and other photogs who regularly covered sports events.

While working the annual media golf tournament at La Costa Country Club after the policy directive, Olender spotted Shirley in the clubhouse, where gifts were being distributed to the press.

"He was in line getting golf shoes and other stuff," Ben told me, "so I took his photo. He looked at me, turned red and walked away. I nailed him good."

I don't know if Olender printed that negative or if Shirley's violation of the policy was reported, but the editor maintained a low profile for some time until the incident was forgotten.

Not as quickly forgotten was a more serious incident involving another Times photographer, Art Rogers. It occurred during pre-game warm-ups for the 1973 Rose Bowl game between Ohio State and USC and made national headlines.

Ohio State Coach Woody Hayes, known for his fierce temper tantrums, became angry when Rogers pointed his camera at him and began snapping photos. In an explosive rage, the coach barged forward, shoving the camera into Rogers' face.

"That'll take care of you, you son of a bitch," Hayes was quoted as saying.

After the game—won by USC, 42-17—Hayes was grilled by the biased media. He again exploded, cursing the reporter who questioned him before storming out of the interview room.

Even in victory, Hayes could lose his temper. While working at the Hollywood Citizen-News, I covered the Buckeyes in two Rose Bowl games, in 1955, when they defeated an outclassed USC team, 20-7, and in '58, when they hung on to beat Oregon, 10-7.

It hadn't rained in Pasadena on New Year's Day for 50 years, but the 1955 game was played in a quagmire. Hayes was furious that the field had no tarp and outraged that the pageant had allowed the band to perform on the turf at halftime. Those complaints ignited a feud with the Trojans that lingered for years.

The Big-10 champions were such prohibitive favorites against Oregon in 1958, Ohio State's narrow win embarrassed Hayes and his team.

I don't know what the coach told his players after the game while the press waited outside locked doors, but when we finally were admitted, it was unlike any winning locker room I had ever entered. The scene was morgue-like. Hayes was in no mood to tolerate controversial questions from hostile reporters. He left town with another Rose Bowl win, certainly not a triumph.

After the Art Rogers incident, he left with a subpoena.

Hayes was fired in 1978 after striking two of his players and a Clemson linebacker named Charlie Bauman who intercepted a pass to clinch the game for the Tigers in the Gator Bowl.

At the time, I wasn't interested in Woody Hayes.

I was the Times boxing writer, having replaced Dan Hafner, who previously covered the Dodgers.

Not an especially polished writer, Hafner was, however, fast and accurate. He dug for interesting angles and came up with good quotes. One of his last ring assignments was the Muhammad Ali-Ken Norton rematch Sept. 10, 1973, in Los Angeles, when Ali won a split decision.

Six months earlier, Ali lost to Norton in San Diego, an important fight Shirley elected not to staff. Why he chose to rely on wire coverage instead of sending Hafner remains a mystery.

It was a mistake even Shirley must have realized. Not only did Norton register a stunning upset, he broke Ali's jaw in the process. Associated Press adequately reported the facts but little more. Hafner would have covered it like a blanket covers a fly.

Dan was devastated when pulled off the beat.

"I never figured why Shirley had it in for Dan Hafner," Hall told me. "He rode him all the time with nasty notes after some of his Dodger coverage.

"Shirley would get jealous of anybody getting any praise. He particularly made life miserable for Dwight Chapin, Jeff Prugh and Ron Rapoport after they (Times beat writers) had books published. Whatta guy.

"After Chuck Curtis died in 1964 after the USC-Notre Dame game and Zim retired in 1968 after the Olympics, Shirley was on his own to set new standards in being rotten."

Chapter 31

Breaking Out

Relatively new on the boxing beat, I was surprised when Bill Shirley sent me to San Diego in late November of 1973 to interview Jesse Freitas, Jr., a sensational quarterback who was making national headlines at San Diego State.

I surmised this assignment was a test. My article could become a feature that could end up anywhere in the paper or in the wastebasket.

Son of a pro quarterback who backed up Frankie Albert for the San Francisco 49ers in 1946 and '47, young Jesse was an all-around athlete who starred in football, basketball and baseball in high school in the late 1960s.

I caught up with him in the collegiate ranks when he was leading the nation in passing and total offense in his senior year at San Diego State.

In his final game that clinched the conference championship with a 41-6 drubbing of outclassed Fresno State, Freitas completed 33 passes for 450 yards and had been within striking distance of the NCAA completion record of 42.

To avoid total embarrassment for Fresno State, Freitas was pulled from the game with about four minutes left in the first half and benched for good with more than 11 minutes remaining in the game.

"I was aware of the NCAA record," Jesse told me. "During the game, I felt I should be taken out. I felt it would've been in bad taste. Their best defensive back was out and they had a receiver coming over, trying to play cornerback.

"After the game, after talking to others, I thought it would've been nice to have had the record. But I still think my first impression was right. It would've been in bad taste."

A backup for Jim Plunkett at Stanford, where he played sparingly before transferring to San Diego State, Freitas went on to a solid pro career with the San Diego Chargers.

Shirley apparently liked my story. It was my first published on the sports cover page.

But it was back to the boxing trenches the next few years, while continuing to make up Sunday's early edition.

Despite having a surplus of good editors, Shirley hired Jack Quigg, a middle-aged Associated Press word-saver who disliked adjectives and tightened sentences until they almost strangled.

Solemn-faced, dull and almost non-communicative, Quigg quickly became the most unpopular person in the department. Like a CPA facing an approaching tax deadline with a stack of unfinished returns in front of him, he labored all day long on a never diminishing pile of copy, slashing, trimming, rearranging, rewriting...

Quigg's desk was the last stop before publication. His pencil moved swiftly, never sensitively, not always accurately. Columnists complained about changes that affected their style of writing or the flow of the piece. Usually it was to no avail.

To avoid Quigg's tinkering, I always dummied my Sunday boxing column somewhere in the back of the section and tubed it straight to composing. No one seemed to notice or care, until Shirley happened to read one.

Although I never heard him compliment anyone about anything, it was clear he found my column about a deaf-mute boxer unique, perhaps even worthy of better exposure than where he had found it. Had the column been previewed, it might have come to Shirley's attention. Thereafter, the editor ordered me to run my columns past Quigg before I dummied them.

That interview with the deaf mute was my most challenging as a sportswriter.

Thanomjit Sukhothai, the bantamweight title contender from Bangkok, Thailand, sat erect in the booth, an orange drink in front of him. His adviser, Devit Chatikavanija, was on his right; his trainer-manager, Prayoon Panungpon, on his left. Watana Sadsonboon, a Los Angeles resident who represents the local Thai community, sat opposite them.

Sukhothai, whose real name is Somchit Chindasi (at least, that's the name on his passport) and who is known in international boxing circles as Super Thai, has been a deaf mute since birth.

Panungpon speaks no English; Sadsonboon speaks some English, and Chatikavanija speaks good English. It was not clear how well each speaks the Thai language, but, at times, they appeared to have some difficulty communicating among themselves.

Sukhothai, a solemn, round-faced young man with black, darting eyes that seem to pierce whatever they focus on, attended school only four years. He cannot read or write except to sign his name. However, his senses, as one might suspect, are extremely keen.

The interview was not so keen. It went something like this:

Is this his first trip to the United States?

Chatikavanij, the adviser: "Yes."

How does he like it here?

The adviser translated the question. The local representative contributed something in Thai. The trainer-manager addressed Sukhothai with a few words and gestures. And the fighter, his stony face cracking slightly, replied with an abrupt sound which apparently the trainer-manager understood. The communication process reversed itself, and Chatikavanij, the adviser, ultimately unraveled it all in good English:

"He likes it."

There was considerably more, a time-consuming process that proved of little value in determining the outcome of the challenger's bantamweight title fight with champion Alfonso Zamora of Mexico, held Aug. 30, 1975, at the Anaheim Convention Center.

Does Sukhothai have any predictions?

After considerable discussion among the three Thais, the adviser replied:

"He thinks he will win."

An obvious mismatch, the fight ended in the fourth round when Zamora knocked out Super Thai and sent him back to Thailand, never to be heard from again.

Had that column been touched by Quigg, well, who knows

how it might have ended up in print? He altered plenty of others in ensuing months until he finally eased up. To his credit, he saved me and other writers more than a few times with his perceptive eye.

Eventually, Jack Quigg unveiled a dry sense of humor and ultimately gained the respect of most of the staff.

"Quigg was actually a pretty good guy," John Hall later said, "but miscast as a copyreader reading about subjects completely foreign to him."

However, he was a quick learner and, I believe, even became somewhat of a boxing fan. Certainly enough boxing stories ran across his desk, such as the buildup for a heavyweight title elimination fight between Ken Norton and Dwayne Bobick.

Early one May morning in 1977, my wife and I headed for the Los Angeles International Airport for a flight to New York, where I would cover the bout.

The freeway was jammed. Worse, it was drizzling rain.

"I told you I had a bad feeling about this trip," Charlene reminded me as we inched toward the airport. "It's like I have ESP."

Late taking off aboard a TWA flight, the plane sped down the runway but never got airborne. Suddenly, we pitched forward in our seats as the plane skidded off the concrete and came to a jolting stop. The pilot announced he had aborted the takeoff because of a faulty air speed indicator.

After taxiing back, the plane moved into position for a second takeoff an hour later. The pilot apologized and said the problem had been resolved.

A second takeoff attempt also was aborted at the last moment much like the first. The pilot again apologized, saying he had decided to have the instrument replaced. He said anyone who wished to switch to another plane, particularly those with connecting flights, might do so. Many did, but most remained on board.

We loosened our seat belts, read, daydreamed or peered out windows. Nothing was served unless ordered.

Charlene again needlessly reminded me.

"I told you—ESP."

A new speed indicator in place, the plane finally lifted off into the dark clouds for a bumpy ride to New York.

"It'll be about 20 minutes before we can get into line to land," the pilot announced, again with an apology.

No more than five minutes later, with no warning, the aircraft suddenly started losing altitude.

I don't know how other passengers felt, but Charlene was terrified. I wasn't exactly relaxed. Finally I realized we were descending for a landing.

Safely on the ground, the pilot explained that he had been given approval to land but didn't have time to notify passengers.

No longer circling above the city, the aircraft began circling on the ground while someone searched for a key to unlock the TWA gate. And we taxied…

"I told you…"

I thought that would end reminders, but no, Charlene hadn't finished. She added an exclamation mark a short time later when our cab driver got involved in a fender-bender en route to our Manhattan hotel.

Eventually settled, we shrugged off my wife's ESP and decided to enjoy the Big Apple. This was Charlene's first visit, my second. Although I would write advances, there was ample time to be wide-eyed tourists.

Obligatory drum-beating began at Gilman Hot Springs in California more than a week earlier when my wife and I spent a few days watching Norton work out.

Charlene's favorite boxer, heavyweight champ Ken Norton.

Charlene had come to know a few fighters she liked, among them Norton, a handsome lady-charmer who also found Charlene attractive. He gave her an ugly workout shirt with his name emblazoned across the back.

My coverage from Gilman began like this:

A gleaming, marshmallow-white Rolls-Royce enters the Massacre Canyon Inn parking lot and heads turn as it stops in front of the coffee shop.

Ken Norton slides out of the 1965 Silver Cloud, straightens his muscular 6-3 frame and glides through the front door. Wearing a western-style hat and chomping on a toothpick, the 220-pound, No. 1 heavyweight contender spots a reporter and joins him.

Norton smiles when a woman in her 40s comes to the table, gushes over him and places his wide-brimmed hat on her head, saying:

"Now I can say I've worn Ken Norton's hat."

"That's my car-washing hat," replies Norton, who owns four other flashy vehicles.

The woman wishes Norton luck in his May 11 fight with Duane Bobick in New York and leaves.

A young brunette a few tables away asks Norton for his autograph.

"Are you for real?" he says, his tone suggesting they might have met before and that perhaps she isn't serious about her request.

She holds up a pen and asks, "Have you got a minute?"

"For you, yes ma'm," he replies. "Have you got about an hour?"

Norton joins her and is shown a photograph of himself, seated on a luxurious white sofa, next to the brunette. He autographs the snapshot, shows it proudly to the reporter and returns it.

"Man, I'm tired," he says. "I'm going up and crash."

He saunters out, climbs into his Silver Cloud and sails off for a few hours sleep before his 1 p.m. workout—his last before leaving for New York.

Fifteen minutes away in Beaumont, Duane Bobick is crudely lumbering through a rough workout with an amateur, Marin Stinson, who has had more than 100 fights.

Trainer Eddie Futch, who was with Norton for 5½ years until he joined Bobick two years ago, watches intently, jerking his head slightly with Bobick's various moves, none of which is particularly fast. In fact, Stinson seems to have an edge.

227

A handful of spectators applaud politely after the round.

The unbeaten (38-0) contender looks bulky with a sponge pad under his jersey. He had displaced some rib cartilage while sparring with his brother, Rodney, in February, causing the fight to be postponed from March 2, and Futch isn't taking any chances.

"This is a precaution," he said after the drill. "He got hit with a terrific shot there yesterday. Nothing. We know it has healed...."

And so it went...

Across the street, a bartender pours a beer and tells his customer:

"I sure hope Bobick wins."

The customer asks why.

Slightly annoyed that he should have to explain, the bartender says, "If he beats Norton, he's got a shot at the title. I just think it'd be nice to have a white champion for a change."

Duane David Bartholomew Bobick. It's a name for the chairman of the board, or maybe a bank president—certainly not a pugilist, even a former choir boy from Minnesota. So, they modified it and called him "The Great White Hope."

Muhammad Ali, meanwhile, had a date May 16, five days after the Norton-Bobick match, to defend his crown against Spain's Alfredo Evangelista in Landover, Maine.

An impressive victory over Bobick seemingly would give Norton, who had beaten Ali once and lost two controversial rematches—another crack at the title. Eight months earlier, the morning after he was robbed of a 15-round decision over Ali, he told me, "I'll probably never fight again."

But a $500,000 purse to fight Bobick was too tempting. So, there he was, again on the doorstep to the world heavyweight championship.

Predictably, the Madison Square Garden weigh-in attracted a sizeable crowd, including promoters, managers and big-name boxers, past and present. Former heavyweight champ Floyd Patterson, a member of the New York Boxing Commission, conducted the weigh-in.

While Ali was keeping 'em laughing 200 miles away in Maine, Norton and Bobick were approaching that night's scheduled 12-rounder as if their lives depended on the outcome. Fistically speaking, at age 31, Norton's did.

"Ken's got to win and he knows it," Manager Bob Biron said

after his rock-hard heavyweight, fortified by six eggs and a steak for breakfast, stepped on the scales and seemed happy with the reading, 222 ¾.

Bobick, who had gone from 3-1 underdog in Las Vegas to 11-5, was expected to enter the ring at no less than 9-5, according to locally published odds.

The unbeaten Great White Hope was conceding nothing to Norton (37-4 with 30 knockouts). "This is not for a payday ($250,000), not for prestige," Bobick said after stepping off the scales at 215 ½. "I'm going out to beat Kenny Norton."

Everyone, it seemed, was quick to make a prediction, except ex-champ Joe Frazier, once Norton's stable mate.

Asked whom he liked, Frazier replied, "Both of them."

"Joe and I are very good friends," Norton said, "but Joe and I aren't fighting. This will be the first time we've been in opposite corners. He told me, 'May you have all the bad luck in the world.'"

Luck, as it turned out, had nothing to do with what took place in the ring that night. Those who blinked might have missed it.

Earning $8,621 a second for less than a minute's work, Norton made it look ridiculous. The beginning of the end came spectacularly when he landed a long overhand right to the side of the head. Bobick never recovered. Slamming blows from every angle, Norton attacked with devastating accuracy.

He landed at least a dozen solid blows to the head that rocked Bobick, then fired the *coupe de grace,* a couple of rights to the head, that put him down, seemingly for good. However, he was on his feet at nine, dazed, wobbly, braced against ropes and in no condition to continue.

Amazingly, the referee motioned for action to resume, took a second look before a punch could be thrown, then ended it, declaring Norton the winner. The time was 58 seconds.

I could have predicted what Bill Shirley would say about paying my expenses to New York for a fight that lasted less than a minute. Of course, he laid it on thick. I suppose he decided not to waste any more of the Times' money by sending me 200 miles away to Landover, Maine, to cover Ali's title defense five days later. Instead, he again opted for wire coverage. That fight went 15 rounds before Ali's hand was raised.

229

After I returned, I updated readers on the activities of Joe Frazier, who hadn't fought in almost a year since being knocked out by George Foreman. At 33, Smokin' Joe was well entrenched in his new career—music.

After rushing away from the Norton-Bobick weigh-in to rehearse for the opening of his new show at the Riverboat, Frazier stopped to sign autographs outside the Felt Forum on the corner of 8th Avenue and 32nd Street. I nabbed him for a quick interview while his driver went for Joe's car.

Almost shouting over a gusty wind as a cluster of fans encircled us, Frazier was still a man on the run. "Boogie, boogie, boogie," as he liked to say.

"I don't have any regrets about retiring," he told me, "because of the situation. I retired. The main thing about it, if I want to come back I can come back. I just retired because I wanted to change the pace a little, you know, do something different."

He meant showbiz. He really wasn't much of a singer or hoofer, but he had assembled a lively act that seemed to appeal to the late crowd opening night, mostly a gathering of friends and acquaintances.

"I sing, I talk to the people, I move about," Frazier said. "I make everything snappy."

His most popular song was a parody of the Sinatra hit, *I Did It My Way*, which Frazier said Paul Anka wrote for him. The key phrase: *I'll fight 'em fair. I'll fight 'em square, but I'll fight 'em my way.*

Smokin' Joe's way wasn't bad. It took him to the top and gained him a million fans.

Charlene was among them, but to her, Frazier didn't compare with Norton.

That ugly sweat shirt he gave Charlene remains neatly folded in her dresser drawer to this day.

By the late 1970s, Shirley had loaded me down with assignments. In addition to boxing, I was handed the prep and small college beats, occasionally worked the desk and cranked out features.

Covering preps was drudgery.

Sent to a high school football game in the San Fernando Valley, I was told to keep a close eye on a young quarterback who was a hot college prospect. Not having any interest in the preps, I knew little or nothing about the player before I arrived. I wrote six paragraphs, which began like this:

"Quarterback John Elway, a 6-3, 175-pound senior, threw six touchdown passes Friday to lead visiting Granada Hills to a 58-29 victory over Crenshaw but neither coach was particularly impressed.

"'We're capable of doing this (scoring frequently) any time with our offense,' Granada Hills coach Jack Neumeir said. 'I'm not happy with our defense to tell the truth'....

"Crenshaw coach Earl Smith merely shrugged when asked his opinion of Elway, who completed 27 of 36 passes for 382 yards and sat out much of the fourth quarter. 'He's a good quarterback,' Smith said grudgingly, 'but I was more impressed with the El Camino boy last week (John Mazur).'"

Elway, of course, became a pro football legend with the Denver Broncos, while Mazur, son of a legendary coach, starred at the University of Southern California but never attained the level of John Elway.

An important high school basketball tournament in San Francisco was a nice diversion but basketball was not my thing. I struggled through the tournament and filed adequate game stories.

My least exciting high school assignment was the 1978 California Interscholastic Federation State Track and Field Championships in Bakersfield.

I had never covered a track meet and was unqualified. For Charlene and me, the timing couldn't have been worse.

Seated in the stands perspiring under a hot June 2 sun along with about 8,000 others, predominantly teenagers, we sipped alcoholic beverages in paper cups and toasted each other on our 27th wedding anniversary.

At one point, I left the stands, stepped over a rope and started to interview a star pole vaulter. An official, who spotted me taking notes, came hurrying over.

"The press is not allowed on the field," he said as if I had just entered a ladies' room. "You'll have to go back to the stands."

It wasn't so much what he said that irritated me; it was his authoritative, arrogant manner. When I began to argue, he smelled liquor on my breath, became belligerent and threatened to call a security officer.

231

With that, I stepped back over the rope.

"I'm going to report you to the Times," he shouted as I headed back to the stands to share another anniversary drink with my wife.

If he did, I never heard about it.

Junior college sports was a step up from the preps, but covering events, scattered as they were around the sprawling Southland, was next to impossible. I wrote features and drove to key games near the end of the football season, but mostly I produced week-end roundup stories from the office.

Shirley, however, approved an overnight trip to cover a league championship game between Whittier and Redlands. I remember nothing about that football game other than when it took place, Nov. 18, 1978, a date recorded in history.

After shivering for more than two hours in an open wood-frame press box on that bitterly cold night, I returned to the motel. I found Charlene sitting up in bed watching live coverage of an air strip ambush in a South American jungle in British Guyana.

I joined her and watched intently.

California Congressman Leo J. Ryan had gone to investigate complaints from his constituents about family members who followed American cult leader Jim Jones.

After the plane landed, Ryan was killed along with four others by a hail of gunfire, apparently under orders from Jones. A day or so later, Jones orchestrated one of the deadliest massacres on record when he persuaded his followers to drink poison.

The horror of seeing those 912 dead men, women, young children and babies on TV sprawled in that jungle compound is unforgettable.

For Charlene and me, the Jonestown massacre remains forever linked to a meaningless, long forgotten football game.

Chapter 32

Hollywood and Dead Reality

Seldom had a movie generated as much controversy over its technical credibility as had "Rocky," a United Artists film nominated for 10 Oscars, including best picture of 1976. Not only is it remarkable the movie was made, but also that it even approached technical excellence.

It was produced from a freelance script by relatively unknown Sylvester Stallone, the 30-year-old star who never attended a boxing match until he was 29. Director John Avildsen never liked the "barbaric" sport and saw his first fight at the Olympic Auditorium after beginning work on the film. Actor Burgess Meredith, who played Rocky Balbo's scrubby, hard-boiled trainer, said at 67 he could find nothing in his past to prepare for the role.

Yet, among many prominent boxing people I contacted—the most critical viewers—comments generally were complimentary.

"It was very realistic," world featherweight champ Danny Lopez said, "except for training in a meat locker. That was the only thing that stood out as unrealistic...."

Stallone and Avildsen had a lot to say, but my interview with Meredith proved the timeliest. It occurred only a week or so after 72-year-old Howie Steindler was murdered.

A strict vegetarian, Meredith selected a clean, cheerful place for lunch near his Malibu home that specialized in salads.

Seeking an Oscar in a supporting role for the second straight year, Meredith had high hopes after nearly half a century before the cameras. I was pulling hard for him because of his on-the-money depiction of Steindler, with whom the actor had spent two weeks studying his mannerisms.

As Mickey Goldmill, an ex-fighter who ran a broken-down gym in Philadelphia, Meredith fit the role perfectly. Small and wiry at 5-5 ½, he jumped sprightly in and out of ring corners and handled the part as if he had lived it his entire life.

Describing the atmosphere while filming as "insalubrious," Meredith recalled that he had "slept in subways in my day, but I had never seen some of the squalor that I saw in those gyms. When I went into the dressing rooms of some of those crummy places, it was all I could do to stop from gagging; they're so filthy and bug-ridden."

Meredith met with two men to create his character. He combined the physical aspects of a "kindly, rather timid" old-timer in a Philadelphia gym—a man with a deep gravel-throated voice—with the "fierceness" of Howie Steindler, who ran the shabby Main Street Gym on Skid Row, a few blocks from the Times.

"I prepared very hard for this part," he said. "I didn't find much in me that really got down to the nitty gritty, I mean the more gritty than nitty part of this man."

The movie scored a stunning upset by winning the Best Picture award, Avildsen got a statue for directing it, and the film captured an editing Oscar. But the other nominees, including Stallone (Best Actor and Best Original Screenplay) walked away empty-handed.

Meredith, who lost out to Jason Robards for his work in *All the President's Men*, died in 1997 at 89 without ever winning the coveted trophy.

I had rubbed shoulders with Steindler for years in his smelly, decaying second-floor gym, at ringside and socially. A Runyonesque character who talked out of the side of his mouth, Howie was feisty, cantankerous and hot-tempered. He may have been bantamweight in size, but he had a giant heart, was honest and genuine.

The long-struggling trainer and manager dreamed of one day handling a world champion. When Ernie (Indian Red) Lopez failed to fulfill that dream, Steindler focused on Ernie's kid brother, featherweight Danny (Little Red) Lopez.

A sensational knockout puncher who attracted large gates, Danny quickly climbed the fistic ladder to title contention. Eventually, he got a shot at David Kotey's 126-pound crown on the champion's home turf in Ghana.

But Steindler would not be in his corner. A smoker most of his life, he had a weak heart and was so frail he carried oxygen.

Lopez scored a shocking upset, winning the title Nov. 6, 1976, and catapulting his beloved manager into boxing's national spotlight.

With his share of the purse, Howie bought a new gold Cadillac and strutted around town like a proud peacock. Stopping at the Redwood for drinks, as he usually did on his way home from the gym, he entertained reporters and friends with a taped radio broadcast of the Lopez match.

His dream finally realized, Howie's glory was short-lived.

On March 9, 1977, four months almost to the day after Lopez became champion, Steindler's battered body was found in the back seat of his Cadillac on the shoulder of the eastbound Ventura Freeway in Studio City.

He had been savagely beaten in the head and there was a puncture wound in his temple. It wasn't immediately determined whether the wound was made by a bullet or sharp instrument. A report two days later said Steindler may have been smothered by having his face held against the car's seat cushion.

Earlier that evening, about 7 p.m., a witness had observed Steindler at the corner of Lindley Avenue and Killion Street in the San Fernando Valley community of Encino, only a block from his home. The witness said Steindler was involved in a confrontation with three unidentified black males who began beating the manager, then forced him into his own car, driving him from the scene. Within an hour, his body was discovered.

Steindler was known to carry hundreds of dollars in his wallet which was missing along with personal papers, distinctive rings, a gold necklace and watch, but detectives did not consider robbery a motive.

I wrote a 10th anniversary story saying Steindler argued with two men the night he was killed, rather than three, and for the first time reported minor damage to the back of his car—cut rubber on the bumper and a dent. That evidence led police to suspect Steindler had been the victim of a "bump and rob" style of holdup after a minor traffic accident.

On Aug. 4, 2007, TV host John Walsh featured the 30-year-old murder on *America's Most Wanted,* and thereafter, the Los Angeles City Council offered a $50,000 reward for leads in the case.

Equally puzzling to the police was a case two years later that also affected me deeply because of my personal connection with Vic Weiss, a wealthy, free-spender who managed welterweight title contender Armando Muniz.

I'll never forget the afternoon I drove into his Van Nuys auto dealership in my new 1979 Thunderbird. Spotting me, he emerged from his office and leaned into an open window.

"Any problems?"

"Oh, no," I replied. "I was driving by and thought I'd stop to say hello. You know my wife. This is our grandson. Big guy for two, huh?"

Weiss acknowledged Charlene but paid little notice to our daughter Linda's son Christopher, seated on my wife's lap.

"How do you like it?" he asked.

A marshmallow-white made-to-order gem with less than 100 miles on the odometer, the car was the first new one I owned. I had called Vic three or four months earlier, inquiring about used Lincolns I could afford.

"I can put you behind the wheel of a new T-Bird for a lot less money," he suggested. Soon the deal was sealed.

A high-roller with lots of irons in the fire, Weiss, it seemed, was seldom available at his Ford and Rolls-Royce dealership. At 51, he had a busy lifestyle. Besides managing Muniz, whose contract he bought in 1973, he socialized with celebrities, flew regularly to Las Vegas for boxing matches and rubbed shoulders with gamblers linked to organized crime. Vic also visited his former high school buddy Jerry Tarkanian, who coached the University of Nevada basketball team.

Well-liked and extremely generous, Weiss was noted for grabbing dinner checks, large and small, and taking under-privileged kids to sports events. He always had time for small talk, particularly with a reporter, and enjoyed a reputation as "Mr. Nice Guy."

That's why my wife and I were surprised when he ignored our grandson and ended our conversation so abruptly, as if preoccupied.

About a week after our chat, Weiss' body was found in his maroon-and-white Rolls-Royce, parked in the garage of the Sheraton-Universal Hotel in North Hollywood.

A story written by Larry Muro in 1980 and posted on the Internet gives a dramatic detailed account of what occurred that Sunday evening of June 17, 1979.

According to Muro, a hotel guest told a desk clerk, "That Rolls-Royce in the parking garage is a good looking car, but it sure stinks."

"What do you mean?" the clerk asked.

"Just what I said. It smells—*bad*—like something's died in it."

The clerk called a bellman. He instructed him to check on the car on the second level of the parking structure adjoining the hotel.

The bellman located the car, found that the guest had not understated the odor but looking through the windows saw nothing inside that might explain it. A parking ticket indicated the car had been there since 6 o'clock on Wednesday. The putrid smell seemed to come from the car's trunk.

When the bellman reported back to the desk clerk, Muro's article continued, the clerk wondered if the car belonged to Vic Weiss.

"I saw a television news broadcast a couple of days ago showing the police looking for him and his car," the clerk said. "They were using a helicopter, thinking he might have run off the canyon road going in to San Fernando."

When police arrived and opened the trunk, they found Victor J. Weiss' body. His hands were tied behind his back. He had been killed with two gunshots to the head.

The investigation yielded no suspects.

Ten years later, a 1989 article by Michael Connelly, a Times crime reporter, disclosed other details leading up to Weiss' death.

"The meeting with Jack Kent Cooke and Jerry Buss had gone well," Connelly's story began. "Vic Weiss was close to a deal that would bring University of Nevada, Las Vegas, basketball coach Jerry Tarkanian to Los Angeles to lead the Lakers, the team Cooke was selling to Buss.

"Briefcase in hand, the stocky but energetic Weiss…left the meeting room at a Beverly Hills hotel, hopped into his Rolls-Royce and headed over the hill to his house in Encino. But Weiss never made it home…."

Connelly reported what boxing writers, including me, had known, talked about among ourselves but never wrote about before Weiss was killed.

"Detectives were able to learn much about the secret life of Vic Weiss," the story continued. "They learned that while he publicly hobnobbed with legitimate names in sports and business, he privately rubbed shoulders with criminals, ran up huge debts on sports betting and skimmed off the top of laundered money he delivered to mobsters in Las Vegas.

"It is believed by police that those latter indiscretions cost Weiss his life. But who ordered the killing and who carried it out remain unknown…."

Not long after the murder, I had an occasion to interview manager Harry Kabakoff, a close associate of Weiss who often accompanied him to Las Vegas.

The interview was unrelated to Weiss, but when I diverted from the subject to ask about the killing, Kabakoff clammed up. He kept a loaded gun in his room, was terrified at the mention of a possible mob killing and refused to talk about his relationship with his former friend.

Only about 3 ½ miles separated Weiss' Rolls-Royce parked in the hotel garage from Howie Steindler's Cadillac parked on a freeway shoulder that contained his body two years earlier.

Homicide Detective Ron Lewis acknowledged there were similarities in the two murders, but I quoted Detective Marvin Engquist in a 1987 anniversary article saying he doubted there was a connection.

"There were not many parallels except that both were found in vehicles."

The murders remain two of the Los Angeles Police Department's most baffling cases, most likely never to be solved.

Chapter 33

The Heavyweights

Muhammad Ali sat at ringside, watching Leon Spinks lumber through 10 frustrating rounds before winning a unanimous decision over durable, relatively unknown Alfio Righetti. The fight took place Nov. 18, 1977, at the new Hilton Hotel Pavilion in Las Vegas.

It wasn't that Ali had nothing better to do that night. He was there to size up his next opponent, who as most experts expected turned out to be 24-year-old Spinks.

At 36 and near retirement, Ali was unimpressed with the 1976 Olympic light-heavyweight king who improved his unbeaten professional record to six wins and one draw.

"He's young, he's strong, he's busy, he keeps coming," Ali told me, "but he don't know how to pace himself. The longer the fight goes, the better it is for me. If I can get myself in shape I'll be all right."

He had three months to accomplish that before Feb.15, when he would face Spinks in the same ring.

Also unimpressed was my editor, Bill Shirley, who had sent me to Sin City for the elimination bout, allocated all of 10 inches of inside space for my story and would reluctantly assign me to cover Ali-Spinks in February. But there would be no hype and almost no pre-bout coverage in the Times sports section.

239

It was, after all, another mismatch. Shirley hadn't forgotten my expensive New York junket six months earlier for the Ken Norton-Duane Bobick fiasco that lasted 58 seconds.

But this was Ali. Mismatch or not, this was for the most prestigious title in sports — the world heavyweight boxing championship.

Moreover, the card included a long-awaited rematch between Danny (Little Red) Lopez, the popular Southern California knockout specialist, and David Kotey, whose world featherweight crown Danny won 15 months earlier in Ghana.

And this was the Times, which could afford sending an army to Las Vegas for such a major event.

Instead, Bill Shirley sent me. Period.

The pressure of night-event deadlines from Las Vegas was no less intense than from local venues. It was a challenge I didn't relish.

**Muhammad Ali,
lost for words.**

Ali, whose mouth seldom closed leading up to title defenses, treated reporters to a refreshing change before this one. The gushing Louisville Lip was zipped. He literally stopped talking.

It had been a subdued, serious and sometimes brooding champion going through the motions in training. With three days remaining before the opening bell, he had sparred only four rounds in Las Vegas, but, according to trainer Angelo Dundee, had worked harder for Spinks, his 20th defense, than for any in the previous seven years.

"He boxed in Miami, a hundred, hundred and fifty rounds before coming here," Dundee said. "He came down from 241 to 221 in four weeks. If he was fighting Kenny Norton tonight, I wouldn't be worried."

Two nights before the match, Charlene and I spotted Ali dining alone a few tables away in the Hilton steakhouse. Ali glanced over, then looked away. The champ was so tight-lipped he refused to even say hello to Lopez, who introduced himself when he came in for dinner.

Ali agreed to only two pre-fight interviews—for *Time* and *Sports Illustrated* magazines—but those articles would be published after the fight.

In one interview, Ali explained his prolonged silence with this comment:

"I woke up one morning and was tired of hearing myself talk. I knew if I was tired of it, so was everybody else."

I can still recall the anxiety I experienced when the ring announcer introduced Lopez and Kotey as they stared at each other, bouncing lightly on their toes in the middle of the ring.

"...and from Alhambra, California, the World Boxing Council's world featherweight champion, Danny (Little Red) Lopez..."

Thunderous applause and shouting filled the pavilion. It was electric.

As usual when covering a fight on a tight deadline, I had compiled a list of facts and figures to incorporate in my story—career records, ages, dates and results of recent fights, key adjectives, anything useful. Joe Somebody was standing by to grab my typewritten pages to transmit to the Times.

I began a round-by-round account of the action, which ended in the sixth, when Lopez exploded with a combination to the head that staggered the African, followed by another right that dropped him. Kotey regained his feet at seven but was on rubbery legs and virtually defenseless. Moving in for the kill, Lopez unloaded a barrage of blows before the referee intervened.

A 2 ½-to-1 favorite, Lopez dominated the one-sided bout, unlike their fierce 15-rounder in Ghana. Having gained a few minutes on the clock because of the knockout, I hurried to Danny's dressing room for quotes and returned just in time to hear introductions for the main event.

While keeping a watchful eye on the headliners and scribbling notes, I resumed grinding out the Lopez-Kotey story, handing more pages to Joe for transmission. I also was maintaining close telephone contact with Chuck Garrity in the Times sports department.

"Forget Lopez," Garrity said. "You can come back to it if there's time. Get going on Ali. We'll do a rush replate for the makeover. Relax. You're doing fine."

I wasn't relaxed. Three-minute rounds seemed interminable as Ali and Spinks battled ferociously, and rest periods seemed never to end while the clock ticked toward my deadline.

Finally, I filed the story. The following are excerpts:

"LAS VEGAS—As the world was saying, Leon Spinks doesn't stand a chance.

"There's a new heavyweight champion," a ringsider remarked moments before the decision was announced.

"I'll bet anyone right now Muhammad Ali walks out of this ring as the heavyweight champion," another said. "I gave the fight to Spinks but..."

The roaring began to subside as a Hilton Pavilion crowd of 5,298—a flea speck among the millions watching on television—awaited Wednesday night's decision.

It was split. Ali got the nod on one card, 143-142; Spinks on another, 145-140. The announcer continued, *"Judge Harold Buck: 144-141. The new..."*

And that was it. Justice finally prevailed, the crown has fallen off the head of a legend and a virtual amateur is king of the world of boxing—Leon Spinks...a believer of miracles.

It was "Rocky" in full bloom in the 15th round as the 10-1 underdog battled toe-to-toe with the 36-year-old man and it was one of Ali's most electrifying finishes.

Still, all three officials gave the final round to the new champion, a former marine from St. Louis, now living in Philadelphia....

Ali knew the end was at hand long before the official verdict was rendered. After the 14th round, he sat wearily on his stool, his head heavy, his eyes on the floor. It was pathetic, actually, as he contemplated what he must do to retain the crown he had successfully defended 19 times. His only hope was to knock out this brash young man who had shown such unexpected endurance.

Ali, huffing and puffing as he lumbered into action, gave it one of his most honest efforts, ripping hooks and firing jabs and taking equally damaging blows in return. It was a slugfest in which both were close to going down. But they continued punching dramatically as the crowd roared.

It was past deadline, but Garrity, bellowing over the phone, instructed me to "keep it coming, keep it coming." So I ignored

242

the clock and kept it coming.

"I didn't know he could fight that type of fight after 10 rounds," Ali said later in an interview room that was not void of laughter or even a bit of wisecracking.

Ali...told the roomful of reporters, "You didn't know it either."

And he smiled. He had proved the press all wrong.

"When I fought Sonny Liston, I upset the world," Ali said, turning to Spinks. "You upset the world, too."

"I gave away too many rounds in the beginning," said the deposed king, his face puffed and hurting, a cut inside his mouth. "It was hard to catch up. He didn't tire...."

"I have no excuses. I wasn't robbed...I did my best. I just lost....The loss can be good if I can ever get it back. I don't know if I can ever get it back, but I'm going to try."

Curiously, it was Ali who still looked like the champion as he sat next to Spinks, elated, of course, but not too talkative.

He was asked how it felt to be the new king.

"It feels good," he said through a gap where his two front teeth should be. "It feels very good."

It also felt good to me days later, when Bob Oates—whose story I mutilated eight years earlier during my tryout—complimented me on my coverage along with some kind words from others.

"You saved Shirley's ass," a colleague said. "I can't believe he didn't give you any help."

I don't recall Shirley commenting directly, but it was clear he was pleased.

"There's a tennis tournament going on in Palm Springs," he said. "I don't have anyone else free to cover it...."

"Tennis?" I replied. "I know how it's scored but I've never written a line about a professional tennis tournament, Bill. I'm really not qualified."

"It's not a big one," Shirley said with a shrug. "We only need four or five graphs a day, then a short wrap-up. Take your wife and rest up."

We stayed a week.

AGAIN, MY story dateline was Las Vegas.

The pre-fight feature described a typical workout for Larry Holmes in the Caesars Palace Sports Pavilion, where the No. 2

contender would challenge Ken Norton for his World Boxing Council heavyweight championship.

The young heavyweight, sleek and sweaty, glided around the ring with the grace of a ballroom dancer.

Like a fastball blazing into a catcher's mitt, his straight, powerful left thumped explosively against the trainer's leather glove. Another jarring jab. Combinations. A hook. Fast, impressive. At 6-4, 210 pounds, he looked lethal.

The showdown, June 9, 1978, was scheduled only four months after Leon Spinks upset Ali, quickly followed by a controversial clash of professional boxing's ruling bodies. The result was a split heavyweight title.

World Boxing Council president Jose Sulaiman awarded Norton a green belt with a gold-colored medallion in March. The World Boxing Assn. recognized Spinks as champion.

"The World Boxing Council is a lot bigger than the WBA," said Norton, who declared himself "90 per cent" heavyweight champion and issued another challenge to "10 per center" Leon Spinks.

"We can settle it with one fight. He has backed out. Now I'm in a position where he has to meet me half way. The easiest way for us to settle this problem is for Spinks to fight me. I don't think that will happen very soon…."

It was a visionary statement. In fact, it never happened.

Flamboyant Don King hams it up with heavyweight champ Ken Norton, left, and unbeaten Larry Holmes at the promoter's announcement of their June 9, 1978, Las Vegas title fight.

Meanwhile, for Norton, there was a more immediate con-cern—Larry Holmes, the unbeaten Easton (Pa.) Assassin, as he was labeled by his manager Richie Giachetti early in his pro career.

Promoted by flamboyant Don King, the fight needed no artifi-cial flavoring; it was a natural. Nonetheless, King kept the media pot hot with his usual drum-beating, predictions and parties.

Las Vegas was King's playground with its glitter, excitement and lavish hotel suites, such as the one at Caesars, with its grand piano at the foot of a spiral staircase with gold-plated railing lead-ing up to I don't know how many bedrooms.

His party was going strong when Ali arrived and elbowed his

Charlene and boxing promoter Don King.

way into the crowded room, brushing near my wife and me, both of us having consumed a few cocktails by then.

Locking eyes with the ex-champ, Charlene greeted him with an out-of-the-blue shocker that left me speechless.

"Ken Norton can beat you," she blurted out, apparently un-aware he had done so five years earlier, breaking his jaw in the process.

Ali smiled and continued inside with his entourage.

Unlike the 10-to-1 spread favoring Ali over Spinks, Vegas oddsmakers listed Norton-Holmes "6-5 pick 'em," and when the officials' scores were announced –all three voting identically, 143-

142—the result remained in doubt. The room hushed.

I can't recall an announcer stretching out a verdict more dramatically or a major fight so difficult to score. Officials scored all 15 rounds 10-9. My card favored Norton, 142-141.

"A split decision," the announcer continued as he reached for Holmes' hand, and, finally, familiar words, "...the new World Boxing Council heavyweight champion."

Certainly not controversial like his split-decision loss to Ali two years earlier, Norton again was devastated. However, a $2.3 million paycheck soothed his pain as he predicted more large purses to come, saying, "I have no plans to retire."

Holmes, who earned about $500,000, ducked a press conference until after a late-night swim in Caesars' pool and a hot bath in his room. He then appeared before the impatiently waiting media and thanked virtually everyone, starting with King.

"I'm 28 years old and 28 and 0," he said. "One thing Norton showed me, he's a man. I don't want to fight him again...."

He never did. For Kenny Norton, it was a fleeting reign atop the world of professional boxing and a steady slide to oblivion thereafter. After being stopped in the first round by Gerry Cooney in 1981, Norton retired with a record of 42-7-1.

Holmes' career flourished. He retained his WBC belt in 16 consecutive matches—including a technical knockout over Ali in 1980—and successfully defended an International Boxing Federation championship four times before relinquishing it to Michael Spinks (Leon's brother) in 1985.

The Easton Assassin lost in a rematch, was stopped by up-and-coming Mike Tyson in a showdown for the world's undisputed heavyweight championship in 1988 and failed in another bid in 1992, when Evander Holyfield outpointed him in Las Vegas. Holmes remained a solid contender and made a final, unsuccessful bid for the WBC crown against Oliver McCall in 1995 before hanging up his gloves in 2002.

Holmes quit with his hand raised after defeating someone named Eric (Butterbean) Esch in Norfolk, Virginia, at age 53.

A largely underrated champion, Larry Holmes posted a record of 69-6. Clearly, he was one of boxing's best, if not "The Greatest."

THE UNDISPUTED champion promoters of that era and decades to come were seasoned entrepreneurs as different as salt and pepper.

Fiery, hot-tempered Don King promoted with gusto. His only major rival, Bob Arum, a conservative, shrewd, low-key attorney, proceeded cautiously, like a bank officer considering a loan application. Both had their stables of champions and top contenders and both were hugely successful in the highly competitive multi-million-dollar business.

Chairman of Top Rank of New York, Arum had locked up a lucrative TV deal for Muhammad Ali's rematch with Leon Spinks and seemed assured of setting a live gate record at the spacious New Orleans Superdome.

The Big Easy was alive with local fans and out-of-towners who had come early to party, argue and bet on the fight. There was plenty to write about before Ali, a 2-to-1 favorite, would step into the ring the night of Sept. 15, 1978, attempting to become the first man in history to win the heavyweight title three times.

Even Bill Shirley recognized the importance of the rematch. Besides the incomparable Jim Murray, Skip Bayless—a young prolific columnist recently hired away from a Dallas daily to upgrade our section—was on hand to assist in the coverage. He had lofty credentials. A Vanderbilt graduate, Bayless attended the university on a prestigious Fred Russell-Grantland Rice Sportswriting Scholarship.

A roaring crowd of about 70,000 contributed to a live gate of about $6 million, easily eclipsing the record of $2,658,660 set by the second Jack Dempsey-Gene Tunney bout Sept. 22, 1927, in Chicago.

Ali got his record, too.

Hard and trim after five months on a rigid training regimen in Deer Lake, Pennsylvania, Ali took command early and never relinquished it.

Floating, stinging and shuffling, the Ghost of Cassius Clay swooped down on the outclassed ex-Marine to win a lop-sided 15-round decision, making Spinks look like the amateur he appeared to be while engaging in only his ninth pro fight.

Murray's column was titled *Ali Puts Some Teeth Back Into Heavyweight Title*, and Bayless, who had filed a pre-fight feature, wrote a sidebar headlined *Ali Reveals Training in Secret*.

I guess Skip hadn't read about Ali's "secret," which I disclosed in my column two weeks earlier. If anyone on the copy desk that handled Bayless' feature remembered seeing it, so what? Secret

Ali regains heavyweight title Sept. 15, 1978, in New Orleans

or no secret, no one was going to make any major alterations on deadline.

"I went to Deer Lake and chopped trees and ran every morning and I tricked you all," Ali told Bayless and other reporters in the interview room while I was busy writing at ringside. "I started training three months before you knew it. I had it all set up. I made suckers out of all of you all. I'm from the House of Shock."

Ali, I suppose, hadn't read my column, either. No surprise. It was well-hidden, buried on Page 19.

My report of the fight was straight-forward, few adjectives, dull reading under 48-point type that told it all—*Ali Turns Back Clock and Wins Title Again, Becomes Champion Third Time...*

Excerpts from my follow-up article published a day later:

NEW ORLEANS—The aftermath. It's boxing's hangover. The day after, when they rehash it all, gripe and cheer, threaten and promise, count the money and start mapping plans for the next one that will be "even bigger."

It's a cab driver complaining about missing out on $50 fares for a five-minute ride to the Superdome because his transmission had gone out on fight night.

"It's an enraged, bleary-eyed fan in the Hilton Hotel lobby (fight headquarters) creating an ugly scene and daring security officers to take him to jail.

It's Muhammad Ali, unprecedented three-time heavyweight king, back in control, chatting on the phone with President Carter and telling the world he'll ponder for up to eight months before deciding his ring future.

It's Leon Spinks, deposed champion, back in the pack after a dizzy seven-month reign, wealthier in many ways, perhaps (including a purse of $3.75 million).

It's Top Rank promoter Bob Arum making announcements, considering offers and basking in the glory of one of the richest promotions in boxing history—a record gate that still was being counted.

It's all of this and more as the city began to thin out Saturday....

For Charlene and me, it was a nude late-night swim in an indoor hotel pool a few floors above its gourmet restaurant, where we had dined.

The pool area and adjacent room where a meeting had just broken up were dimly lighted and deserted when we decided on a quick dip. Giggling like school kids doing something naughty, we quickly shed our clothes, left them on a nearby chair and stepped off the ladder into the deep end.

At that moment, a pair of footsteps headed toward us. We backed against the ladder, ducked down and held our breath. The footsteps continued to a counter, where a briefcase had been left and was retrieved. The footsteps again passed above our heads and continued out the door.

"Let's get out," Charlene whispered. "Maybe someone else will come in."

"We've still got a lot of time to kill," I replied. "Are we going to just sit around the airport?"

"I'm getting out."

That, of course, settled it. We got out, picked up our bags, hailed a cab and headed to the airport for our Delta red-eye back to Los Angeles.

THE OFFICIAL word finally came. With 56 wins and only three losses marring his record, Muhammad Ali announced his retirement.

Two years after proving to millions of fans he truly was "The Greatest," he ignored Father Time, again attempted to rewrite history and was stopped by Larry Holmes in the 11th round in

Jack Hawn

Las Vegas. Fourteen months later, December of 1981, Ali suffered another ignominious defeat in the Bahamas, where he was out-pointed by hard-hitting Trevor Berbick in a 10-rounder.

It was Ali's final curtain call. Sadly, it was over.

Chapter 34

Freelancing

When I walked into the Times sports department for my tryout in 1970 and saw my former colleague on the boxing beat, Cal Whorton, in the copy desk slot, I never suspected I would be filling his chair a decade later.

But it happened, and I never saw it coming.

Without warning, another young import from Bill Shirley's list of potential replacements for aging beat writers suddenly materialized. He introduced himself as Richard Hoffer and demanded the keys to my kingdom.

That's not really the way it happened. But it was devastating, nonetheless. One day I was solidly entrenched as the L.A.Times boxing columnist, the next an expendable morning desk chief responsible for producing the bulldog edition.

Covering boxing wasn't merely a job. I had nurtured a lifestyle I shared with Charlene. We had good friends, enjoyed good times. I had acquired valuable contacts, not only locally, but around the country. I could telephone Muhammad Ali and expect him to pick up the phone.

Suddenly, I knew how Dan Hafner felt when I replaced him. It was as if Bill Shirley had sent me to prison. I detested him for his insensitivity and struck an immediate dislike of Richard Hoffer.

Quiet, reserved, seemingly miscast, Hoffer's lofty attitude

coming into the job was reflected in choices of adjectives published under his byline — words like *pugnacious*, for example. The grungy fight mob was not impressed, nor was I.

Hoffer, however, authored many front-page features and eventually proved a capable boxing reporter before moving on to cover other major sports. He ended up as a staff writer at *Sports Illustrated.*

Meanwhile, my 9-to-5 desk job had become drudgery, and I could see nothing in the future that would alter it. No sense appealing to Shirley. I was stuck for what seemed like the duration of my employment at The Times.

I wasn't looking for revenge. I simply wanted out.

Early on I had sold three stories to the Times' Sunday supplement, a 50-page tabloid insert called *West.*

In describing its contents in the issue dated Dec. 12, 1971 (our son's 15th birthday), Editor Peter D. Bunzel enticed readers with a few words about dreams, the dominant theme.

Most, he said, never see the light of day.

"You may recall them fleetingly as the alarm clock rings, but by the time you've struggled to a standing position, they've pretty much evaporated. This week's 'West' proves that some dreams don't have to do that."

He cited diversified examples, including those long harbored by "a most curious outdoorsman named Jefferson Spivey."

A succinct paragraph in the table of contents pretty much told his story: "The Long, Hard Ride: To promote his dream of a cross-country horseback and hiking trail, Jefferson Spivey blazed it out himself. Page 33."

My article expanded it to more than 130 column inches covering most of five pages with photos of Spivey being honored by Mayor Sam Yorty in Los Angeles and Supreme Court Justice William O. Douglas in Washington, D.C., among other photos.

An extraordinary young man obsessed by a boyhood fantasy to ride horseback under the sun and sleep beneath the stars, Spivey lived his dream in 1968, when he set out from Santa Barbara, California, on a borrowed 4-year-old Arabian gelding for a six-month 3,850-mile coast-to-coast journey that ended on the sands of the Atlantic.

In the process of that unprecedented ride, the 33-year-old

Oklahoma adventurer gave birth to a dream far greater in scope and considerably more idealistic—a prodigious plan to establish a giant trail across the heart of America, connecting 14 states from coast-to-coast with north and south feeder trails to be used exclusively by hikers, horsemen and bicyclists.

It's true Spivey was a dreamer, romanticist, crusader and restless wanderer, but his concept made sense to many powerful politicians who supported his plan. Yet, it fell short of being adapted as he conceived it.

Rereading the article published almost 40 years ago, I realize how prophetic his words were.

"If today's hip generation did nothing else," he said, "it got people to think about ecology. You don't realize the decay in America until you actually see it, until you go over it foot by foot, slowly, like I did.

"I have this feeling that someday it's all going to be parking lots and junkyards and fenced-in super highways that transport you across country like water in a pipe and keep you from seeing what America is like."

Handed the written proposal Spivey had submitted by an editor who expressed interest, I was offered an opportunity to write the story with no guarantee it would be published.

The great outdoors wasn't my cup of tea, but it was a chance for a good paycheck and a foot in the door.

Spivey's dream was infectious. I joined his mushrooming list of supporters, wrote about another of his treks across the heartland, a different route, and couldn't shake him. He even showed up at my urban home one day unannounced, his Arabian gelding tied to a small curbside tree.

Jeff asked me to co-author a book he had been working on for years. I looked at his huge rambling manuscript that would require a complete rewrite. I didn't have the time or interest. As gently as possible, I turned him down. Then one day, Jeff Spvey faded from my life, as did his dream.

West magazine paid contributing writers handsomely, and I was eager to start my next feature. I didn't wait long.

"We're running a two-page spread of boating and fishing ads in the coming issue and need a story to go with it," the editor said. "Think you can come up with a good angle?"

Fishing? I had dropped a few lines into lakes during my

lifetime and once hauled in six dolphins off the coast of Mexico, assisted by two commercial fishermen who did most of the hauling and drinking of the beer I bought.

I was not qualified to write a feature about fishing.

It mattered not.

The Great Fish Debate: Fresh-water man Fred MacMurray takes on old salt Richard Boone appeared on Page 36 of the magazine's April 30, 1972, issue.

Illustrated by full-page centerfold mugs of villainous-looking Boone, star of the popular TV western *Have Gun-Will Travel*, and gentle Fred, with his mom-and-apple-pie expression that seldom changed, the two articles ran side-by-side.

I met Boone for lunch at a noisy restaurant near Universal Studios. His drink, served in a thick, stubby glass, was gaudy blood-red; his steak sandwich, precisely as ordered—a naked hunk of rare meat, bare on the plate, *"no nonsense."*

His penetrating black eyes sparkled as he talked about the sea and the great fighting fish that challenged rugged sportsmen like him—*hard strikers that will tear the back off your boat, wreck your equipment and burn up your reel.*

Fresh-water anglers?

"They're hikers and trail walkers," he replied, condescendingly. *"Fresh-water fish are just too dammed small. I can't get with it."*

MacMurray chose a quiet dining room at the Beverly Wilshire Hotel for lunch—soft violin music, soft lights, expensive wine.

Told Boone's opinion of tying flies and casting lines into rippling mountainous streams—MacMurray's lifelong passion—Fred bristled...slightly.

"Let him tie into a nice, big steelhead with light tackle, and he'll see how 'damned' small they are."

Quickly regaining his composure—congenial, easygoing, imperturbable—the 62-year-old actor recalled a terrifying experience when, as a youth of 19, he nearly drowned while swimming alone in the Pacific Ocean. It left him with an intense dislike for the sea.

"There are all kinds of salt-water fish," he said. *"You don't always tie into a big one. There are all kinds of fresh-water fish, too, and they're not all small."*

I can't say who won the debate, but I came away from those

interviews convinced personalities have a lot to do with where a fisherman casts his line.

West magazine didn't last long. After it folded, I sold a travel piece to Jerry Hulse, one of America's most authoritative and respected travel editors, a couple of articles to the equally renowned and award-winning entertainment editor, Chuck Champlin, and a feature to the TV editor, Aileen McMinn that, for me, was a natural—the transition of a retired pro quarterback to TV actor.

The long-forgotten 1978 sitcom starred Joe Namath as a high school basketball coach in a series called *The Waverly Wonders.* It was a one-season flop directed by former *Laugh-In* star Dick Martin.

"He's far beyond the jock-turned actor," Martin said. "He's actually a very good actor now. He did a picture with Ann-Margret years ago and they cast him as his Broadway Joe macho image, which is not Joe at all. He's a very laid back, cool, very shy type of guy.

Interviewed on the set, Namath—35 at the time—focused on football.

"My senior year in college was the first time I tore my knee up," he recalled. "But in high school I separated my left shoulder in a game. I separated it on second down, came out on third down and went back in on fourth down, punted and played the rest of the game.

"It wasn't a bad separation. I separated my right shoulder against the Colts in '72 or '73. I had a total separation. All three ligaments tore. We healed that well. That doesn't bother me at all now. Broken wrist doesn't bother me. Broken ankle doesn't bother me. Broken cheek bone doesn't bother me. Broken finger doesn't bother me. Everything's healed."

That was Broadway Joe...Super Bowl superstar, not much of an actor.

One of the hottest series on TV about that time was *CHiPs,* a weekly drama about the California Highway Patrol, which starred handsome Erik Estrada, who portrayed motorcycle cop Frank Poncherella.

Two familiar names were listed among the credits—William D. Gordon and James Doherty—neither of whom I had heard from for years.

"I finally got out of Jack Webb's doghouse," Jim said over the phone. "Cy Chermak hired Bill and me to co-produce the show. So far, so good..."

After some catching-up, I told Doherty I had spoken to the View editor about writing an article on the series, specifically about the stunt drivers who risk their lives filming scenes of police pursuits, rolling cars, fiery freeway crashes....

"He liked the idea. Can you set it up?"

"I'll have to run it past Chermak, but I don't see a problem," he replied. "He's a nut for publicity."

The feature, illustrated by photos of spectacular car crashes on a new unopened section of a Pacoima freeway, was published on Page 1 of the View section Aug. 14, 1979.

"The marshmallow-white concrete cast a harsh glare under a morning sun. Steaming, rust-colored water dripped from hot automobile radiators and there was a scent of burning rubber.

Stunt man Paul Nuckles, sleeveless and dripping sweat, was conducting a briefing on a major accident to be filmed. Surrounded by technicians, director John Flores and other stunt people, Nuckles lined up eight miniature vehicles of various types and colors. Moving the toys, he explained his concept of a dangerous, complicated stunt. Even for him, it's always an experiment with no guarantees of success.

Before sunset, the film would be in the can and Nuckles in a hospital — not the first injured on this series and, as subsequently proved, not the last.

The stunt involved a three-car collision that was supposed to culminate with an airborne sedan falling into a moving convertible. Instead, the convertible flipped, landed upside down and skidded on the concrete for several feet.

Huddled in an incredibly small space under the dash board, Nuckles was helped out by paramedics who treated his injuries. Blood gushed from an arm and flowed down his face from a head wound.

Obviously dazed, but unwilling to be pampered, Nuckles admitted with a forced smile, "That's about as close as I've ever come. That's as close as I want to come."

The stunt man was hospitalized overnight, but was back on the set the following day.

"We've said all along we were afraid someone might get killed," one source confided, "but we never thought our star would get hurt."

The reference was to Estrada, who was hospitalized with critical injuries following "a freak accident while doing a routine piece of business.

A real CHP guy wouldn't have had any problem. Erik just doesn't have the experience.

"*...I studied for six weeks, three hours a day, learning how to ride,*" *Estrada said, munching on a greasy chicken breast. "It was so rough, so tough. I used to get so mad. When I can't pick up something right away it frustrates me. Anybody can go fast on a motorcycle. It's the slow stuff, stopping for stop signs without putting your feet down, figure 8's, that's the tough stuff.*"

Estrada, 30, suffered a broken sternum, collapsed lungs, three broken ribs and a broken wrist while engaged in "a routine piece of business" in an alley off the freeway. He was hospitalized 10 days.

Chermak was not pleased by Estrada's quotes nor the reference to his star's riding inexperience, but generally liked my story.

While working on it I had renewed my close friendship with Doherty and Gordon—the former *12 O'clock High* producer who had hired me away from the Citizen-News—and came up with a story notion for a *CHiPs* episode. They liked it, cleared it with Chermak and I went to work on the outline.

During its development, I conversed with Chermak on the phone about Estrada's condition. I didn't inform him his comments were "on the record," as perhaps I should have. The next day, Aug. 30, 1979, a five-inch update appeared in the Times' Calendar section, for which I received about $100.

In the article, Chermak stated that Estrada was making a fast recovery but his return to work remained uncertain.

"He's been sneaking out onto the streets," he added, "but I don't know when we can get him back on a motorcycle."

The same day the article ran I received a call from Doherty.

"Looks like your deal's off, buddy," he said. "We're going to have to scratch it. Chermak was furious about that story. He didn't know you were going to quote him. The network called him and asked what the hell was going on with Estrada."

After a week of refusing to accept my calls, Chermak picked up the receiver.

Stopping short of an apology, I pointed out that I quoted him accurately and that he shouldn't have commented about Estrada if he didn't want it printed.

"I didn't know you were going to quote me," he said. "We were just talking."

"You knew you were speaking to a newspaperman, Cy. That's what I do. I quote people."

When the conversation ended, all was forgiven. My deal to write a *CHiPs* episode was back on track.

A number of my stories were syndicated by the Times, for which I was well paid when publications picked them up. The timing for my syndicated Estrada update couldn't have been worse.

Published in the National Enquirer under my byline, the story was rewritten, strongly hinting that the series was in jeopardy. A sensationalized headline drove the final spike into my coffin, sending my *CHiPs* deal to its grave. I never spoke to Chermak again.

I received $600 from the Enquirer for that five-inch "update" and lost a potential $6,182 for the TV script—the Los Angeles Writers Guild minimum for a one-hour drama at the time—plus residuals.

Not having an agent, I hadn't seen a contract, but assumed one would be forthcoming in due time after getting Chermak's approval to proceed.

"I did have a verbal commitment," I reminded Doherty. "Do you think I should appeal to the Guild?"

"It wouldn't do me any good," he said matter-of-factly.

I doubt it would have done me any good, either. I dropped it.

Later that season, possibly the next, Doherty refused to produce an episode about young people using drugs—a story Chermak wanted. Predictably, the stubborn Irishman lost the argument as he had with Jack Webb when producing *Adam-12*.

Not only was Doherty fired, but also his partner, Bill Gordon.

EARLY IN 1980, shortly after my 50th birthday in January, a vacancy occurred on the View copy desk. I applied for the position and a few weeks later walked down the lengthy third-floor corridor into a new life.

Chapter 35

Ivy Leaguers and Me

Anchored by two oblong copy desks in the closed end of a horseshoe-shaped wing on the third floor—a world away from the hard news and sports departments—writers and editors produced the guts of the newspaper, if not its heart.

Don Alpert, a sprightly bantam-sized executive who idolized the Los Angeles Angels, always found time for a good joke and laughed out loud at the daily comics, never took life too seriously despite carrying a heavy load.

In addition to supervising the View and Calendar desks, dummying pages and overseeing composing room paste-ups, he also was in charge of real estate, travel, books, food and, in his words, "other odds and ends." His title, I believe, was executive news editor.

When arriving to begin my new job, I rounded an open end of the horseshoe into a cloud of smoke exhaled by Dick Roraback, another devoted baseball fan seated at a far end of the View desk. Life on a copy desk can get boring year after year and a new face—particularly an ex-sportswriter's—was welcomed.

"Have a seat," he said, rolling out a cushy chair equipped with casters. "You stay out of trouble down here."

I thanked him, introduced myself and accepted his invitation, not dreaming that seat might be mine permanently. During the

259

brief period I sat there—before the Times banned smoking inside the building—we became good friends.

A graduate of Dartmouth University, Roraback lived for a number of years in Paris, where he studied at the prestigious College of Sorbonne and became fairly fluent in the French language.

When talking about the country's cuisine one day, I mentioned my favorite French dish—*bouillabaisse*—which I mispronounced as, I'm sure, do most Americans. Roraback cringed.

"It's *bwee-ya-bess*," he said over and over. "Remember, like Bess Truman.—*bwee-ya-BESS.*"

After a bit of practice, I proudly nailed it.

The next time I ordered the fish soup at a French restaurant, the waiter looked puzzled. He scanned the menu, then smiled and looked up.

"An excellent choice, sir. *Bulla-base* is our specialty."

A gifted and prolific journalist, Dick wangled his way off the desk from time to time to pursue some weird stories, including a weeklong trip to the Midwest to investigate the source of some ancient love letters; a 12-article series on the Los Angeles River which took four months to produce more than 15,000 words, and a stint as the Times' food critic.

The "river," which wound through the city and outlying neighborhoods, passed directly behind our walled-in backyard. We called it a wash. When it rained heavily, water from surface streets gushed into it, swelling it to high levels.

During summer, young skateboarders and bicyclists wheeled up and down the sloped concrete sides, dodging various forms of debris on the bottom, including, no doubt, a few champagne corks.

Among Roraback's many stops while researching the series was my Reseda home, where he interviewed Charlene and me.

"We pop corks over our wall to test the quality of the champagne," I told my friend. "The farther the cork goes, the better the champagne."

The quote, which I exaggerated, never made it into print. According to Roraback, the View editor at the time—there was a steady turnover—deleted it along with sizeable chunks of his lengthy article.

As a food critic, Roraback usually chose restaurants near his San Fernando Valley home to review, some of which he revisited more than once. Occasionally, I appeared in print as his unnamed dinner companion. When I requested A-1 sauce at a prominent steakhouse, Dick was appalled.

His review suggested my steak was so tasteless it needed seasoning, surely costing the restaurant numerous dinner reservations. Later I told Roraback the steak was tasty enough; I simply liked A-1 sauce.

Unable to tolerate Dick's smoking any longer, I moved ten feet down the desk into a vacant seat facing two other baseball fanatics — prankster Vic Johnson inches away on the opposite side, and beyond him, my boss Don Alpert, sequestered in his small office.

Sociable Jean Wudke, a capable middle-aged editor who processed Jack Smith's column, sat to my left; easygoing, imperturbable Stan Williford to my right. Among other editors who had strong influences on my life during that decade was Ed Sakamoto, a fledgling playwright marking time while reaching for the brass ring.

"Before diversity became a popular rallying cry," Alpert recalled 20 years after he retired, "I had integrated the copy desk with women and people of color. I'm actually proud of that. We had a very good desk and worked shorthanded much of the time."

Alpert was particularly complimentary about George Kelly, an eccentric Harvard graduate.

"George was a terrific editor," he said. "He was early almost every day and worked solidly until all the copy had been processed. When George edited a story there was never anything wrong with it, including punctuation."

Alpert was not exaggerating. George could spot a typo in a word a foot long, almost extinct in the English language. Yet, he was stunned to learn the copyrighted trade name, Dr Pepper, contained no period.

No big deal? Such trivial things *were* big deals on the copy desk, including President Harry Truman's middle name —S— which stood for nothing. Truman's parents chose "S" as his middle name to please Harry's grandfathers, Anderson Shippe Truman and Solomon Young. No period.

I once got a nasty letter from the Levi Strauss Company for omitting the apostrophe in the phrase *a pair of Levi's*, mentioned only once in a feature I wrote—obviously not edited by George.

One hot summer afternoon, I spotted Kelly in the men's room washing his white T-shirt in cold water, which he put back on dripping wet, then returned to the desk to resume work. On another occasion, when rising to get coffee, I nearly stepped on him. George was lying on his back at the foot of my desk, meditating.

"He was undoubtedly a character," Alpert agreed, recalling Kelly's habit of watching TV dramas, turning the set off 10 minutes before they ended, then supplying his own endings.

Alpert also praised Bob Work, "an outstanding editor and slot man who did the work of three or four people."

Like Kelly, Work had a sharp eye for details. He could zip through a lengthy article, fix whatever needed fixing and write a clever headline in record time. Quiet, well liked, never abrasive, Bob was the most important cog in the wheel. He kept a photo of a scene from his favorite movie, *Gunga Din*—a 1939 release that starred Cary Grant, Victor McLaglen and Douglas Fairbanks—next to his computer.

Virginia Tyson—another bright Ivy Leaguer, a Yale graduate—was delighted to be in Los Angeles after leaving a wire-service job in Omaha. Asked how she liked living in Omaha, where I had relatives, she replied, "I suppose it's all right if you're over 50, a Republican and white."

Tyson and Wlliford, both black, sat near each other and bickered frequently, sometimes about their racial attitudes.

One afternoon, Stan retuned from his lunch break and told me he had just witnessed a bank holdup while waiting in line to cash a check.

"He ran right past me and out the door."

"What'd he look like?" I asked.

"It happened so quickly I didn't get a good look," he answered with a disparaging shrug, "some black guy."

Although harboring no real hostility toward Stan, Virginia disliked it immensely when he seemed to forget his heritage. She once became so irked she called him an "Uncle Tom"—an offensive term for a black man thought to be subservient to white people.

I don't remember Stan's response, if any, probably something akin to a sleepy late-afternoon yawn.

It was, indeed, a unique, diversified staff.

"Some transferred from other departments (like you) and some like Vic Johnson were not wanted by their boss at the time," Alpert said. "I always tried to hire editors with varied backgrounds and play to their strengths. Some were good with copy, some with headlines, some with makeup and so forth."

During 11 years in that department, I remember only one inept copy editor—Steve Whitmore, son of veteran actor James Whitmore. A pleasant young man, eager to learn and fit in, Steve was hired as a part-timer.

"He had a good resume and a great personality like his dad," Alpert recalled. "I thought he could bring some insight into Calendar, with his background. He had worked for the Glendale News Press and seemed to know his way around a newspaper. He proved otherwise. I had to let him go when he proved he couldn't handle any of the editing jobs, including working in the composing room."

Although my background had little in common with those of my co-workers, I enjoyed sharing the desk with them and appreciated their help adjusting to the drastic changes from sports.

One of my first front-page headlines, for example, contained the word *Ladies*, a definite no-no in those early days of women's liberation.

"Never refer to them in print as *ladies*," Alpert said with a smile. "They're *women*. In fact, if you want to stay out of trouble, don't even call them ladies to their face."

I inadvertently did so one evening when bidding a group goodnight as they waited in the hallway for an elevator. I got no reply, merely a smirk or two.

While editing a View feature that included the term *significant other*, I sent the author an e-mail, asking what she meant, embarrassed to admit my ignorance.

For me, it definitely was a learning process.

Each section operated independently with its own editor and staff writers, making Alpert's supervisory role somewhat thorny at times, particularly since he also had to appease Times Associate Editor Jean Sharley Taylor.

Constantly striving for a smooth consistent flow of copy from writers through various desks and finally into print, Taylor out-ranked everyone. Egos being what they were, it was a day-to-day challenge for her.

"What did you do in sports to get writers to observe dead-lines?" she asked me shortly after I joined the team. "Some of our writers don't seem to pay much attention to them."

"Bill Shirley put them on the desk for awhile," I replied. "They soon got the message."

"Oh," Jean said, shaking her head, "we couldn't do that."

There was, of course, a distinct difference. View and Calendar deadlines usually were flexible—unlike the rigid ones in sports. If a story wasn't ready on time, a standby feature would fill the space. In rare instances, Taylor would kill a piece that arrived past deadline or she didn't like, to the mortification of its author.

Producing readable daily Calendar and View articles required more writers than those on staff, opening the door to freelancers, which included me. I had barely warmed my seat when another View feature bearing my byline appeared on the front page April 24, 1980.

It was headlined "Life on the Tour: The Greening of the Pro Golfers' Wives."

An attractive brunette—prominent among the gallery—hurried off the golf course, pausing long enough to autograph several programs thrust in her face. Then she apologized for having to limit an impromptu interview to half an hour.

"I have an appointment for a massage at 4," Linda Watson said.

The following afternoon, a television cameraman would zoom in on her beaming face after recording the final tap-in that gave her husband, Tom Watson, another tour victory... and $54,000, boosting his career winnings total to almost $2 million.

That was the beginning of my in-depth feature on the wives of the top PGA pros during their pampered, luxurious week at La Costa Country Club, site of the annual Tournament of Champions. It was the only tournament in which players' fami-lies received a free ride. La Costa picked up the tab for every-thing.

But, as those I interviewed readily pointed out, La Costa was an exception to a life considerably less glamorous than what most people perceived.

As the wife of the game's No. 1 superstar, Linda Watson has no financial worries, but agrees that "It's a difficult life... trying to get airline reservations to suit you, being late in an airport and having to spend the night, especially with a baby. You have to worry about her food. I travel with a day's worth of food, a day's worth of diapers, a day's worth of clothes in my carry bag.

"You go to Laundromats in towns, have to eat in a restaurant three meals a day. You don't have the privacy with your husband you would like..."

I can't say life on the tour caused Tom and Linda to split, but as discontented as Linda professed to be, it clearly contributed to their eventual divorce.

Times Editor Bill Thomas, an avid golfer, liked the story, and soon thereafter, Jean Taylor called me into her office.

Her bottom line: "Do you want to write or be an editor?"

Those weren't her precise words, but whatever they were came as a surprise. I wasn't prepared to make an on-the-spot decision and avoided a direct answer.

I returned to the copy desk to ponder my future.

THE FOLLOWING is part of a Times obituary, published Aug. 26, 1998:

Dick Roraback, a colorful feature writer and copy editor at The Times for 22 years, has died. He was 68.

Roraback, who retired from The Times in 1995, died Saturday in Woodland Hills of throat cancer, after a yearlong battle.

He also had been sports editor of the International Herald Tribune in Paris from 1957 to 1972. His verse ode to an expatriate's longing for baseball, "The Crack of a Bat," is reprinted by that paper every year around opening day.

An adventurous soul, Roraback helped refugees escape from Hungary after the 1956 uprising against Communist rule. He was captured by Hungarian authorities and imprisoned for several weeks until the U.S. State Department negotiated his release.

He returned to the United States at that time but was soon drawn back to Paris, as he put it, "by hearing an Edith Piaf song."

After study at the Sorbonne, Roraback edited and wrote for the

Herald Tribune. In one 1970 series, he retraced the journey of newspaperman Henry Morton Stanley to find missionary David Livingstone in central Africa.

Roraback moved to Los Angeles in 1972 and joined The Times the next year. In a memorable 1985 series, he followed the route of the Los Angeles River, telling its history to residents who scarcely knew of its existence.

He served as a U.S. Navy lieutenant in the Korean War and later as a Lutheran church missionary to refugees in Jerusalem in the 1950s.

He is survived by his wife of 33 years...

Chapter 36

Changing of the Guard

On Jan. 14, 1981—less than a year after I left sports—a front-page expose about "Big Profits in Super Bowl Ticket Deals," written by Times staffers Mike Goodman and Al Delugach, ignited a monumental scandal that had the entire newspaper buzzing.

Like a bomb dropped from the sky, the story made a direct hit on a nationwide black market Super Bowl ticket operation involving professional scalpers, National Football League players, coaches and team officials.

Curiously, two Times sportswriters—Charles Maher and Mark Heisler—contributed to the explosive article that cast a dark cloud over their own department, mainly over their boss, Editor Bill Shirley.

Sportswriters and editors from The Times and other newspapers and publications have been recruited by ticket brokers to get them tickets from the teams they cover, Goodman and Delugach wrote at the beginning of the story. The news media receives thousands of tickets each year from the NFL front office and league teams.

In some cases, the sports press got personal vacation travel.

Buried near the end of more than 100 column inches, the writers expanded on that teaser, providing details that may have shocked thousands of readers, but came as no surprise to those who worked closely under Shirley. An excerpt:

Times Sports Editor Bill Shirley said that three or four times during the last 10 years he has sold Super Bowl tickets not used by The Times to Surl Kim, a Los Angeles travel agent who packages Super Bowl tours.

Shirley said he sold Kim about 20 tickets a year at face value and the money was used to reimburse the newspaper for the initial ticket purchase. He said Kim also handles his personal travel and has given him discounts on vacation trips abroad. Kim declined to be interviewed.

Shirley said he has asked one of his writers, Bob Oates, to get more tickets for Kim from the Rams. Oates covers professional football for The Times.

Oates said he bought 12 to 15 pairs of tickets a year for Kim from former Rams owner Carroll Rosenbloom, who died in 1979.

"I just did it for a couple of years," Oates said.

"I've been a sportswriter for 40 years and I can't remember the time when people didn't want tickets. The pressure to get tickets comes with the beat," Oates said. "I've never sold a ticket for a nickel over face value."

Citizen News Sports Editor Bob Panella and I frequently stood in front of the Coliseum before a kickoff with an extra pair of football tickets. Bob would offer them to skeptical people who thought we were scalpers, ignore us and walk on.

"Here," Panella would say, "you can have them. No charge."

Reactions sometimes were hilarious.

After I became editor and controlled press tickets, I followed Panella's example. I never sold a ticket to anyone—except a pair of Rose Bowl tickets each year to a Hollywood travel agent for considerably more than face value. Times were tough then, especially during the holidays.

In 1966, when Charlene and I accompanied boxing publicist Don Fraser and his wife to Europe for a month, the trip was arranged by Surl Kim, a friend of Fraser. It was not free nor was there any ticket swapping involved. It was however, *almost* free—slightly more than $1,000 for the two of us, as I recall.

During my years in sports, Shirley never offered me a Rose Bowl ticket.

"Surl Kim fixed Shirley up with trips for favors other than Rose Bowl tickets," columnist John Hall said. "Surl paid all staff

members at least double face value for their comps that were issued by the Tournament of Roses committee—two to each staffer.
Shirley's deal was to hold back tickets from the staff and sell them
himself to Kim."

Speculation throughout the newspaper was running high
that Shirley would be fired following that front-page expose. He
wasn't.

Bill Dwyer ultimately became only the fifth sports editor in
the history of the Times, following Bill Henry from 1928 to 1932,
Paul Zimmerman, Chuck Curtis and Shirley, who reigned for two
decades, from 1961 to '81.

"I was hired by Shirley and started as his No. 2 on April 27,
1981," Dwyer told me. "Garrity had just left to work for the pro
football magazine. I knew little about the ticket scandal stuff until after I arrived. Then, I was told that was why I was brought
there—to give Otis and Cotliar and Bill Thomas an option."

Dwyer was referring to Publisher Otis Chandler, Managing
Editor George Cotliar and Editor Bill Thomas.

"In the months after I arrived until I replaced Shirley in June,"
Dwyer continued, "a steady stream of visitors came to see me—
mostly when Shirley took a Surl Kim trip to China on his own
after Cotliar told him not to. Otis stopped by, then Cotliar, then
Thomas."

A week after Shirley returned from China, he asked Dwyer to
join him for lunch in the Picasso Room.

"He told me over dessert that I was to be the new sports editor," Dwyer remembered. "I took over as acting sports editor in
mid-June of '81 and had the 'acting' portion of the title erased a
few months later."

Shirley was given a private office and wrote, among other features, a number of travel pieces.

"He worked for me, right through the '84 Olympics," Dwyer
continued. "Our relationship was fine. He did some good work
and Otis let him retire with dignity—something that isn't even
pondered in this day and age.

"In the end, Shirley had hired me, treated me well, and gave
me a tremendous boost, simply because I was replacing a guy
who was so hated by staffers that I could have been an axe mur-
derer and been welcomed with open arms.

"I was 37 years old then, green and unsophisticated, and the whole thing left me amazed. But that turn of events turned out to be what the section needed—somebody from the outside who would start anew and leave all the old wounds and anger behind."

Ironically, while sailing somewhere off South America—said to be a free cruise—Bill Shirley suffered a fatal heart attack. His body was kept in a freezer until the ship reached its final destination.

Two years after Dwyer took over sports, fate again would dictate my future.

Chapter 37

The Gamut of Freelancing

The city bus, which I used daily for 11 years, provided a good source for my off-beat articles published in a column that appeared periodically in View.

After years of fighting bumper-to-bumper freeway traffic, I didn't mind the 90-minute stop-and-go rides. I used the time to transcribe taped interviews, rough out stories and read the daily newspaper.

Looking out, I noticed the smile on the young attendant's face.

Perhaps it struck him as rather humorous that a Los Angeles Rapid Transit District bus driver had parked at the curb, left his engine idling, the door open and 50 or more passengers waiting while he disappeared into the men's room.

The young man seated next to me was unconcerned about the delay. Arms crossed, chin on his chest, he dozed comfortably. Others read or merely gazed out, observing this and that.

It was about 9:30 a.m. on Ventura Boulevard in Studio City. A prominent sign across the garage portion of the small, six-pump station read, "Service Is Our Business."

The attendant seemed to take the words seriously as he waited on a customer.

Gas pumps partially obstructed my view of the man behind the wheel, but I noticed the car—a white, 1978 Ford Thunderbird—and was virtually certain the driver was its only occupant.

Minutes later, my eyes flicked up from the book I had been reading and focused on the scene outside. It resembled a scene from a Keystone Kops comedy.

The attendant, an empty cash drawer in hand and shouting, was scurrying toward the driveway, looking incredulously after the fleeing T-Bird as a man lathered with shaving cream—the owner—emerged from the men's room, followed by the bus driver.

The attendant, wild-eyed and using sweeping gestures, gave the two men an account of the holdup after which the driver boarded the bus and asked his passengers: "Anybody get that car's license number? The guy just robbed the station."

"I did," a young woman replied.

Thanks to the observant passenger, the thief, who got away with $1.70, was arrested after a lengthy pursuit by three squad cars, a couple of motor officers and a helicopter through downtown Glendale and a residential area.

I NEVER got back to Jean Taylor but decided not to accept her offer to become a full-time staff writer at a fixed salary. As it turned out, she didn't seem to mind that my articles were appearing all over the paper—short news items to in-depth features.

Most ran in Calendar and View. I also was paid extra for book reviews, television and travel pieces, even articles for real estate and business pages.

I conducted phone interviews in Don Alpert's office during lunch breaks and wrote at the copy desk while others read books, worked crossword puzzles or engaged in computer fun following the relatively new transition from typewriters.

Sneaking onto computers to send fake messages bearing the names of co-workers who had stepped away usually generated a few laughs during dull afternoons after the section was put to bed.

Even Alpert sometimes dashed out of his office, sat in front of Vic Johnson's computer, typed a quick message to someone with Johnson's name on it, scurried back and awaited the reaction.

Johnson replaced Alpert when he was out of the office, and when both were gone at the same time, I was in charge. I got along well with my boss, but not with Vic, who resented my writing on company time. He once opened my files and deleted a story in progress when I left for coffee without shutting down my computer. I reported the incident but nothing came of it.

"There was always downtime on the desk and it didn't bother me if someone did some writing on the side," Alpert told me. "If it did, I would have said something."

Always swamped with heavy workloads, editors generally had little time to discuss story ideas. Consequently my brief electronically transmitted proposals often sufficed. Soon, editors began offering me assignments staff writers couldn't cover—such as one on Sarah Ophelia Cannon.

I interviewed Sarah, a kindly looking, tastefully dressed woman of 68, in her seventh-floor suite at the elegant Beverly Wilshire Hotel.

She didn't look at all like Minnie Pearl, who wore that flat, garish straw bonnet adorned with all those multicolored flowers and a $1.98 cardboard price tag dangling from a safety pin.

"This hat is very important," she said as she handed it to me. "Girls in Grinder's Switch would wear hats like this to shade their faces. In those days they never thought about getting a tan."

Sara Cannon bought the prototype of that bonnet in Aiken, South Carolina, in 1939—that and a yellow organdy dress, white stockings and a pair of white shoes, all for about $10.

Thus, Minnie Pearl, the friendly, homespun character of country music fame, finally got her long-awaited wardrobe.

When I met her, Minnie was celebrating her 40th anniversary on Nashville's Grand Ole Opry, and the following evening she was in full, story-tellin' bloom on a CBS TV special titled *A Country Christmas.*

That assigned feature was published in the television section because of the CBS special. It could easily have appeared in View, which targeted women readers.

As a freelancer, I proposed story ideas with angles I knew would appeal to the various editors.

The Ladies Professional Golf Association was a natural for View. I had no trouble getting an okay to cover the women's 1982 tournament in Las Vegas.

Headlined *Will ERA Bring Lady Golfers Up to Par in Purses,* my feature focused on the disparity of prize money offered by the

PGA and LPGA.

As several thousand spectators surrounded the 18th green at the Desert Inn Country Club course, Nancy Lopez-Melton bent over her golf ball, lining up her final birdie attempt. Only the roar of a jet overhead disturbed the silence.

Striking the ball firmly, she missed by an inch, tapped in and flashed a $30,000 smile. That was the amount she received for winning the J&B Scotch Pro Am tournament by five strokes.

About three hours earlier, at Ponte Vedra, Florida, Jerry Pate was making a similar birdie attempt in the $500,000 Tournament Players Championship.

Pate sank his putt, the crowd reacted and the former U.S. Open champion dived into a nearby pond to celebrate his two-stroke victory. His prize: $90,000.

Lopez-Melton's win catapulted her into the Ladies Professional Golf Assn. money lead with 1982 earnings of $52,743, while Pate took over the No. 1 spot on the men's list with nearly $160,000—three times that of the top woman professional.

I interviewed 20 LPGA players that week, asking their views on the Equal Rights Amendment three months before the deadline for ratification by Congress. Ten opposed it, eight supported it and veteran pros Amy Alcott and Pat Bradley expressed no opinions.

Lopez-Melton, who was against the amendment, noted that the men's tour had been around much longer and that "It will take time; maybe we can get there."

More than a quarter of a century later, the LPGA is still fighting for comparable prize money and as of 2010, the ERA amendment, first proposed in 1923, had not been ratified.

Nancy Lopez—with a new hyphenated name and a baby on the way—successfully defended her J&B Scotch Pro-Am title the following year when she sank an eight-foot putt to avoid a playoff with Laura Baugh Cole, who had never won a tournament nor earned more than $10,000 in a single event.

My angle that year centered around the hardships women pros dealt with while competing on the LPGA circuit—pregnancies, raising children, sporadic weekend rendezvous with husbands, travel, health and dietary concerns, what to wear, maintaining the proper image and, for many, financial difficulties.

"I wouldn't be playing if it was me," Cole said. "When I miss a three-footer I get emotional. Maybe Nancy's cooler than me. I don't know. I just know that when I played, I lost my baby."

A year earlier, Lopez was married to Tim Melton—a Houston sportscaster who sulked inconspicuously in the gallery while the spotlight shone on his wife.

"I'm old-fashioned, maybe closed-minded," Nancy said at the time, "but I believe men should be the supporters, even though I make more money than my husband. It's difficult for him to accept it…. He has his pride and I'm proud of that. But he *has* accepted it."

Really? In a matter of months they were divorced and in September of that year Nancy married Houston Astros infielder Ray Knight. It seemed a match made on the links, if not in heaven. A low-handicap golfer, Knight proved a good competitor but seldom, if ever, defeated his wife.

I came up with a totally different angle for the 1984 Bob Hope Classic—his 25th annual—in Palm Desert, California.

Played on four courses, that year's five-round charity event drew a whopping field of 408 amateurs and 136 professionals. The tab for rubbing elbows with top pros, 80-year-old Hope, former President Gerald Ford, Speaker of the House Thomas P. (Tip) O'Neill and other famous entrants approached $9,000.

Most amateurs, however, never played with anyone on the "A" list. The vast majority competed in relative obscurity, their "galleries" composed mostly of friends and neighbors, far removed from the crowds.

Among the celebrities were Glen Campbell, Foster Brooks, Victor Mature, Gary Morton, Scatman Crothers, Vic Damone, Tom Jones, Andy Williams, Joey Bishop, Fred MacMurray, Hal Linden and Telly Savalas from the entertainment world and from baseball, Johnny Bench, Mike Schmidt and Joe Morgan.

A personal friend who suggested I write the article—Tom Stevens, a Hollywood film editor who maintained a home in the desert community and was a member of the Bermuda Dunes Country Club—competed in his sixth consecutive Hope tournament, but said that year's probably would be his last.

He was unhappy about escalating entry fees, unimpressed with tee prizes and would've seen more celebrities play golf had he been on the other side of the ropes.

275

For Charlene and me, it was a fun event. Hope kept the one liners flowing, starting on the first tee when his remark about a small wager with Ford caused the President to suddenly abort his backswing. When he struck the ball, the shot sliced onto an adjoining fairway.

Still fresh in the minds of those lining the first tee, no doubt, was Ford's errant shot in an earlier tournament that hit a spectator.

"He's in jail over there," the comedian said.

Bob's tee shot didn't fare much better, but overall, he played well.

With Ford in the passenger seat, Hope occasionally stopped his cart for both to sign autographs and chit-chat. He continued to host his tournament long after he no longer could swing a club.

One late afternoon in 1987, I phoned Hope's local office, hoping to get a few anecdotes to include in an article I was writing about bandleader Les Brown. I was told Bob was in a meeting and would return my call when it adjourned.

Waiting by the phone and watching the clock tick past 6 p.m. without hearing from him, I left the paper and hurried to the bus stop, arriving just in time for my long ride home. Early the next morning, Hope's associate called.

"Bob phoned your office right after the meeting," she said. "He was sorry he couldn't get back to you right away. He said for you to call him this afternoon in Washington, D.C."

She provided a number and told me when he would be expecting my call.

Excerpts from the Les Brown feature:

The band rates high on VIP social calendars, having played for inauguration parties for Presidents Richard Nixon and Ronald Reagan, Gov. George Deukmejian and a gala for Queen Elizabeth II, arranged by Frank Sinatra.

But primarily it has been Brown's close 40-year association with Hope that has kept his orchestra in the spotlight. Brown has provided musical accompaniment for 18 of Hope's Christmas tours, three of his around-the-world junkets and still is committed to six specials a year for the 84-year-old comedian.

"Now we prerecord all of our music for Hope," Brown said, "and he takes it with him. We don't travel with him out of the country."

When Hope was touring in the Middle East a couple of years ago, a U.S. Navy band sat in for the Brown orchestra, purely for visual effects on camera.

Later someone who had seen them on TV remarked that the sailors sounded "pretty good."

"They should've," Brown told him. "It was our music. They weren't blowing a damned note. If they had, they would've ruined the whole thing."

Speaking to me from Washington, Hope recalled when Brown and his Band of Renown were with him overseas.

"In North Korea it was so cold they could hardly put their trumpets to their lips," he said. "And in Vietnam, it was so warm it was hard for them to play.

"He's very easy to get along with, he's a good performer and he's got a very popular band."

The comedian occasionally plays golf with Brown, but Hope had a small complaint.

"He cheats a little on his handicap (27)," he said, "but who doesn't?"

Because of my desk schedule, I sometimes had to arrange interviews at odd hours. When I made an appointment to meet Edie Adams for an early morning breakfast at a Valley coffee shop, she was thrilled and never questioned the time.

An attractive actress who had signed to play the lead in a Long Beach Civic Light Opera production of *The Merry Widow*, she may be remembered as the Muriel Cigar Girl, whose TV commercials swept the airwaves for years.

Looking as if she had just stepped out of a beauty salon (she once was in the cosmetic business and wrote a book about beauty), Adams had arrived home from a rehearsal about eight hours before joining me that morning.

She covered a lot of ground between bites.

In May of 1982, two decades after her husband Ernie Kovacs was killed in an auto accident, her 22-year-old daughter, Mia Kovacs, died when her car drifted off Mulholland Drive and overturned. They were painful memories.

Edie didn't smoke, and when asked to hold a cigar for the commercial, she said it didn't look right, so she invented a ring to hold it.

"It never actually touched my finger and never touched my lips," she said. She remained under contract to Muriel until 1994.

About her age: "I will never tell anyone. I always say I'm older than Liza Minnelli and younger than Rose Kennedy."

Subjects of my articles occasionally were a bit heavy. Two, published a month apart early in 1983, generated a lot of response from sympathetic readers.

One, headlined "Helping to Make Wishes Come True," was an emotional piece dealing with terminally ill children whose simple and sometimes wildest dreams materialized, thanks to a relatively new organization called the *Make-a-Wish Foundation*.

Incorporated in November of 1980, the foundation was staffed by volunteers and funded by financial donors. At that time, about 50 terminally ill kids got their final wishes—from attending a Super Bowl game to basic requests.

One youngster, bedridden with a kidney disease, asked that someone might send him a birthday card. A Phoenix woman he had never met purchased "the biggest card I could find for $1" and mailed it, along with a stuffed animal.

A few days later, Tommy died at age 9.

The second feature bore the headline "Life Flights: When Minutes Count."

My coverage began on a Friday when a Times photographer and I spent a dull afternoon at the Northridge Hospital—five miles from my house—waiting for a call for a helicopter to rescue someone, but none came. The following morning while brushing down my backyard pool I got a call.

"If you can get here in 15 minutes, you can go with us," a nurse from the hospital said. "We're going to pick up a baby in Ojai and transfer her to Childrens Hospital in Los Angeles. We can't wait."

The rotor blades were whirling when I ran across the rooftop to climb aboard.

"No time to get a photog," I told the nurse. "I brought this."

Flashing my $30 Instamatic—a gift from our daughter Barbara—I began snapping shots of the liftoff and continued taking pictures throughout the transfer of a pathetically frail 2-year-old redhead named Kelly.

Afflicted with a congenital heart disease, she had suffered an apparent stroke the night before. It was decided Kelly should make her third trip to Childrens Hospital, where she had undergone open-heart surgery six months earlier.

As I click-clicked at Childrens Hospital while a medical team was tending to Kelly, I overheard a nurse whisper to the nurse from Northridge.

"I would think the Los Angeles Times could afford a better camera."

Although a bit fuzzy, a large photo of the baby that accompanied my article dominated the front page of the View section— the only photo credit I ever received. In a subsequent edition, however, it was replaced by a less dramatic in-focus picture of a copter touching down on the Northridge Hospital roof.

That same day, an accident occurred at Big Bear Lake, where snow-covered slopes were crowded with weekend skiers, among them a 34-year-old woman who had suffered a serious head injury when she collided with another skier. With me aboard, the copter transferred her to San Bernardino Hospital.

By then, I had exhausted my supply of Instamatic film.

Other stories, proposed and assigned, ran the gamut of free-lancing:

Jack's 1988 feature on Rosemary Clooney focused on her annual fund-raising tribute to her sister Betty, who died of a brain aneurism at 45. Shuffling through old photos, Rosemary occasionally wiped away a tear. "It's still difficult," she told Jack 12 years after her sister's death, "very emotional. We always sang together, from the time Betty was 2 and I was 5."

279

—Female singers Rosemary Clooney, cresting on a new career 15 years after being hospitalized for an emotional breakdown, former recording star Roberta Sherwood, at 69 performing for showbiz friends at Horace Heidt's retirement complex, and Virginia O'Brien, the striking, dark-haired beauty of the '40s with the expression of a wall clock and a voice that could bellow like a jackass, showcasing a new album that included her biggest hit, *The Donkey Serenade.*

—A beautiful female boxing referee, a hard-as-nails pistol-packing woman bounty hunter, and a resurgence of roller derby action featuring ex-models and cosmeticians.

Jack, Charlene and other dinner guests were asked by host Rudy Vallee to line up for an autographed copy of his studio photo. Almost unreadable, the scribbling reads: "To Charlene in friendship, Rudy Vallee, 12/17/85." Earlier, he showed one of his old movies on TV.

—Nearly forgotten Rudy Vallee minus his megaphone but not his enormous ego, showing up in a music rock video. He invited Charlene, me and several others to dinner at his mountain-top home where we were forced to tour his trophy room, watch one of his old movies and stand in line for him to autograph his 8-by-10 glossies.

Good heavens. What would they have thought down at Mory's, where all those Whiffenpoofs assembled with their glasses raised on high? After all, wasn't it Vallee who gave that Yale drinking group some class with his *Whiffenpoof Song* back in the '20s, when he was a student at the university? Of course, it was.

—Jazz pianist Frankie Carle, on the road again at 79, booked for shows with the Russ Morgan band and others in 55 cities and 27 states.

"I won't ever quit playing," he told me, "but I doubt I'll do another tour."

—Lina Romay, bandleader Xavier Cugat's sexy singer in the '40s, known as the Latin Doll, discovered at Hollywood Park, where she provided radio listeners with racing information in Spanish.

—A shocking use of the "F" word on national TV during NBC's Friday night boxing series.

—A Laurel and Hardy look-alike contest.

—Mother Angelica, the broadcasting nun.

— Former FBI agent, ex-singer and TV host Joe Graydon, who employed many of those entertainers and others of that era for cross-country big-band bus tours popular in the mid-'50s.

Graydon recalled a particularly thorny problem he faced when receiving a phone call from the troupe's road manager. It was a Friday, payday for the 22 entertainers.

"They were somewhere between Albuquerque and Hobbs, New Mexico, in a blizzard, averaging 30 miles per hour," he said. "There was no way they were going to get to the bank in Hobbs before it closed, and the manager was the only one authorized to withdraw the money."

Describing the group as *22 starving musicians*, Graydon not only had a payroll problem but also faced the possibility that the concert, scheduled that night in Hobbs, might have to be postponed.

But it all ended well.

"I got the bank to release the funds to the guy who was putting on the concert," Graydon said, "and the storm cleared in time for the show to go on. They got in town at 6:30."

HIS SPORTS colleagues called him the Silver Fox because of his distinguished silver hair and wide-ranging reputation as a principled, uncompromising editor, but I called George Kiseda my biggest supporter when I covered boxing.

A devout Catholic who lived alone, intensely private and un-waveringly honest, Kiseda joined the Times in 1972 after working at several papers in Philadelphia.

"Could you drop by when you get a few minutes?" George asked when he phoned one day in late summer of 1983. "Bill Dwyer would like to talk to you."

Dwyer? I hadn't even popped my head into the sports department in more than three years, never even met him. Why would Dwyer want to talk to me?

I dropped what I was doing and headed down the third-floor hallway.

Chapter 38

Road to the Olympics

Some 50,000 people jammed St. Peter's Square waiting for at least a glimpse of Pope John Paul II, one of history's most loved religious leaders.

As his Pope Mobile approached, I leaned over a wooden barrier, pointed my Instamatic (yes, that one) and pressed the button. Immediately, I discovered my horrendous mistake.

I had loaded a roll of 12 exposures into the camera before leaving the hotel, not 24. While awaiting a close-up of John Paul II, I had taken a dozen pictures of the vast square of worshippers and famous Vatican structures.

No more exposures, no more film. Oh, oh...

"Don't worry," my Times colleague Earl Gustkey said as he aimed his expensive-looking device at the Pope. "I've got him covered."

Click, click... click.

Like everyone else lining the papal route along the barriers, I extended my hand as his vehicle passed, but John Paul couldn't grab everyone's. Of course, he missed mine.

I didn't get nearly as close to the pope on two other occasions in Los Angeles, but at least had film in my camera and managed almost recognizable photos of the pontiff.

My meeting with sports editor Bill Dwyer and George Kiseda

a month earlier lasted all of 10 minutes. As a result, Charlene and I were back in Rome 17 years after I frivolously tossed a penny into the Trivi Fountain, said to assure a revisit. I never believed that but like most tourists joined in the silly custom.

"Earl will be covering boxing for us at next year's Olympics," Dwyer had told me. "We need a Number Two man. George suggested you."

I was ecstatic.

Dwyer, who appointed Kiseda his deputy to coordinate coverage of the Olympics, had others on his staff qualified to work with Gustkey, including the beat writer I replaced—Dan Hafner. Again, I attribute my good fortune to fate.

"You would be going to Rome right away for the World Boxing Championships," Dwyer continued, "then join Earl in Fort Worth next summer for the Trials. Of course, you also would be gone two weeks covering the Games. Do you think Don Alpert will give you the time away from the office?"

Having accumulated some vacation weeks and knowing Alpert as I did, I was certain he wouldn't object. He didn't.

A robust, full-bearded workaholic, Earl Gustkey was a perfect fit for the profile of a rugged outdoorsman who loved fishing, hunting and all that goes with the great outdoors. He had been the outdoor editor before being assigned to boxing.

Anyone who ever read *anything* under Earl's byline couldn't help but be impressed. He was a consummate pro—well versed in all major sports, thoroughly prepared for interviews after extensive research and an accurate reporter.

Ten years older and more experienced as a boxing writer, I was expected to offer Gustkey some guidance in his Olympic coverage, but I soon discovered he was in complete control.

Boxing was Earl's passion. He owned a large library of fight films he delighted showing friends and had vast knowledge about the sport's greatest boxers.

After being offered the job, I had only one important question for Dwyer: "Can my wife go with me to Rome?"

"You would have to pay for her flight and meals," he said, "but that's fine."

Charlene was excited about returning to Rome, this time for a full week, but she's never been adventurous and had no desire to extend the trip.

"We shouldn't pass up this opportunity to see Spain, honey," I suggested." The Times is paying my way. We could fly into Madrid, then take the train to Rome."

"Okay," she finally agreed, "one extra week."

Not having a map of Europe handy, my wife didn't consider that Madrid was a long way from Rome, in fact a country away.

It took more persuading before Charlene agreed to our itinerary. It covered five weeks of travel with stops in Spain, France, Italy, Athens and a cruise through the Greek islands. The Times paid my expenses only in Rome.

I bought Euro rail passes that entitled us to hop on and off trains, booked accommodations at hotels in Madrid, Rome and Athens and pulled two large suitcases thousands of miles across the continent.

To Charlene's credit she proved surprisingly durable those first two weeks of that warm Indian summer. Despite a partial train strike in Spain and a desperate late-night phone call using my limited Spanish vocabulary to rent a decent Barcelona hotel room, she would have to agree positives far outweighed negatives.

Particularly memorable were two romantic nights in a cozy second-floor rooming house on the edge of Cote d' Azur in San Rafael, France, near Nice.

And now Charlene was back in the Eternal City, looking into the eyes of the passing Pope and toward an exciting week while I covered the *Three A Coppa del Mondo Roma.* It was the final major international amateur boxing competition before the '84 Los Angeles Olympics.

Nearly 100 modern-day gladiators from Africa, Asia, Europe, North and South America, Oceania and Italy would battle in the shadow of the Colosseum, where musty ruins still stirred images of bloody centuries-old "games of sport."

Isolated somewhere removed from the crush of bodies in St. Peter's Square that morning were the Soviet boxing team, its head coach and chief of the delegation, and a female interpreter.

Asked his impression of the large turnout, the coach replied, "It is good that people have someone to believe in."

The interpreter was less diplomatic.

"It would have been nice," she said, "if there had not been so many people."

Earl had arrived in Rome a few days before his wife Nancy Yoshihara, a staff writer in the Times business department, joined him. After she checked in, the four of us took in some of the city's famous sites and dined together at restaurants. For Earl, it was a rare escape from his typewriter. His stay in Rome was mostly business.

Dwyer sent me to familiarize myself with boxers expected to compete in the Games, not file secondary stories. Consequently, I wrote only a few sidebars, providing more quality time with my wife. I wasn't unhappy about that abbreviated work schedule, nor was Charlene. We were in Rome only three nights in 1966. There were plenty of sights left to explore.

The week passed quickly. Charlene and I said goodbye to Earl and Nancy. We boarded a train to Brandisi, on the heel of Italy, and despite threatening weather, set sail in a small ship across the Adriatic Sea.

Soon, the full brunt of a major storm unleashed its fury. Rolling violently in the turbulent waters, the ship tossed furniture around, made passengers ill and arrived at our destination, Piraeus, Greece, when it was nearly dark, long overdue.

Heavy rain, swept by fierce winds, drenched the area. Worse, a money-exchange booth had closed and taxi cabs were on strike. I had a hotel reservation in Athens, but didn't know its location or how we would get there.

"What are we going to do?" Charlene asked as she eyed a bus loaded with tourists about to depart, her eyes welling. "I wish we were with them."

"I don't have any Greek money," I replied, "but might have enough liras to get a bus ticket to Athens, if they will accept Italian currency. If not, maybe they will cash a traveler's check."

"Where's the bus station?" she asked.

Looking out from the edge of the terminal through the sheet of rain, across an open area, I pointed to a small structure where a group of young travelers wearing back packs huddled outside under cover.

"Over there, I guess."

Charlene squinted, her mouth agape.

"Clear over there?"

"It's not much farther than the length of a football field, honey. We don't have a choice. Open your umbrella and grab the strap. Let's go."

Wind immediately inverted our umbrellas, making them useless. Missteps into deep potholes soaked our shoes and tipped over our luggage as we trudged forward. The station was closed, and none of the young people spoke English. But they saw our concern and tried to assure us there was no need to panic.

Soon, a window opened. After a futile attempt to communicate, we were able to buy two tickets with the Italian lira. Rain was letting up when we finally climbed aboard a warm bus, squished down the aisle and wearily sank into our seats.

I can't remember exchanging conversation with Charlene during that 20-minute bus ride. We were both exhausted and she had been fighting tears for an hour.

Glancing out, I suddenly saw it. Constructed on a large hill directly above us was a surreal, majestic sight I'll never forget.

"Wow! Look at that!"

Charlene lifted her head and looked out the window.

It was breath-taking, almost eerie against the gray clearing sky—the illuminated ruins of the ancient citadel of Athens, the crumbling, historic Acropolis.

A few miles later, the bus stopped on a side street. It was, incredibly, *our stop*. Before I realized what was happening, we and our luggage were deposited on a shadowy block somewhere on the outskirts of the city. The bus rolled away, leaving us stranded.

Was that as far as our Italian lira would take us? I can't explain it. I tried to console Charlene, grabbed both luggage straps and motioned toward a semi-lighted street a few paces ahead.

"Come on, dear. That looks like a main drag. Maybe I can find a place to get a check cashed."

Pulling our suitcases up a hill, I saw a small cafe. We entered and immediately drew open-mouth stares from diners shocked by our disheveled appearances. It was obvious no one understood our dilemma. We quickly exited.

Continuing up the deserted street, I glanced back and saw two nefarious-looking men on the opposite side hurrying across, toward us.

I alerted Charlene.

"Come on, hurry."

We began half-running with our luggage up the hill to the corner. A group of young people were standing under a street light looking at a map. We crowded near them. No one spoke or understood English.

Momentarily, a middle-aged Greek appeared from behind. I couldn't be certain, but he may have been one of the men pursuing us.

"You look like you're in trouble," he said in good English.

After explaining our situation, he offered to drive us to our hotel, which he said was only a couple of miles distant.

When we balked, he insisted.

"You're in Greece," he said with a disarming smile. "You are with friends. I want to help you."

He seemed sincere, and, of course, we had exhausted our options.

"I'll get my car," he said. "Wait here."

Within minutes, a sedan pulled alongside the curb and parked. Our "friend" stepped out from behind the wheel.

"Oh, oh," Charlene whispered as he loaded a piece of luggage into the trunk. "There's another man in the car. I'm not getting in."

When the driver reached for the second suitcase, I stopped him.

"My wife's uncomfortable about going with you," I said. "We don't know you or your friend."

With that, he pulled out his wallet and showed us a photo of a young female relative he claimed resided in Southern California.

"You're in trouble," he repeated. "The taxis are on strike. How are you going to get to your hotel?"

I looked him in the eye, at his companion, then turned to Charlene.

"Honey, we don't have a choice. We'll have to trust him."

It was a short, uneasy ride to our hotel, where I immediately cashed a traveler's check. I hurried back to the car and handed our Greek friend a generous tip despite his reluctance to accept payment for his good deed.

After three nights in Athens and seven days in the Greek

Isles, we flew home. I returned to the View copy desk, but not for long.

A FEW days after Charlene and I celebrated our 33rd wedding anniversary, I boarded a flight from Burbank, California, to Dallas to cover the Olympic Trials.

Nothing went well after I landed and began roaming that huge airport in search of Dick McCrillis, my high school buddy who was to meet me. Eventually we connected and headed for his home in Rockwall, a Dallas suburb, where his wife Joanne had planned dinner much earlier. It was great seeing my old friends after so many years.

Returning to the airport after a short visit, I rented a car and set out for Fort Worth, where the Trials would begin the next day, June 6.

After missing a freeway turnoff, I eventually spotted the Fort Worth Hilton and other buildings in the distance, illuminated by bright lights and spectacular flashes of lightning.

Suddenly, I whiffed a hint of burning rubber and instinctively reached under the dimly lighted dash for the emergency-brake release. I pulled.

S-w-i-s-h!

Up sprang the front hood. It whipped back forcefully against the windshield. The effect was terrorizing, as if suddenly going blind while speeding down a freeway at 55 miles an hour.

Headlights from a large truck directly behind me reflected in my mirror. I could only guess what was ahead. I hoped the far right-hand lane was free and beyond that, a shoulder wide enough to pull over and stop.

Activating the turn signal and reducing speed, I began slowly edging over.

Apparently, the truck driver was aware of my problem, as he, too, changed lanes, staying close enough to prevent other vehicles from getting between us.

As cars whizzed past on my left, I blindly eased onto what turned out to be a shoulder and slowed to a stop. Getting out on the passenger side, I slammed the hood shut. I took a deep breath and continued to the hotel. The burning smell had vanished.

Shaking as I checked in, I soon joined Earl Gustkey in a large suite and related my story.

Gazing out a huge picture window, he was preoccupied with the spectacular show—jagged lightning streaks and intermittent crackling of thunder.

To Earl, a seasoned traveler on a Times expense account, such an experience probably didn't qualify in his top-10 horror stories. I think he might have mumbled something as he continued to stare out the window. He had come to work and was excited about it.

"Think this storm is going to last through tomorrow?" he asked. "I doubt they'll sell out in this kind of weather."

COMPETITION THAT week produced numerous stories about those who made the U.S. team, but it was a loser who impressed me more than anyone—heavyweight Mike Tyson, the future professional champion.

Excerpts from my feature about Mike and his crusty 76-year-old manager, Cus d'Amato, published June 8:

As if turning back the clock, D'Amato again has his adrenaline gushing, his dreams laced with gold.

D'Amato, who guided Floyd Patterson to a 1952 Olympic gold medal as a middleweight and to the world heavyweight championship four years later, is back with another prospect.

He's heavyweight Michael Tyson, one of boxing's most devastating punchers....

At 17, Tyson, indeed, is awesome. But making the Olympic team is a different matter. If he does, it will be an upset.

Like Patterson, Tyson grew up on the streets of Bedford-Stuyvesant in Brooklyn, New York, where he battled on concrete long before his feet ground resin on canvas.

"I had a lot of street fights when I was around 10," said the muscular youth, who looks mature beyond his years. "I would just fight to fight, no reason. I got my share of getting beat up."

Predictably, he got into trouble. Sent to a boys' detention center, he met a counselor named Bobby Stewart, a former professional fighter who knew D'Amato. Stewart asked D'Amato if he could help the boy, as he had helped Patterson and others.

Soon, D'Amato was lacing gloves on Tyson and training him. But it was a relationship far deeper than boxer-manager. D'Amato gave Tyson a home....

At 14, Tyson—who never knew his father and whose mother died of cancer two years ago—was placed in D'Amato's custody.

Not eager to be interviewed, Tyson spoke in a low, guarded voice, almost inaudibly. When asked if he had any hobbies, his reply was a one-word mumble, which I didn't understand. I asked again, then a third time.

Eyeing me as if I were an idiot, he jumped up from the table in the hotel lobby and joined a cluster of friends.

The manager said Mike's hobby was *"pigeons,"* which he raised and trained.

He's outgoing under certain conditions," D'Amato said, as if apologizing for his abrupt departure, "but an introvert in others. I'll go talk to him."

He persuaded Tyson to resume the interview, but he had little to add and said nothing more about pigeons.

Before Tyson faced his first opponent in the Trials—favored Avery Rawls of Los Angeles—talk centered on his awesome punching power.

"I don't think there's a man alive, including the pros, who can hit as hard as Tyson," said the father and coach of one of the boxers.

Officials didn't dispute his punching ability, but unanimously agreed he lacked good technique and boxing skills.

Bob Surkein, a referee and judge and former chairman of the Amateur Boxing Federation who had been associated with the sport for 40 years, was especially critical.

"He's a strong kid," he said. "He's been taught all the pro rules. Twice disqualified for fouls. He was fighting super-heavyweights and didn't belong there. No question he can bang. Whether he's overcome those stinking pro tactics Cus has taught him, we don't know."

Tyson surprised Surkein and others, easily defeating Rawls and "making mincemeat" of Princeton graduate Henry Milligan, in the published words of Gustkey, before losing to Henry Tillman of Los Angeles.

Later, in Las Vegas, Mike spotted Charlene and me and greeted us warmly. Exposing two gold front teeth, he said they were replacements for decayed ones.

"Hi, buddy," he said as he draped a bulging bicep across my shoulders. "How ya doin'?"

As D'Amato had said, the young man was capable of extreme mood swings. At that moment, he definitely was "up." I can only surmise Mike had seen a copy of my feature and was pleased.

That was before Tillman beat him a second time in the Vegas box off, ending Tyson's hopes for a berth on the U.S. squad.

Chapter 39

Let the Games Begin

*T*here no doubt were countless times when even the most stout *and hearty of the Los Angeles Olympic Organizing Committee figured that if they could pull this one off, then this must really be the City of Angels.*

That was Randy Harvey's lead paragraph of his Times article published July 28—Day 1 of Olympics '84: The Games of the XXIII Olympiad—in the 44-page edition of a special section launched six days earlier.

The story behind that section was never made public. Now, more than a quarter century later, former Times Sports Editor Bill Dwyer, responding to my request for information, provided the following:

"When I was named sports editor in June of 1981, I quickly received a visit from (Times publisher) Otis Chandler. He was kind and friendly and made one thing very clear: we would cover these Olympics like never before.

"I quickly ascertained several things. I was 37 years old and well in over my head. The distance from Milwaukee to Los Angeles, in miles and perception, was light years. I shared this with nobody except my wife, who already knew.

"Despite this, I made several fortunate decisions—one of them being to fight off several Metro-type attempts to take over

293

the entire Olympic coverage authority. Once I won that, which was no small battle, I was able to take the next steps:

"First, I decided to swallow as much pride as I needed to and yield on the initial content concepts to George Kiseda, who was brilliant and had the respect of the entire staff—unlike me, who was from Milwaukee and neither had, nor had a chance to earn, the respect of anybody. Kiseda was smarter and more experienced and more full of story ideas and vision than anybody I had ever met. I also realized that he had no political instincts, hated all authority and would blow up the ship in mid-stream over the smallest matter.

"So I drew the lines: Kiseda was my co-Olympic coordinator, and he would design the concept of what we would do and how we would do it. I would get the money commitments, schmooze the bigwigs, pep-talk the staff, and get George all the money he needed for the assignments he wanted to make. I fought the battles with the local organizing committee for more credentials, and got budget and space increases, as well as working with Vance Stickell (executive vice president of marketing) on advertising positions.

"When it came to beat assignments, Kiseda had a big role in that, but we did do it together. There was little anger over who got what, because everybody got something and several of the sports staffers wanted to stay with the sports (section) and not be involved in the Olympics.

"Kiseda knew people from other departments who had some sports background, such as you, and we got some applications from other people, such as religion editor John Dart, that impressed us. So we made it a newspaper-wide thing, and there seemed to be little dispute over any of the assignments. We knew you knew boxing and could work with Earl and that is exactly how it came to pass and how it worked out as well as it did."

Full of impressive facts and figures, the Day 1 issue gave the Games a dynamic sendoff with its half-page photo of a gold medal atop a sprawling downtown skyline. Below the fold, Harvey's story noted myriad problems confronting the committee during five years of planning—not the least of which was the Soviet-led boycott by 14 nations.

According to Harvey, the committee had "worked hundreds

of millions of hours, spent hundreds of millions of dollars and suffered hundreds of millions of headaches."

As if the LAOOC did not have its hands full taking care of things that it can control, it also has been asked to make the impossible possible—clean the air, create a cool breeze, reduce the traffic and make sure there is plenty of parking for everyone.

It also has been forced to think, and plan for, the unthinkable, a terrorist attack such as the one that resulted in the murder of 11 Israelis in the athletes village during the 1972 Munich Olympics.

Meanwhile, Earl Gustkey was confronting a problem of his own.

"This won't work," he told me as he checked out our room at the New Otani Hotel, where the Times, two blocks away, had booked accommodations for writers covering the Games. For Gustkey, sharing a room—particularly a bathroom—was unthinkable. "We're going to need separate rooms," he insisted.

Not surprisingly, Dwyer approved Earl's request.

I wasn't happy about sharing a room with Gustkey either, but was delighted to share it with my wife. During our first week apart, Charlene joined me for dinner one night and returned home the next morning. The following week, we repeated our romantic rendezvous. But that visit ended badly.

Discovering an earring nestled in a shag rug as she was leaving, she exploded.

"I don't know *where* it came from," I said defensively. "It must have been there quite a while. I guess the sweeper didn't pick it up."

Whatever else I said mattered not. She left in tears. Nothing I could say would alleviate the situation.

The following morning, my phone rang.

"I solved *your* mystery," Charlene said matter-of-factly.

"My mystery?"

"The earring. It matches one I had at home."

Typically managing to gloss over the facts, Charlene offered no apology for her impulsive outburst and insinuations. At least, I clearly was exonerated even though such words never crossed her lips.

The simple explanation: Charlene had lost the earring during her first conjugal visit without realizing it, and upon discovering the one in the rug the following week, failed to recognize it as being hers.

"Well," I said. "I'm happy you found the mate, dear."

"I am too. I love these earrings."

Dining with my wife at two upscale restaurants during her visits was a treat.

The Otani restaurant, where Earl and I ate most of our meals, had a limited menu with basic dishes. Earl insisted on sizzling hot dinners and sent many back to the kitchen until servers got the message.

The hotel was conveniently located near Olympic venues, mainly the Coliseum and Sports Arena, where boxing was held daily between 11 a.m. and 2 p.m. and from 6 to 10 p.m.

Earl and I sometimes remained on the job until late at night, depending on when important matches were scheduled. We wrote at our Sports Arena desks, fought tough deadlines, and often grabbed quick meals nearby when time permitted.

Boxing writers Earl Gustkey and Jack take a break at the 1984 Olympics.

The Day 1 issue included two Gustkey articles and two photos that covered a full page, but his first four paragraphs summed up what fans could expect.

It was to have been a boxing tournament for the history books, the biggest amateur tournament in history. And two of the powerhouse boxing countries represented, the United States and Cuba, were to have suited up possibly their best teams ever.

And it was to have been the grand finale, the final curtain call, for one of the sport's legendary figures, Cuba's Teofilio Stevenson

It's something less than that now, of course. The Soviet-led boycott has removed one team, Cuba, which seemingly had a chance of winning up to half a dozen gold medals, just as it did in Moscow. And the Soviet Union might have won a couple of golds.

It's still the biggest tournament ever held—more than 400 boxers from 84 countries are expected—but it shapes up as an All-American show.

And, of course, it was.

During the Aug. 11 finals, the public address announcer asked the audience to rise nine times for the playing of America's National Anthem, when gold medals were awarded to nine U.S. champions. A silver and bronze also were presented to two other Americans, with only one medal ceremony devoid of a U.S. boxer. Americans won 52 of their 55 bouts.

Unquestionably the most controversial incident occurred on Day 13, when Evander Holyfield—a strong favorite to win gold in the light-heavyweight division and solid choice for the outstanding-boxer award—was disqualified by a Yugoslavian referee for failing to obey a command to "stop" punching with five seconds left in the second round.

Holyfield's outclassed opponent, New Zealand's Kevin Barry, hit the canvas after absorbing a devastating left hook, arose shakily and took a standing eight-count. But the fight was over and Holyfield's gold-medal hopes gone as well.

The disqualification ignited a near-riotous crowd of 11,729 as paper cups, popcorn boxes and assorted trash were hurled toward the ring. An official protest failed to overturn the referee's decision, and Evander ended up with a bronze medal.

Coincidentally, my story on the page opposite Gustkey's coverage also was controversial, but had a happier result when a jury overturned a verdict that gave Henry Tillman a win over Italy's Angelo Musone in a semifinal bout. Tillman went on to be draped in gold.

Holyfield became a four-time professional heavyweight champion who forever will be linked to his 1997 encounter with cannibalistic Mike Tyson when Iron Mike chewed off a one-inch piece of cartilage from Evander's right ear, spit it onto the canvas and, moments later, nibbled on his left ear.

Tyson's disqualification was announced by Jimmy Lennon Jr., son of the Olympic Auditorium's hugely popular announcer among Mexican crowds because of his command of the Spanish language. Jimmy Sr. was the uncle of Lawrence Welk's famous vocalists, the Lennon Sisters.

Holyfield lost a small piece of his anatomy during that re-match but retained his title and, in a sense, gained retribution for that unjust 1984 disqualification that robbed him of Olympic gold.

Gustkey's perceptive eye seldom missed anything important in the ring, his reports almost always unquestionably accurate, but his scoring was suspect.

He frequently scored rounds considerably different than the officials. We usually disagreed on the numbers as well, if not the verdicts. A colleague covering for Associated Press, Ed Schuyler, also questioned Earl's final tallies.

Gustkey, however, steadfastly maintained that his view of the match was correct. Eventually, Bill Dwyer decided to stop pub-lishing Times scorecards, invoking a rule prohibiting journalistic involvement in the outcome.

"I figured it exposed us to more ridicule from the know-it-all boxing fans than we were already getting (from writers)," the edi-tor said.

When Gustkey was assigned to cover USC football, the move was watched with special interest by Schuyler, a nationally ac-claimed ring expert who also was voted into the International Boxing Hall of Fame in 2009.

As the story goes, Schuyler was in Las Vegas for a fight the day Earl covered his first Trojan game. When Schyler saw the game had ended, he called Earl in the press box and was told USC had won, 21-10.

"OK, Earl," Schuyler replied, "but how did you have it?"

At ringside, Earl scored fights his way. And that was that.

As the secondary Times reporter, I had more opportunities than Earl to interview spectators and file notes.

Former Oakland Raiders head football coach John Madden,

whose broadcasting career was in its infancy, could generate as much excitement watching a good fight as he could seeing a bruising linebacker sack a quarterback. Seated prominently in the stands, Madden was hard to miss.

California's Golden Boy, Art Aragon, wasn't far from a spotlight, either. Asked about his amateur ring career, Aragon said, "I had 13 fights, won all but 12."

Actor Ryan O'Neal and his glamorous companion, actress Farrah Fawcett, cuddled near the ring in a roped off VIP section reserved for celebrities, off limits to the media. Nonetheless, I managed to squat beside them briefly.

Asked if he had ever boxed as an amateur, O'Neal replied, "I had 12 fights and won the majority of them."

Majority?

"That's right... more than half."

One published report listed O'Neal's amateur record as 18 wins, four losses with 13 knockouts—yes, a majority.

O'Neal managed professional boxers in previous years and hoped to sign Canadian heavyweight Willie deWit to a pro contract after he competed in the Olympics. His partner, O'Neal said, would be rock music promoter Shelly Finkel of New York.

DeWitt, heavily touted going into the Games, brought home a silver medal. As a pro, he won the Canadian title and retired in 1988 with only one loss after defeating Henry Tillman—the man who beat him for gold in Los Angeles. DeWitt opted for a career in law and became a successful attorney.

Other ringsiders spotted included singer Andy Williams and former champions Carlos Palomino and Sugar Ray Robinson, whose ring career—including more than 200 amateur bouts—was legendary.

The most famous observer was Muhammad Ali, seated quietly with his wife in the VIP section, guarded by two uniformed police officers. His bout with Parkinson's disease was readily apparent although not acute.

I asked Muhammad if he regretted throwing his 1960 Olympic gold medal into the Ohio River in Louisville, a story documented in his book and on film. He nodded slowly but said nothing.

Pressed for a reply, Ali almost whispered, "I do now. I wish I'd kept it."

Twelve years later, the champ received a replacement during the opening ceremonies of the 1996 Games in Atlanta.

In the last installment of National Public Radio's series on *All Things Considered*, Ali talked about his life with help from his wife Lonnie. An excerpt:

"Early in 1996, I was asked to light the cauldron at the Summer Olympic Games in Atlanta. Of course my immediate answer was yes. I never even thought of having Parkinson's or what physical challenges that would present for me.

"When the moment came for me to walk out on the 140-foot-high scaffolding and take the torch from Janet Evans, I realized I had the eyes of the world on me. I also realized that as I held the Olympic torch high above my head, my tremors had taken over. Just at that moment, I heard a rumble in the stadium that became a pounding roar and then turned into a deafening applause.

"I was reminded of my 1960 Olympic experience in Rome, when I won the gold medal. Those 36 years between Rome and Atlanta flashed before me, and I realized that I had come full circle.

"Nothing in life has defeated me. I am still 'The Greatest.' This I believe."

I, too, realized I had come full circle with the young man Charlene and I met so many years earlier—from the glib, affable Cassius Clay to the sedate 42-year-old warrior seated below that Olympic ring, hands quivering, virtually ignored.

Don Fraser employed countless promotional gimmicks during his long career as a boxing publicist, but pinning that cheap button on Clay may have been his "greatest."

COUNTING PRE- and post-Olympics coverage, Dwyer and his staff produced 24 issues of that special section, each consisting of about 44 pages of event schedules and results, columns and in-depth features, on-the-spot news stories and photos, many of them spectacular. At a post Games party, Dwyer gave contributing writers and editors a box of each issue, labeled Olympics '84, fresh-off-the presses.

The Times, it seemed certain, couldn't miss winning a Pulitzer. The question was in what category.

As it turned out, none.

"I couldn't figure out why," Dwyer said, and, no doubt, neither could anyone else at the paper.

"Years later," Dwyer confided, "Dave Laventhal became our publisher, coming from New York Newsday. One day, shortly after he arrived, he dropped into my office and said he had a story to tell me.

"He said that, in 1985, he had been one of the Pulitzer judges. He said that when the process began, The Times entry of Olympic sections, in the box that we handed out afterward, had been put on a table as things were being discussed, and the sentiment in the room was that it would have to win something, but they'd just decide on the category later.

"Then, they got involved in the process and got all the way to the finals and had all the categories filled when somebody looked up, saw the box still sitting there, and realized they had forgotten about the entry. They decided it was too late to do anything—finalists had all been notified—and so we just got screwed."

Dwyer punctuated his remarks with bitterness.

"Ever since," he said, "I have had little regard for the credibility of the awards or what they allegedly stand for."

Chapter 40

Nostalgia Editor

While the Times had plenty of critics among its readers, it also had an abundance of them in the Calendar section. Because of limited space, critics on the "B list" often groused about their stories being trimmed, sometimes killed. But when articles bearing the bylines of Chuck Champlin, Martin Bernheimer and Robert Hilburn came across the copy desk, makeup editors found sufficient room at the expense of most everything else.

Champlin, a Harvard graduate who had written for *Time* and *Life* magazines before becoming the Times' entertainment editor in 1965, specialized in the motion picture industry and soon became the paper's top film critic. Nonetheless, Kevin Thomas no doubt holds the record for most Times movie reviews, reportedly 16,000 during his 43 years at the paper and four additional years as a freelancer.

Chief music and dance critic Martin Bernheimer, who started at the Times in 1965 and won a Pulitzer for criticism in 1982, focused on opera. No editorial changes in his copy were made without his approval. Howard Rosenberg's TV column also was sacrosanct, especially after his 1985 Pulitzer.

Thanks mainly to Bob Dylan and the Beatles, pop music was becoming an exciting art form that inspired Hilburn to freelance for the Times for four years before being hired by the paper as a full-time critic in the summer of 1970—the same year I arrived in the sports department.

Hilburn became a nationally recognized and highly respected critic—the only music writer to accompany Johnny Cash for his landmark Folsom Prison concert. Hilburn also joined Elton John when he became the first Western rock figure to play in the Soviet Union, was with Paul Simon on his "Graceland" tour stop in Zimbabwe, with Dylan for his first concerts in Israel and with Michael Jackson on much of the Jacksons' Victory tour. Bob also spent a week on the road with the Sex Pistols during their turbulent 1978 U.S. tour, after which the English punk rock band disbanded.

In my mid-50s when I rejoined View and Calendar following the Olympics, I regrettably sloughed off the Beatles, hated rock and roll and once questioned a writer on the "B list" about something he wrote pertaining to Bob *Dielan*.

"It's *Dillan*," he said disgustedly before embarrassing me further.

The generation gap worked both ways, I discovered, when an editor rejected my request to cover a gala event celebrating Bob Crosby's 50th anniversary in show business. The youthful editor's reply left me momentarily speechless.

"Who's Bob Crosby?"

Of course, he had never heard of Bing's brother or Bob's popular big-band orchestra, the Bobcats. I assumed he had heard of Bing, but decided against arguing my case. The event was well covered in other papers, not the Times.

Fortunately, Hilburn and others in power were more supportive.

"We'll call you the Nostalgia Editor," Hilburn said.

With no objections from Jean Taylor or Don Alpert, I began churning out features regularly while working full time on the desks and in composing.

Occasionally I needed to clear interviews with Leonard Feather, a London-born freelancer who learned to play the piano and clarinet as a youngster, started writing about jazz and film by his late teens and served as the Times' chief jazz critic for more than 40 years until his death at age 80.

Leonard focused on traditional jazz singers and musicians, while I wrote about entertainers making comebacks at such places as the intimate Vine St. Bar & Grill in Hollywood.

For a number of years in the mid-and late '80s, that club booked a steady run of aging singers that packed the place—among them 6-foot-4 Herb Jeffries who turned back the clock with his biggest hit, "Flamingo," and hard-luck vocalists Ella Mae Morse, Eartha Kitt and legendary big-band vocalist Anita O'Day.

Blues and boogie-woogie singer Ella Mae Morse fingered a glittering pendant encircling her neck. Shaped like theatrical masks, it was made of gold and brilliantly studded with eight large diamonds.

"My ex-husband gave it to me," she said proudly, "one diamond for each year I've been sober."

For Morse, a top recording star in the '40s and '50s, life took some miserable turns after she stepped out of the spotlight in 1957 to have her fourth child.

Partly responsible for her premature retirement at age 30, she said, was another birth: rock 'n' roll.

"I thought, 'If I record one of those monsters and it becomes a hit, I will leave the country.' I couldn't make head nor tails of it. But a lot of kids grew up on that and thought it was great."

Ella Mae, who had six children along with countless hangovers before giving up alcohol permanently, appeared with Ray McKinley's orchestra each year at Disneyland since 1971 and had spot engagements elsewhere before I met her. But she hadn't worked steadily in years and after her 25-year marriage to her fourth husband ended in 1983 (she married her first at 13), she was on her own and desperate.

Morse cut her first record for Capitol in 1942 when she was only 15. Her recording of "Cow-Cow Boogie," backed by Freddie Slack's band, proved a huge success. She recorded many other big sellers for Capitol over 15 years, including "Blacksmith Blues," "House of Blue Lights" and "Mister Five by Five."

A thank-you note expressed her sincere gratitude "from my heart" for that 10-inch 1985 article buried on Page 2. She died in 1999 at 75.

Charlene and I met Eartha Kitt when she, too, was headlining at that Vine Street dinner club.

Almost terminating the dressing-room interview before it

Former amateur boxer Tony Danza, star of the TV hit "Who's the Boss?" shares a laugh with Jack, who featured the actor in a 1985 L.A. Times article.

Patti Page revisits Jack and Charlene backstage after her 1995 concert at the Sundome in Sun City West, Arizona.

Jack visits singer/actress Suzanne Somers after her performance in Sun City West, Arizona.

Singer/actress Anna Maria Alberghetti shares a moment with Jack and Charlene at a play's intermission in Long Beach, California. Jack holds a photo taken at the singer's home during an earlier interview.

began, the singer disliked a racially-charged question which taught me to save controversial ones for last. An excerpt of the story that ran on Page 1 of Calendar March 20, 1986:

Her hair was pinned up at weird angles, and a makeup artist was darting in and out with brushes and eye pencils between her words—no simple task.

For Kitt's words often come with machine-gun rapidity, particularly when the subject is heavy. And sometimes they get her in trouble, such as the celebrated incident in 1968, when she spoke out against the Vietnam War at a White House luncheon during the Johnson Administration. She still claims she was blacklisted in the industry as a result.

Then there was the report a few years later that the CIA had a long dossier on her, and again her career suffered.

Eartha Kitt doesn't mince words about much of anything—racial prejudices, civil rights, even her age...

"Numbers are for a calendar. What matters is how you feel."

On more important subjects, the turmoil in South Africa, for instance, Kitt—born on a cotton plantation in South Carolina—left no doubts about her feelings.

"I was the first artist to break the apartheid rules," she said, recalling her trip to South Africa in 1974, when she refused to perform in front of a segregated audience.

She remembered drinking champagne on stage, then passing the glass to front-row spectators, black and white; each took a sip and passed it on.

"It was not permitted," she said, "but I did it. Once you break a precedent, the precedent is broken. When I first worked in Las Vegas, we could not go through the front door. We had to go through the kitchen. The people of South Africa need a Martin Luther King. (She marched with him in Atlanta.)...

"Hatred is going to be passed on. In the end, the people themselves will have to do it (gain their freedom). They will have to help themselves."...

The interview ended perhaps prematurely, but after all, it was show time.

Minutes later, the singer stepped on stage, her personality—and appearance—having changed as effortlessly as shifting gears.

Makeup in place, hair suitably styled, a sexy, black-sequined gown and heels replacing the drab robe and sneakers, Kitt batted her lashes and began purring those familiar sounds heard for decades.

After an enduring career that spanned theater, cabaret,

television and the recording industry, Eartha Kitt died on Christmas Day, 2008, at age 80.

Anita O'Day, interviewed at the Hollywood club in 1988 before her closing show, also told it like it was after almost 55 years of ups and downs.

Singer Anita O'Day reminisces with Jack and his wife in her Hollywood night club dressing room.

Signed by drummer Gene Krupa as a virtual unknown in 1941, O'Day remained five years before joining Stan Kenton and other bands.

"The big-band years," she said, smiling, "I really miss them."

Asked about her health generally, she didn't mince words. "I'm old," she replied pungently, "sixty-nine, and spell it out—s-i-x-t-y n-i-n-e."

Born Anita Colton in 1919 in Chicago, she changed her name to O'Day early in life. Her reason: O'Day was the pig-Latin pronunciation for the word dough, of which she expected to accumulate considerable. And for a period, she did.

"I made $100,000 a year for nine years with Verve (Records)," she said, but "my partner took it, my manager took it, my husbands took it, my road manager took it, the government got it and I helped spend some of it.

"Four years ago, I had $200 to my name. Now I have $300, but I don't owe anyone."

Single since 1952, with no living relatives, she lives alone in the desert community of Hemet because "it's quiet, I get a lot of rest and the price is right, $138 a month.... I own my trailer, I own my '68 Pontiac, and I own my dog, a Yorkie terrier. What else do you need?"

For O'Day, there was one other need.

"The stage," she acknowledged, *"that's my life. I come alive when I have that going."*

O'Day's 1981 autobiography, *High Times, Hard Times,* focused on her heroin addiction two decades earlier. She died in 2006 at 87.

For Charlene, my transfer to entertainment fulfilled much of our social life together more so than ever before, now that our kids had grown and had their own families—dinners at the Bar & Grill and other restaurants and occasional out-of-town junkets, such as a particularly interesting Las Vegas assignment.

The McGuire Sisters: The Las Vegas Hilton Hotel elevator opened on the 15ᵗʰ floor, where a burly armed bodyguard greeted my wife and me, escorted us down the empty hallway and admitted us to the suite for my interview with the three bubbly sisters who had reserved the entire floor.

The McGurire Sisters—from left, Christine, Phyllis and Dorothy—with Jack and Charlene during the trio's 1986 comeback at the Las Vegas Hilton Hotel.

Making a showbiz comeback that year, 1986, the sisters, particularly Phyllis, were still edgy about previous ties to organized crime—specifically Mafia kingpin Sam Giancana. During the interview Phyllis recounted in detail her affair with Giancana, saying, among other things, *"I'm still close with his family, his three daughters."*

Three years later, during an interview in Los Angeles, she quickly dismissed the subject that still fascinated the media 14 years after Giancana was murdered.

Simply stated, she had no regrets. She loved him. Period.

Singer Kay Starr: *The voice is distinctive—strong, earthy, familiar to millions over the last half-century as a country singer, big-band vocalist, recording artist, concert soloist, lounge entertainer...*

Kay Starr and Jack beam for L.A Times photographer George Rose during Jack's 1988 interview. Starr's rendition of Wheel of Fortune helped make her a top pop star in the early '50s.

Seemingly, Kay Starr has covered most of the musical bases, highlighted by her No. 1 hit record, Wheel of Fortune, *which made her one of the top female pop stars of the early '50s.*

Despite her acclaim as a singer, she is, in her words, simply a storyteller, an actress playing a role, set to music.

But, once upon a time, something happened in the musical world that disturbed Starr—or, at least, frustrated her. Someone picked up an electric guitar and, suddenly, there were no stories.

"I sing things that have a beginning, middle and end," she says. "Rock, hard rock and acid rock didn't tell a story, just, 'I got you, Babe. I got you, Babe.' I was too old to be standing up there doing 'I got you, Babe.'"

Kay decided to step down. For a full year she became involved in a variety of activities, including an exciting six-week African safari in Mozambique, where she killed a greater kudu, whose spiraled horns were large enough to get her name engraved on a wall in the Safari Club.

But singing was what she enjoyed most, so she returned to work and forged ahead, full-throttle.

Interviewed at the edge of her Bel-Air home pool in 1988, Kay sipped white wine and reminisced, acknowledging matter-of-factly that her personal "Wheel of Fortune" was spinning as profitably as her hit recording did more than 35 years earlier.

Besides her home—which she bought for about $65,000 in 1955—she listed a Rolls-Royce, a Mercedes and a million-dollar profit on the recent sale of a home in Honolulu among her assets.

On the downside, she declined to list the number of her failed marriages.

"Yes, I've been married a number of times. I've been married enough. Let's put it that way. I want to tell you I'm not proud at my age (66) to be turned out in the traffic again."

Singer Perry Como: Speaking from Portland one lazy summer afternoon in 1985, Perry had a lot to say about his life and coming engagement at the Greek Theatre in Los Angeles, where Charlene and I visited with him after the show.

You could almost envision the scene: Perry Como stretched out on a long sofa, belt loosened, shoes off, eyes closed, the phone propped up on a pillow next to his ear....

At 73, he seems to be cruising along smoothly as ever at half-speed, feeling fine and enjoying life...

He recalled an accident in 1971, when he fell from a stage while taping a Christmas show in Los Angeles, broke his knee and was laid up with a cast on his leg for six months.

"I got up to 210 pounds. My cocktail hour was 7 o'clock in the morning... ate pizza, waffles, pancakes. I had a helluva time—looked like a sumo wrestler...

"I feel like George Burns. What is it he says? When I get up in the morning, I look in the paper and if my name isn't in the obituary column, I shave.

"I once asked George why he didn't chase after women his own age, and he said, 'Hell, there aren't any my age.'"

311

Como laughed.

"That," he said, "is the attitude I want to have when I'm 89."

Como died in his sleep in 2001—six days before his 89th birthday.

Actress Ann Blyth: *A waiter led the way—skirting the edge of the busy dining room and on through an iron-grate opening to a secluded nook, where a single VIP table had been reserved.*

Actress Ann Blyth craved a Cobb salad

Ann Blyth had insisted on the Brown Derby for lunch because, she said, she yearned for a Cobb salad....

But it was more than salad that appealed to the actress. It was the atmosphere of an earlier era—the caricatures of former Hollywood greats on the wall, the soft music and special attention—a nostalgic, familiar setting for a brief rendezvous with yesteryear.

Like a scene out of the Twilight Zone, *Blyth suddenly appeared at the table, her star image of the '40s and '50s untarnished by age.*

At 57, she verily glowed—hair meticulously styled atop her head, long, polished nails, fluttering lashes, makeup tastefully applied, pearls, a few diamonds, a blue jacket, a brightly colored size-4 dress and white hose and heels..."

She spoke reluctantly about an osteomyelitis operation as an infant, about being abandoned by her father at age 10, a broken back suffered in a tobogganing mishap at 17, studio suspensions, the deaths of her mother and, more recently, an aunt who helped raise her, the serious illness of her husband about four years ago, difficulties raising her own family and a current hypothyroid problem involving 'my grandbaby.'

Eyes moist, Blyth preferred to change the subject. She finished her salad and stepped outside, leaving the memories behind. Once again, it was Hollywood, 1985.

Just then a young fan approached the actress, extended a pen and asked, "May I have your autograph?"

Smiling, she graciously obliged. The timing, it seemed, was perfect.

Actress Dorothy Lamour: The last time I saw the once curvaceous film star—best remembered, perhaps, for cavorting around the islands in a dazzling Tahitian sarong with Hope and Crosby—she was performing at Marriott's Santa Barbara Biltmore Hotel, a luxurious 21-acre resort sprawled along the seashore. She was celebrating her 50th year in show business, closing fast on age 69.

There was nothing pretentious about Dorothy, a feisty gal who pulled no punches. She died in 1996 at age 81 at her modest, three-bedroom North Hollywood home, which—at the time I met her—had a grass shack but no swimming pool.

She had few secrets. Her autobiography, *My Side of the Road*, published by Prentice-Hall in 1980, *sank almost without a trace*, according to a librarian at *Publisher's Weekly* in New York.

"It was too clean...," said Lamour, who provided the media with little if any gossip during her 35-year marriage to William Ross Howard III, who died in 1978.

A capsule of her life: Born in a charity ward of a New Orleans hospital in 1914... "Miss New Orleans" at 14... Chicago department store elevator operator... married 2 ½ years to band leader Herbie Kay, who discovered her... singer, actress, the Bond Bombshell who sold $300 million worth of World War II bonds, etc.

Although Dorothy Lamour appeared in about 60 other movies, it was her *Road* pictures with which she was most closely identified.

"We only count six," she said, "because 'Hong Kong' created such a bomb."

313

Singer Helen Reddy: *Although seldom quoted about her strong beliefs in reincarnation, psychic phenomena and "out-of-body" experiences, Reddy said she talks about such things if asked. But apparently, she maintains a profile somewhat lower than that of Shirley MacLaine, for example.*

"I believe we switch back and forth constantly," she said. "I've had more male lives than female."

Singer/Dancer Sammy Davis, Jr.: Interviewed on the phone before his 1986 Christmas concert in Long Beach that included a cast of more than 1,200 singers, dancers, musicians and gospel choirs representing 22 countries, Sammy was in the twilight of his career.

Sammy Davis, Jr., hosts Jack's daughter and grandkids in his dressing room after a Long Beach concert. From left are Sarah and Jennifer Mann, their mom Patty and Charlene, lost in the background.

He's 61 now, finally a grandparent, and doesn't pretend to be younger.

However, there are times the energetic "Candy Man" who has brightened stages all over the world for more than half a century may feel much older.

A year ago, for instance, he underwent a hip reconstruction operation that put his golf game on temporary hold, among other activities.

His dancing shoes have been gathering dust for some time, and earlier this week, dental work was temporarily affecting his speaking voice, if not his singing.

Davis had three titanium screws inserted into his jaw during oral surgery last week and on Tuesday he was feeling less than good.

"I've been slowing down considerably," he said matter-of-factly through a swollen jaw. "Last year I worked 29 weeks and this year about the same.

"I'm not hiding in a cave, though. I work Vegas and Tahoe, Reno, occasionally Atlantic city…"

Normally Davis takes the Christmas season off, he said, but agreed to do the Long Beach show because it is being produced and directed by a longtime friend and will include performances by "500 to 800 kids from all over the world who now live here.

"*It's their baby," he added. "It belongs to the kids of the world as opposed to Sammy Davis Jr."*

When Charlene, our daughter Patty and two of her four youngsters—Jennifer and Sarah—visited Davis in his dressing room after the show, he bounced our grandkids on his knee and sipped on A & W Root Beer he had ordered before his performance.

He said he allowed himself a glass of wine occasionally, but not when working. A heavy smoker most of his life, Sammy said he was trying to cut down and stopped smoking on stage.

"Trying?"

"Hey, man," he replied, "one thing at a time."

Sometime later, Davis invited Charlene and me and our other daughters, Linda and Barbara, and their husbands to a dinner show he headlined at Harrah's in Reno. Typically, his rousing performance brought the audience to its feet with bursting applause. Sammy showed no signs of fatigue on stage, but I suspect by then the disease was taking effect to some extent. In any event, he was not up to another dressing room visit.

Sammy lasted three years after that Long Beach concert, finally losing his battle with throat cancer at 64.

I'll always remember that half-hour dressing room chat with "Mr. Bojangles"—a showbiz dynamo of small stature, gold dangling from his neck, glittering rings, a booming voice and a giant heart.

Singer Dinah Shore: One of my favorite entertainers, Dinah placed a dozen brownies she had whipped up on the coffee table when I interviewed her at her country club home in Rancho Mirage, Calif., where she was hosting her 14th annual Nabisco Dinah Shore LPGA golf tournament in 1985.

Singer Dinah Shore joins Jack, her golf partner, on a patio overlooking the 18th green following Nabisco's Media Golf Day at Rancho Mirage, California, in 1985.

Author of two best-selling cookbooks, a gifted painter whose work was exhibited at the California Museum of Science and Industry among other places, no stranger to large-corporation board rooms as a director and involved in numerous other activities unrelated to showbiz, Dinah seemed happiest swinging a golf club.

"Admitting to a 24-handicap when I shared her cart for 18 holes in a pro-am event at the plush Palm Desert, Calif., layout, she added, "but it's going down. I've become a real golf bum."

The singer said she granted few interviews dealing with her personal life, believing "numbers and statistics" unimportant.

"But your fans would like to know, Dinah," I said when trying to clarify her age. "I have two books that don't agree on when you were born."

"I'm not going to tell you," she said as she grabbed a club from her bag with a broad smile. Now tell me if I'm swinging this thing right."

Born Frances Rose Shore Feb. 29, 1916, in Winchester, Tenn., Dinah died Feb. 24, 1994, after a brief battle with cancer. She fought her illness with the same dignity and privacy that she had lived with in her life.

Dancer Mitzi Gaynor: Published on the front page of Calendar June 25, 1988, my feature focused on Mitzi's return to a Southern California venue after a 16-year absence.

At 55, the perky entertainer danced up a storm at the Valley Music Theatre, an intimate Woodland Hills theater-in-the round. Her act included a slapstick comedy routine, which noticeably detracted from her sizzling, sexy performance.

"Stick to dancing, Mitzi," I suggested, with a smile, of course.

Admittedly a ham, she enjoyed playing a goofball role on stage, probably a refreshing diversion from decades of pounding the boards. Despite my criticism, we became friends and exchanged Christmas cards for years.

When I first interviewed Mitzi, also a gourmet cook, at the Beverly Hills home she shared with her husband—an incurable sports fanatic—I spent much of the evening talking to him while she prepared a snack in the kitchen.

"I'm Mitzi Gaynor on the road and Mrs. Jack Bean at home," she said when she arrived with a tray of hors d'oeuvres. "Jack says I'm a cook who can sing and dance."

Accordionist Dick Contino: After rediscovering the musician performing at a small restaurant/bar in the San Fernando Valley in 1982, I wrote an in-depth feature published on the cover of the Sunday Calendar.

The article probed Contino's disappearance on the eve of his induction into the Army that led to a $10,000 fine, 4 ½ months jail time in a federal penitentiary and, he claimed, being blackballed as an entertainer.

During interviews, his dramatic life story evoked tears from his eyes when he talked about his actress/wife dying of cancer.

My feature rejuvenated Contino's career, which had been in shambles for decades. Las Vegas bookings, however, didn't last. His famous version of *Lady of Spain* and other former hits failed to capture the attention of younger audiences. But for Contino, the Times story was a high point in his troubled life.

Singer Jo Stafford: One of my most enjoyable interviews was in 1986 at the Bel-Air home of a member of the original Pied Pipers, and her husband, arranger-composer-conductor Paul Weston—but the assignment was difficult.

Recommended by Chuck Champlin, I was hired by a New York freelancer to write Stafford's biography and liner notes for her forthcoming album, listed as the 14th in a *Time-Life* music project called Legendary Singers. His name was Harvey B. Loomis, whom I never met. We spoke on the phone and corresponded by mail.

The first of his lengthy letters emphasized strict requirements for brevity.

"The space for the bio is so limited that you'll barely have room to turn around," he wrote. "Nevertheless, it should:

1—"Establish why Stafford belongs in this series, i.e., why she is legendary, and catalogue her historical niche in the popular music world.

2—"Present a roughly chronological biography, mostly highlights, but including just enough details for an intimate feel; not avoiding, but not dwelling on down-side events.

3—"Essay a short and serious, if not technical, analysis of Stafford's talent and particular musical strengths. What you say here should be reinforced where possible by specific references in the Notes of the songs.

"That's a full bill for 225 40-character lines, which is what the Bio runs. I'd be glad to have you go over that a bit, though, and I'll trim to size. The Notes run 210 44-character lines, including the byline. That comes to about nine lines per song—there are 22 cuts in each album. Each song gets one paragraph, which can vary depending on the importance of the song or the richness of the material on it.... The paragraphs don't form a continuous narrative, but of course any inter-references and lead-in transitions that you can work out will improve the whole..."

Etcetera, etcetera, etcetera...

My work was rewritten extensively—by me and Harvey—before it was approved by Stafford, her husband and the *Time-Life* people, none of whom ever contacted me directly.

An excerpt of the final product:

Jo Stafford virtually retired from her professional career in the mid-1960s, but the lustrous memory of her singing stays bright for the millions who knew her as the queen of the big-band era. From 1940 to 1955, according to the Billboard charts, Jo was the best-selling female vocalist in the country—the first female recording artist to sell 25 million records, and at one time, the only singer with two separately sponsored weekly radio programs. With the advent of television, Jo was one of the first singers—along with Dinah Shore and Perry Como—to have her own program, **The Jo Stafford Show.**

Flawless intonation and perceptive phrasing are her musical trademarks, and to anyone with half an ear, her voice is unmistakable. Within the music business her reputation is formidable. When Ella Fitzgerald began her first recording session with Paul Weston, she admitted to being nervous, because, as she put it, "if I sing out of tune, you'll go home and tell your old lady."

I was paid $800. I have no idea what Harvey B. Loomis received.

Chapter 41

The Andrews Sisters

E asily my most disappointing writing project during more than two decades at the Times was one that never made it into print. The following is part of that story, written for the Sunday Calendar section in the summer of 1989:

Since they last performed together in the Broadway musical "Over Here" 14 years ago, Patty and Maxene Andrews have scarcely spoken to each other.

Maxene Andrews gives Jack an exclusive interview.

But the bitterness goes much deeper, tracing to the early 1950s, long before LaVerne Andrews died of cancer at age 54.

In an exclusive interview, Maxene speaks about the feud in depth. Patty and her husband Walter Weschler declined to be interviewed for this article, responding to written excerpts of Maxene's taped interview through their lawyer. "...My clients state emphatically that there is not a word of truth in any of Maxene's remarks," attorney Stephen J. Rawson wrote in a letter to the Times. "More important than merely being false, these charges are also a source of great pain and suffering."

Maxene Andrews—saying she definitely has not retired and probably never will—nonetheless recently moved to a "beautiful," sparsely populated area among tall pines, east of Sacramento. She had lived in the Southland for half a century, the last 14 years practically a neighbor of her sister Patty, a Northridge resident. But the physical distance between them—five miles or 500—hardly seems to matter. They have been estranged for years.

"I have intentionally stayed away from talking about the feud," Maxene said, "because I had hoped that maybe in just the silence there would be a time that Patty and I could get back together again and just become sisters. But it seems the longer it has gone on, the bigger the breach has become."

When first contacted, Maxene and Patty both agreed to Calendar interviews, but after Maxene had gone on record, Patty and her husband had second thoughts and canceled.

Since recovering from a near fatal heart attack and quadruple bypass surgery in 1982, Maxene, 73, has kept busy—concerts, tours, cruise ship bookings, PBS appearances, one-nighters and TV commercials here and abroad.

Now, however, she is recuperating from surgery in April—an operation to relieve pain that had been intensifying for 15 years as a result of an injury. It occurred during rehearsals for "Over Here," the Broadway show that reunited her with Patty...

"At one point I was in such pain that at intermission, I just sat on the stage and wept," Maxene remembered. "And Patty came over. She was very concerned. I said, 'Honey, I can't do it. I just can't do it.' So I was off for about two days, I think, or three days. And she showed concern, but no visits."

The Andrews Sisters' voices had a distinctive, joyful, upbeat sound—a natural blend that captivated audiences around the globe. On

**When the Andrews Sisters—Maxene, Patty and LaVerne, from left—
entertained troops during World War II, servicemen at home and abroad
literally hung from rafters in makeshift showrooms for a glimpse of the trio.**

stage, they created an aura of happiness, a clear impression of what appeared to be a close sibling relationship off stage, as well.

For many years, it was precisely that—until about 1948, when Patty married Marty Melcher, who, Maxene said, caused friction among the singers and other family members.

"I have nothing very good to say about him," she added. The couple divorced after 2½ years. Melcher later married another famous singer, Doris Day, and in 1952, Patty married Walter Weschler, the trio's accompanist-arranger. It was then, Maxene believes, that "attitudes began to change."

Maxene used the words power and control repeatedly in describing how, in her opinion, Weschler came between her and Patty, not only on a professional level but also in family affairs.

Based on numerous interviews, Maxene's opinion of Weschler's influence is shared by others. Typical was a comment by Ken Waissman, one of the producers of "Over Here."

"If he (Weschler) hadn't been in the picture," Waissman said in a recent telephone conversation from New York, "it seems they (Maxene

and Patty) wouldn't have had all the problems they had with their careers and in their private lives. Patty was totally under his influence."

Maxene had been excited about appearing on Broadway when approached about the musical. Bette Midler had revived one of the Andrews Sisters' biggest hits, "Boogie Woogie Bugle Boy," which ultimately brought Maxene out of virtual retirement....

"It was always my dream for the Andrews Sisters to do a Broadway show because we had done everything else," she said, "more than any other harmony group had ever achieved."

Although Maxene and Patty shared equal billing, it was Patty and her husband who attempted to call all the shots, Maxene said—from initial contract negotiations with producers Waissman and Maxine Fox to their stage performances.

According to Maxene, Weschler offered to be her agent along with representing Patty. Instead, she acquired a Los Angeles-based agent affiliated with a New York agency "who merely did the paperwork. Everything had already been decided.

"I was the girl that was to be hired for salary," Maxene continued, her tone reflecting the deep bitterness that hasn't diminished with the passing of time.

Maxene said the sisters had always shared salaries equally, but "Patty refused to do the show unless she got some of my percentage and some of the songwriter's percentage. She had to get more.

"I was on the verge of tears because I was so upset. I couldn't believe it was my sister sitting there saying this."

Maxene's business manager, Linda Wells, said Patty earned $1,000 more a week than Maxene and 7% of the net receipts, compared to 3% for Maxene.

"It became a standing joke (among the company)," said Waissman, who confirmed that Patty received more money. He recalled that someone had drawn a large cartoon and sent it to him after the show closed. It showed caricatures of Patty and Maxene standing in line at an unemployment insurance office. The one labeled Patty was captioned, 'What do you mean your unemployment money is the same as mine?"

Waissman also remembered having to pay Weschler "$500 or $600" to replace the regular piano player for the third act in which the sisters sang a medley of their former hits.

"Patty said it was impossible for her to sing with another pianist," Waissman recalled, "but when Walter's mother was injured in a car accident and he was gone for two days, she had no problem performing with another pianist."

There were times, Maxene remembered, when Patty expressed sisterly love—but not often.

"There would be nights when she wouldn't even touch me, and I knew, instinctively I knew that he (Weschler) must be hiding someplace watching her," Maxene said. "He has done everything he could to ruin the Andrews Sisters. Everything!"

"Over Here" ended its New York run in 1975 after 348 performances, then was to go on the road for another year. However, the tour was abruptly canceled.

After the show closed, Weschler—who was credited for his "creative contribution" to the title number and two other songs—filed a lawsuit claiming he'd written four songs by the play's composers, Richard and Robert Sherman. The case was heard in a New York court in December of 1976. Judge Whitman Knapp ruled in favor of the Shermans....

About 18 months ago, the feud flared anew when an L.A. monthly magazine reported that Patty had reneged on an agreement to work with a writer on her autobiography. Among the details Patty revealed during a taped interview, the article stated, was how the sisters found themselves "practically penniless" because Maxene had mismanaged their financial affairs.

Infuriated by the story, Maxene wrote to Weschler, stating that "as all of us well know, I have never at any time managed your financial affairs." She proposed a meeting "so we can all have our say."

A month later, Weschler responded by letter. He rejected the idea of a meeting.

During the disastrous 1961 Bel-Air fire that destroyed hundreds of homes all but seven of the Andrews Sisters' 19 gold records were destroyed. Decca, Maxene said, wouldn't replace them.

She shrugged, as if the loss isn't important now. But in the '40s, when Patty, Maxene and LaVerne were on top of the pop music world, gold records were important—to them and to millions of their fans.

The hottest singing group in show business from 1938—when their recording of the Yiddish love song "Bei Mir Bist Du Schoen" catapulted the trio to fame—through the 1940s, the Andrews Sisters have recorded, by some counts, 90 hit singles, sold about 75 million records worldwide and appeared in 21 movies.

When they changed into their smartly tailored Class A Army uniforms and marched off to entertain troops during World War II, servicemen at home and abroad literally hung from rafters in makeshift showrooms to get a glimpse of their act.

Patty sang melody, clearly dominating the trio with her bubbly personality, while the more reserved Maxene and LaVerne provided the rich harmony.

"To me and to LaVerne and to the world, Patty was the best lead singer of any girl singer around, any girl singer," Maxene emphasized. "Patty was wonderful. There was never any jealousy in the act.... We were always proud of Patty. Patty was a clown. Patty was a comic. Patty was a happy-go-lucky young girl."

But that was the swinging '40s, an exciting era when they laughed together... and sometimes cried together.

Times changed and so did the Andrews Sisters.

In 1954, for example, they created headlines when they tangled in a Long Beach courtroom over the estate of their late parents.

Patty claimed LaVerne, the executrix, failed to distribute personal property from the estates. Maxene sided with LaVerne, and Patty was backed by her husband, Weschler.

Ultimately the judge denied Patty's petition.

In the early stages of their career, the trio was managed by Lou Levy, who married Maxene in 1941. They had two children.

Levy eventually left the act to devote full time to his mushrooming music publishing business, and the marriage ended in divorce after about 10 years.

Contacted in New York, Levy commented, "He (Weschler) ruined a great, great act, and you can quote me in spades."

Lou Rogers, a former trumpet player who was married to LaVerne for 19 years, agreed.

"Weschler pulled the act apart," he said during a recent phone call. "He ankled the act. That's an old show business expression. He was responsible for breaking them up."

Maxene said Patty left the group to go on her own several times. "The first time, she returned after about a year...."

Meanwhile, the sisters had been going through a lengthy, "financially devastating," fight with the Internal Revenue Service, which began in the early 1950s and lasted almost a decade. Maxene blamed the trio's tax problems—the federal government sued the singers to recover $230,424 in back taxes for the years 1949 through 1953—on bad management decisions by accountants and others they relied upon.

In order to pay their delinquent taxes, the trio had to remain intact to generate enough income. Eventually, Weschler demanded one-fourth interest in the act, Maxene said, and she and LaVerne reluctantly consented.

"Patty was qualified to sing alone. LaVerne and I had not had that experience. She could do a solo; LaVerne and I were unprepared to do anything."

They signed a one-year contract because "He had us up against the wall. Then after that year, it wasn't working. LaVerne and I had no more rights. They weren't discussing anything with us. Wally and Patty were making the decisions. The anger within me kept building and building and building..."

Maxene said her last engagement with LaVerne was in September, 1966—one year before LaVerne died of cancer.

Maxene continued singing with Patty and a relatively unknown replacement, Joyce DeYoung, "who was wonderful." But the strain of working with Patty and Weschler became unbearable, Maxene said, and after about a year she left to teach at Lake Tahoe.

"What this man has done," she said, "is completely isolate Patty from anybody except himself.... So all she hears is the poison that he has been putting in her ear....

"My sister has changed," she added, her voice quavering. "She has changed from a happy, talented, wonderful girl to somebody that I really don't want to know, somebody who is rude, somebody who is very self-centered, somebody who can be ugly and somebody who is very shy of love."

Maxene Andrews, who last resided in Auburn, California, died Oct. 21, 1995, after suffering a heart attack while vacationing on Cape Cod. She was 79.

Patty and Walter, married Christmas Day, 1951, still resided in Northridge as of 2010. Patty celebrated her 92nd birthday, Feb. 16, 2010.

After several rewrites of this article following close scrutiny by Times lawyers, the Sunday Calendar editor, John Lindsay, decided not to publish it.

"Our lawyers say the paper could be sued if we run this," John said. "They say they're confident we would win but wonder if the story is worth going to court over. I'm sorry. We're going to have to scratch it."

I was paid a kill fee of $500—the largest kill fee Calendar ever paid a writer, according to Lindsay.

Chapter 42

A Year of Ups and Downs

Along about 1987, the Times began to tighten its financial belt, sparking rumors that the annual budget for merit raises had been slashed throughout editorial.

I never got a merit raise under Bill Shirley during my 10 years in sports, but never failed to get one in 11 years in View.

Until 1987, the guessing game for everyone on the copy desk, I suppose, was the amount of our raises. But that year, no one felt comfortable when called into Don Alpert's office to get the official word. Since pensions were determined by salaries at the time of retirement, merit hikes were particularly meaningful.

Asked to explain the merit-raise process after he left the paper, Don said that each year Jean Taylor would be allocated a certain sum of money to divide.

"She would ask me to submit my recommendations and the amount," he said. "We often discussed each individual choice, but ultimately it was Jean Taylor's decision.

"I called everyone into the office one at a time and let them know whether they would get a merit raise or not. I would say it was a fair process without too many complaints."

In 1987, however, if not complaints, there were major disappointments.

Upon exiting Alpert's office after an unusually long discussion,

328

Jean Wudke, who worked next to me, was visibly shaken, her eyes welling.

"Did you get a raise?" she asked me bluntly.

Searching for comforting words, I found none and simply answered without comment: "I did."

"I'm not sure why Wudke didn't get a merit raise that year," Alpert said, "but outside of doing a good job editing Jack Smith's column, she didn't do a hell of a lot more. She got her share of raises but once in a while, she slacked off."

Wudke soon transferred to the travel department, and I inherited her duties—mainly processing Jack Smith's column.

After 25 years at the paper, Jean retired in 1992. Seven years later, she died from a heart attack at age 77.

Stock market investors, of which I was one, also will remember 1987 as the year when the Dow Jones industrial average dived 508 points on Oct. 19—"the biggest one-day plunge in history," the Times reported.

"Fear and panic of historic proportions overwhelmed the stock market Monday," the Oct. 20 banner story began. "The Dow Jones average lost almost a quarter of its value, nearly doubling the percentage drop that occurred on Oct. 28, 1929, the crash that preceded the Great Depression."

Even as I write this more than two decades later, memories linger of those dreadful days when I signed a contract for a second loan on our house, paid double-digit interest rates, traded stocks on margin and bought and sold options—sometimes getting in and out the same day.

My propensity to gamble aside, had it not been for that TV monitor on the copy desk that kept editors instantly informed of Wall Street's current ups-and-downs—from the market's opening bell to its close—I doubt I would have been making daily phone calls to Charles Schwab.

The truth is, it was exciting.

I wasn't the only editor mesmerized by that bullish ticker tape. Leading up to the crash, many of us were profiting handsomely.

Among other heavy investors was fellow editor Ed Sakamoto, who became a close friend. Ed didn't trade on margin and steered away from options, thereby escaping total calamity, unlike me. That black Monday and subsequent margin calls all but wiped

329

out my portfolio.

For my wife, those were the darkest of days. Charlene was riding high when sizeable returns on options enabled me to pay off the second loan only days before the crash.

But when telegrams from the brokerage house began to appear in our mailbox, when I arose in the dark to check the opening of the Tokyo exchange and when I wrote large checks to meet margin calls...well, she reacted as if her world had collapsed.

Nothing I could say dried her tears. I was in the doldrums, too, of course. But my optimistic nature gave me hope for a quick recovery.

"Honey, it was mostly a 'paper loss,' not our savings," I tried to explain. "We still have a good retirement fund. I'm still buying savings bonds through payroll deduction. Believe me, the market will turn around. We'll be fine."

My words swept past her like wind-blown winter leaves.

Meanwhile, life at the paper became dreary. Between editing jobs in the morning, I watched the market continue to slide. When work slowed in the afternoons, I drank too much coffee and resorted to unproductive activities.

One day while thumbing through a Writers Guild of America newsletter, my eye caught the name of a TV executive producer I had known when he was story editor for *The Fugitive* and rejected my freelance submission—Phil Saltzman. He planned to conduct a weekly seminar at his Westwood home and invited a small group of writers with a few credits.

Saltzman once suggested I enroll in a writing class to improve my technical skills, but regrettably I never did. Had it been his decision instead of producer Bill Gordon's to buy my *12 O'clock High* script in 1966, I never would have sold it.

In the summer of 1987, however, there I was in Phil's living room with a few others pitching an idea that seemed to drop from the sky like an out-of-control elevator.

It was nothing more than a spur-of-the-moment notion, but Saltzman and others thought it had the potential for an episode of *The Twilight Zone*. The resurrected series was created by one of television's most prolific writers, Rod Serling. It ran from 1959 to 1964 when 148 episodes were televised.

I shared my idea with my friend Ed Sakamoto, who had some

minor success as a part-time playwright. He liked it; we shook hands and put our heads together to develop a shooting script.

With so much down time between editing copy on the desk, we were able to work for long periods each day on the teleplay.

Titled *Going Up,* the story centered on Michael, a fiercely ambitious 26-year-old attorney employed by a firm in a New York high-rise building.

He barely misses a crowded elevator one morning, then finds a weirdly appointed empty one down the hall. It's operated by a pasty-faced butler-type named Jason.

"Going up, sir?"

Michael peers in, looks puzzled but enters.

Stopping at the 12th floor, the elevator doors slide open. Michael steps out and immediately is transformed as a bespectacled, bookish 12-year-old. He relives a horrible experience as a boy victimized by a couple of rowdies.

Young Michael is chased down the hallway. He narrowly escapes through the closing doors of Jason's mysterious elevator. Immediately he becomes the adult attorney again.

Continuing up, Michael eagerly exits at various levels that correspond to his advancing age. At each floor, he resorts to whatever unscrupulous behavior necessary to further his career, divorcing his beautiful wife in the process.

At age 50 on the 50th floor, Michael is a wealthy, high-powered law firm partner, an overweight alcoholic on the brink of a second divorce.

When he suffers a mild heart attack, Michael becomes frightened, realizes he has wasted his life and struggles toward the waiting elevator.

"Down, Jason, all the way… the lobby."

"Oh, no, sir," Jason replies matter-of-factly. "You can't go down. Would you like to go to the fifty-first floor?"

Michael is visibly stunned. It's a death sentence.

After several rewrites, Ed and I felt it was a can't-miss script. It hit the target dead center. We obtained an agent who submitted our work.

And we waited.

Word finally came—in the form of a letter dated Dec. 14, 1987. Signed by Executive Producer Mark E.A. Shelmerdine, it reads, in part:

"…Like all television series, we have only so many slots we need to fill and the competition for those few slots is intense, in part because the legacy of *The Twilight Zone* attracts some of the most highly-respected talents working in the genre today. I hope you will find it some consolation to learn that your material was considered side by side with the work of some of the finest writers in the business.

"Because the volume of submissions is so high and we have filled most of the available slots, I cannot encourage you to submit more stories for this season. If the series is renewed for additional episodes, I hope you will keep us in mind…."

I had become accustomed to rejections, but this one was the *coup de grace.*

At least that was my immediate reaction.

After the shock subsided, Ed and I collaborated on several other unsuccessful TV projects before I finally, *finally* threw in the towel. We severed our partnership, but being considerably younger than me, Ed resumed working on theatrical plays.

As the stock market began inching back while my financial holdings seemed stuck in limbo, I pondered other ideas to bolster my income, including another story for View.

The editor at the time, a young man named John Brownell, had just arrived from *The Times Magazine* with impressive credentials.

Hired by the paper in 1980, he was, in the words of his colleagues and various editorial executives, a "brilliant editor" destined for an extraordinary journalistic career.

He was bright, handsome, had an infectious smile and was preceded by unfounded snickering rumors.

Initially unaware of those rumors, I sent the new editor an e-mail proposing a story about how the LPGA image was changing on the professional golf tour—basically, attracting more family-oriented players, fewer lesbians.

His curt reply came within minutes: "I think not."

It didn't take long before it was clear he was, indeed, a homosexual.

Soon, a series of features relating to AIDS began dominating front pages of the View section. They were emotionally charged, heart-wrenching stories dealing with the horrible disease, then in its infancy, and its tragic victims.

Ugly jokes targeting Brownell and our section circulated throughout editorial as staff writers continued to provide a steady flow of shocking downbeat articles. They quoted dying AIDS victims, photographed in their final days, alarming statistics on the spreading disease and focused on similar angles.

I got my share of them to edit. Always well-written, they sometimes got to me emotionally. Still, I thought enough was enough.

One afternoon, I looked up from my computer to see Times Editor Bill Thomas and Associate Editor Jean Sharley Taylor escorting a man in his mid-40s past our desk, seemingly showing him around the section.

I learned his identity later when he joined the staff. His name was Shelby Coffey III, which, in itself, impressed me. He spent most of his early newspaper career at the Washington Post. I assumed he shared authority at our end of the corridor with Taylor. Within weeks Coffey was in complete charge.

"He wanted to revamp the copy desk," Alpert recalled. "I told him I thought it was fine as it was. He said he wanted two separate desks, one for View and one for Calendar. I told him that was essentially what we had but it all went through one slot. That way, if one desk got loaded down the other could help, and vice versa.

"He said he wanted two separate desks. I said it would take more editors than what we have. He asked me to diagram the operation. I spent a weekend drawing up two plans, the one we had and the one he wanted. The one he wanted required two or three additional editors and was not as efficient. Also, in the new plan, I eliminated my position. That's the one he went for."

In April of 1988, Times Publisher Tom Johnson named Coffey executive editor of the newspaper, succeeding Thomas, who had retired.

Coffey wasted little time sending Don Alpert to the farthest corner of the opposite end of the third floor, where he started and edited Moscow Fax. It was a compilation of top Times stories available in Moscow the same day they were printed in Los Angeles. At least his assignment wasn't in Siberia.

Alpert believes Coffey's insistence on revamping the copy desks was "a ploy to get me out of there and to increase the influence of John Brownell."

In 1989, Coffey promoted Brownell to assistant managing editor of The Times.

It was about that time John took a long vacation to Rio de Janeiro with a friend. Upon his return, he presided at a small meeting I attended. He appeared shockingly gaunt, seriously ill.

On June 10, 1990, the paper reported that "John Brownell, the youngest journalist in the history of the Los Angeles Times ever to become a top newsroom executive, died Saturday. He was 33.

"Before his condition became terminal, he had written a note to his colleagues at the paper in which he expressed gratitude for 'your heartfelt expression of support and caring…both during my hospitalization for complications of AIDS and my recuperation here at home. I am sorry I cannot thank each of you personally, but I want you to know how deeply appreciative I am.…'"

I liked John, but wasn't as tolerant in those days, I guess. A number of people in View boycotted a memorial service for John at St. Vibiana Catholic Church, a majestic old cathedral a block from the Times.

I was among them. It was a decision I've always regretted.

Chapter 43

An Irresistible Offer

Steve Moore, a brilliant (yes, another brilliant) young View makeup editor half my age, suddenly appeared in the slot one day, sat there impassively, doodling on a pad while the clock ticked.

Had it been me making up the section—or my adversary Vic Johnson (not brilliant, but capable) or my black friend Stan Williford (also capable, but agonizingly s-l-o-w)—we would have started making up the section half an hour earlier.

But Moore, who had been hired to fill the vacancy created by Don Alpert's departure, seemed cool and confident, oblivious to the approaching deadline.

It immediately became clear weeklong tryouts for each of us old timers were nothing more than token trials when Moore showed up unannounced and quickly demonstrated his remarkable computer and page layout skills.

Moore's doodling, I suspected at the time, was roughing out a creative idea for his *In the Bleachers* cartoon strip, which appeared periodically in the section while he marked time in his bread-and-butter job.

Twenty years later, when I communicated with Steve on the Internet, I learned how completely wrong my first impression of him really was.

"I have very fond memories of the days at The Times," Steve wrote in an email. "I was one scared puppy who was just trying to learn and grow, but it was (and I hope will someday get back to be) an amazing newspaper. Just for the record, I didn't do any cartoon drawings while on duty. Just sketches of layouts."

Moore also took charge in the composing room, where we immediately clashed, resulting in an incompetent woman copy editor sending me back to the desk. That move quickly backfired when Steve recalled me for a second chance.

More humble and less resentful by then, I gulped down my pride, learned a few things from my young boss and came to realize time had caught up with me like others my age.

By June 28, 1991—the day I stepped down—the stock market had made a significant recovery, Donald Trump miraculously had climbed out of a bottomless financial pit to resume his mega deals, Charlene had dried her tears after celebrating our 40th anniversary on a second Caribbean cruise three weeks earlier, and corporate America was looking to the future by offering generous buyouts.

Like so many other Times veterans, I accepted an offer, perhaps not as lucrative as others, but too tempting to decline—a year's pay at full salary.

At 61, there I stood sipping that inexpensive champagne, accepting those useless gifts from co-workers and listening to Jack Smith ramble on about how he was going to miss me.

Not every gift was useless or unappreciated. Among them was a single-framed comic-strip drawing, especially created by Moore, whose hilarious spoofs on baseball were just beginning to attract attention. It wasn't long before Steve's work was being nationally syndicated and he, too, was gone from the Times.

When I embarked on this long-delayed project, I dug out that View cover page from almost two decades earlier, dusted it off and reread Jack's column. What a fine writer he was. The cover page also includes a reprint of part of a long feature I had written in 1982, about Myron's ballroom. I would like to think that story had been selected for my keepsake because it was well written, interesting and "captured the essence of a Los Angeles institution," as the subhead states.

The truth, I'm sure, is that it fit the allotted space and, in seven graphs, presumably ended well… or well enough.

It's a Friday evening," the article begins, *"and the traffic on the nearby Harbor Freeway is heavy, the city emptying for the weekend. But here at Grand Avenue and Olympic Boulevard, the streets are virtually lifeless—except for Myron's where a searchlight casts a bold beam and neons beckon.*

Patrons wander in—singles, couples, small groups—in stiff tuxedos, lavish gowns, garish getups—mostly the "older crowd," 40s and up, some in their 80s. But they step lively, faces aglow.

Up the stairs, past an inviting lounge and through an arch of flashing bulbs, they walk into yesteryear, where flickering shadows dance across the polished hardwood of the spacious ballroom.

Beneath revolving mirrored globes, dreamy-eyed couples shuffle with the shadows to the romantic strains of "Embraceable You" as Horace Heidt directs his Musical Knights—14 of them—on stage.

For 1½ decades, Al Jarvis broadcast on radio and TV from Myron's—a show he called 'The Make-Believe Ballroom,' and today the name might still apply.

In reality, this night it's Horace Jr. with the baton, launching what's being billed as 'the new big-band policy'…."

His father, then 81, honored at intermission, later added Charlene and me to his permanent guest list for parties at his 170-unit Magnolia Estates in Sherman Oaks, where professional entertainers lived and staged monthly variety shows.

Among residents were Roberta Sherwood, a top vocalist in the '40s, Dick Van Patten of TV's *Eight Is Enough* and Jack Leonard, who recorded more than 200 songs during four years as Tommy Dorsey's featured vocalist before being drafted by the Army at the beginning of World War II.

Jack's hits during his budding career with Dorsey included *Once in a While, Josephine* and *Blue Orchids.*

A few mellow bars of his biggest hit, *Marie*, were re-recorded decades later for his telephone answering machine, perpetuating his bittersweet memories of what might have been. While serving Uncle Sam, Leonard was replaced by another young singer Dorsey hired away from Harry James—Frank Sinatra. Although Jack learned to live with that, he never got over it. He often introduced himself as "the guy who gave Sinatra his start in show business," or something like that.

337

Leonard died in 1988. He was 73.

Heidt's unique 10-acre hideaway was patterned after a typical Hawaiian village on one side, a Palm Springs resort on the other, complete with street names, landscaping and structural designs.

Secluded behind a wall of shrubbery, palm trees dominated the grounds that included swimming pools, waterfalls, an aviary of exotic pheasants, health club, party room and an 18-hole pitch-and-putt golf course—all of it out of place amid the banal setting of that San Fernando Valley area.

Heidt's home, opposite a large waterfall and the aviary, was nestled among heavy foliage near the complex entrance. The sprawling, single-story house, about 4,000 square feet, was filled with eye-catching sights—Christmas decorations, flashing lights, glittering garland strung over doorways, a piñata and a plastic Santa resting against the fireplace collecting dust. Over it hung a portrait of Heidt in his band-leading days.

"Horace," I asked. "why all the Christmas decorations? It's July."

"Why not?" he replied. "I like 'em."

The most impressive room was strictly for show—an enormous trophy room of items Heidt had collected for more than half a century.

Mementos included Nazi Hermann Goering's golf clubs; photographs of entertainers he discovered (Art Carney, Al Hirt, Gordon MacRae, the King Sisters, Frankie Carle, Alvino Rey, Dick Contino and others); crystallized sand from the first atomic-bomb explosion at Los Alamos, N.M., and the original sign U.S. prisoners in Korea saw when they were released in 1953: "Gate to Freedom."

At the time, Heidt played the piano daily for about an hour. One evening he invited my wife and me and a few friends to a marvelous Chopin recital he played from memory.

Single for about six years when we met, Horace lived alone but wasn't far from the influence of the first of his four wives, Adaline, the mother of band leader Horace Jr. and three other children; she rented one of the estate apartments.

"I never could make it with the women," Heidt told me. "I had a one-track mind. When I get my mind set on doing something, I'm completely involved. I wanted my wives to show interest, and if they didn't, I didn't have too much interest in them."

Looking around the room, he smiled and added, "If I was married, my wife would take these decorations down, and she wouldn't burn the eggs."

Although it had been days since Heidt had left the house with a pot of eggs boiling on the stove, the odor had not completely vanished.

"I boil 40 eggs twice a week to feed the birds," he said. "I've got about 50, all pheasants, different species... I felt it would add a lot of atmosphere to have rare birds. I tried pigeons, but they were too messy."

A rare bird himself, Horace Heidt, Sr., not only was a marvelous world-famous musician, but also a kind, caring, ambitious man who in his twilight years immersed himself in his village until pneumonia led to his death in 1986 at age 85.

AFTER THE retirement ceremony, I boxed my gifts, Scotch tape dispenser, Times style book and other useless incidentals, bid my colleagues farewell and left with Charlene and our friends, Jewett and Evelyn.

Still early and not eager to go home and watch TV, we stopped for cocktails at a crowded Ventura Boulevard nightclub—where, in a sense, TV came to us.

A glass of champagne in hand, I spotted Telly Savalas enter and step toward me.

"Kojac," I bellowed as heads turned.

Eyeing me with the disdainful look of an incognito superstar whose cover had just been blown, Savalas brushed past us and joined waiting friends in a booth.

By 1991, the famous actor must have grown weary of his enduring role as the shiny-bald, lollipop-sucking New York detective with a gold chain encircling his open-collar neck.

To this day, I remember my embarrassment after calling attention to Savalas, who clearly wanted to enjoy an evening with friends and not be hounded by overzealous fans.

"Telly," I wanted to say, "sorry about that. I'm with The Times. I merely wanted to say hello and introduce you to my wife and friends. Guess I've been celebrating too much..."

What came out of my mouth was nothing.

Suddenly I had mixed feelings about leaving the paper. At 61, was I really ready to give up my career?

Retirement, I decided, was something I would have to work on.

Epilogue

In 1993, less than two years after relocating in Arizona where my only connection with a newspaper was at the breakfast table, I rewrote an article I had done on Billy Eckstein and submitted it to the publisher of our community weekly after the singer had died.

That short obituary was the beginning of an extended career—a freelance position as a reporter, entertainment editor and columnist that paid $4.50 an hour and lasted 14 years without a pay raise.

As Charlene might have said had she ever heard of Yogi—"It was *déjà vu* all over again."

Author's Bio

BORN JAN. 25, 1930, in Kearney, Nebraska, I was delivered by a doctor across the street from where my mother used to live. Her father, also a physician who still resided there, planned to bring me into the world.

"He was too nervous," my mother once told me, "so he asked his friend if he would do it."

I have seen Kearney listed on maps of Nebraska—once landed near there in Grand Island during a violent thunder storm when traveling with the Los Angeles Dodgers—but have no recollection of those first few weeks of life in that small town. My mother bundled me up and took me to Omaha to meet my father, a hard-working Iowa farm boy struggling to find a job during those lean years of the Great Depression.

At age 5 or 6, I made my first communion at St. Aloysius Catholic Church in Kansas City, Missouri, where my father worked at the Ford Motor Company. He operated a heavy grinder, smoothing out small dents in new models as they rolled along the assembly line.

Major labor problems and union strikes forced him to seek work elsewhere, and in 1939, our family relocated in Richmond, California, where dad found a job at a barrel man-ufacturing company.

My sister Bonnie, born in 1934, and I occasionally greeted our weary dad after a long day on the job with a duet from a popular song at the time, *The Beer Barrel Polka*. At least mom laughed.

Our next California destination was the San Fernando Valley town of Burbank, where Lockheed Aircraft was hiring workers in anticipation of a war.

Early in 1941, dad bought a two-bedroom tract house in Roscoe (later renamed Sun Valley). Asked for a $100 down payment, my father bristled, noting that the house had been lived in for six months. The owner settled for $50 down with monthly payments of $31. Total price: $3,200.

I grew up in the Valley, graduated from San Fernando High School in June of 1947 with a B average and started college that fall at University of California, Santa Barbara.

Asked to select a major, I hadn't given it a thought. Law sounded interesting, so I signed up for such pre-law courses as bowling, football and music appreciation. I doubt my parents, who were footing the bills, were impressed. I obtained respectable grades that semester and next, but nothing akin to law was part of my curriculum.

After a full year at the university, I signed Army enlistment papers for a three-year tour of duty and served almost four—virtually all of it in Public Information offices, where I launched my journalistic career.

Upon my discharge in 1952, my wife Charlene and I returned with our infant daughter to the Valley where our children were raised. I retired from the Times in 1991, when we moved from our Reseda residence of 32 years to Sun City West, Arizona—because a neighbor had purchased a home there and recommended it.

We have four children—Patty, Linda, Barbara and John—14 grandchildren and 17 great-grandkids.

My wife and I celebrated our 59th wedding anniversary June 2, 2010.

CPSIA information can be obtained at www.ICGtesting.com
Printed in the USA
BVOW032051180912

300512BV00002B/3/P